Other Books by Roy Ziegler

History
The Parrys of Philadelphia and New Hope
New Hope, Pennsylvania: River Town Passages

Novels
Requiem for Riley
Dawn's Eerie Light
Twilight of Separation

Children's Literature
Let's Visit New Hope (co-authored with Gayle Goodman)

Unfaltering Trust

*How Pilgrim Edward Fitz Randolph Jr.
and His Descendants Helped Build America*

ROY ZIEGLER

UNFALTERING TRUST
HOW PILGRIM EDWARD FITZ RANDOLPH JR. AND
HIS DESCENDANTS HELPED BUILD AMERICA

Copyright © 2020 Roy Ziegler.

All rights reserved. No part of this book may be used or reproduced by any means, graphic, electronic, or mechanical, including photocopying, recording, taping or by any information storage retrieval system without the written permission of the author except in the case of brief quotations embodied in critical articles and reviews.

iUniverse books may be ordered through booksellers or by contacting:

iUniverse
1663 Liberty Drive
Bloomington, IN 47403
www.iuniverse.com
1-800-Authors (1-800-288-4677)

Because of the dynamic nature of the Internet, any web addresses or links contained in this book may have changed since publication and may no longer be valid. The views expressed in this work are solely those of the author and do not necessarily reflect the views of the publisher, and the publisher hereby disclaims any responsibility for them.

Any people depicted in stock imagery provided by Getty Images are models, and such images are being used for illustrative purposes only.
Certain stock imagery © Getty Images.

ISBN: 978-1-5320-8617-5 (sc)
ISBN: 978-1-5320-8619-9 (hc)
ISBN: 978-1-5320-8618-2 (e)

Library of Congress Control Number: 2019916701

Print information available on the last page.

iUniverse rev. date: 04/09/2020

CONTENTS

Dedication ix
About the Author xi
Acknowledgements xiii
Special Acknowledgements xv
Illustrations xvii
Introduction xxiii

Part 1   Fitz Randolph Origins. 1
Lords of Spennithorne and Middleham, Direct Descendants of Charlemagne

Part 2   The Fitz Randolph Family Emigrates to America 8

Descendants of Edward Fitz Randolph Jr. (1607-1675)
and Elizabeth Blossom (1620-1713)* 27
*Ancestors of George H. W. Bush and George W. Bush
Founding Family of New Jersey (1669)*

Part 3   Descendants of Benjamin Fitz Randolph (1663-1746) &
Sarah Dennis (1709-1747) 28

Nathaniel Fitz Randolph (1703-1780) 28
First Contributor of Land and Funds for the Establishment of Princeton University

Benjamin Randolph (1737-1792) 32
Noted Cabinetmaker, builder of desk upon which Thomas Jefferson wrote the Declaration of Independence

Part 4   Descendants of Joseph Fitz Randolph (1656-1726) &
Hannah Conger (1670-1742) 37

Theodore Fitz Randolph (1826-1883) 38
U. S. Congressman, Senator and Governor of New Jersey

Joseph Fitz Randolph (1803-1873). 44
U. S. Congressman and Delegate to the Peace Conference of 1861

Joseph Fitz Randolph Jr. (1843-1932). 46
Author of Books on State and Federal Laws and Religion

Part 5　Descendants of Nathaniel Fitz Randolph (1642-1713) &
　　　　Mary Holley (1644-1703) 49
　　　　Leader in the Fight for Religious Tolerance in Plymouth Colony
　　　　Ancestors of US Presidents Gerald R. Ford and Barack Hussein
　　　　　Obama

Mary Fitz Randolph (1710-c. 1779) 60
Granddaughter of Edward Fitz Randolph Jr.

Hartshorne Fitz Randolph (1723-1806) 62
Early Leader in the Fight to Abolish Slavery

Captain Nathaniel Fitz Randolph (1747-1780) 67
Hero in the American Revolutionary War at the Battles of Long
　Island, Staten Island

Part 6　Descendants of Capt. Edward Randolph (1754-1837) &
　　　　Anna Julianna Steele (1761-1810) 76
　　　　Hero in the American Revolutionary War at the Battles of Paoli
　　　　　and Germantown
　　　　Early Entrepreneur in Philadelphia

Julianna Randolph Wood (1810-1885). 95
Granddaughter of Captain Edward Randolph and Wife of
　Richard Davis Wood

Dr. George Bacon Wood becomes a Prominent
Physician and Distinguished Author. 95
Son of Richard Davis Wood and Founder of the Wawa Dairy

Richard Davis Wood embarks on a career in industry 97
Leading Industrial Developer in nineteenth-century New Jersey

Jacob Randolph, MD (1796-1848). 112
Prominent Physician and Surgeon

Successor of Dr. Philip Syng Physick (Father of American Surgery) at Pennsylvania Hospital, the First Hospital Established in the United States

Rachel Randolph Parry (1804-1866) 123
*Daughter of Captain Edward Randolph and Wife of Oliver Parry
Co-founder of Early Job-training Program for Women in the United States*

Major Edward Randolph Parry (1832-1874). 135
*Pioneer in the Development of the Territory of Minnesota
Hero in the American Civil War*

Captain Oliver Randolph Parry (1873-1958) 145
Early-twentieth-century Architect and Builder

Evan Randolph (1822-1887). 149
*Grandson of Captain Edward Randolph
Partner with William Pearson Jenks in a major nineteenth-century Cotton Manufacturing Company in Philadelphia*

Evan Randolph Jr. (1880-1962) 165
Son of Evan Randolph, and a Philadelphia Banker

Part 7   The Randolph Family in the 21st Century 167

Evan Randolph III (1909-1997) 168
*Son of Evan Randolph Jr.
Philadelphia Banker*

John Randolph (b. 1947) Architect, Community Activist.... 170
*Philadelphia Architect and Founder of the "Schuylkill River Development Council" for the Revitalization of the Schuylkill River and its Environs
Co-founder of the "Community OutReach Project" for Assisting the Homeless Population in Philadelphia*

Epilogue 177
Appendix.. 181
Endnotes 185
Bibliography 197
Index... 211

DEDICATION

This book is dedicated to all pilgrims, immigrants, and refugees seeking freedom and opportunity.

ABOUT THE AUTHOR

Unfaltering Trust is Roy Ziegler's third book about early American History. His second historical work, *The Parrys of Philadelphia and New Hope* (2011), is a history of five generations of the renowned Parry family. *New Hope, Pennsylvania: River Town Passages* (2007), his first book, traces the history of the fifty most historic buildings and sites located in New Hope, Pennsylvania, a town that played a prominent role in the American Revolutionary War and in the nation's early industrial development. Mr. Ziegler is past president of the New Hope Historical Society, and currently serves on the Historical Society's board of directors.

The most recent of his novels, *Requiem for Riley* (2017), set in New York City and Brussels, explores the mysterious disappearance of the Mozart Requiem Mass fragment that occurred during the 1958 World Expo in Brussels. His previous novel, *Dawn's Eerie Light* (2016), presents three intertwined stories of unrequited love. His first novel, *Twilight of Separation* (2013), tells the story of a young man who loses his faith but finds redemption in love.

Mr. Ziegler's novel *Mozart's Revenge* is expectecd to be released in 2021.

He has also collaborated on a children's book, *Let's Visit New Hope* (2015). Written for nine-to- twelve-year-olds, it presents a colorful look at Bucks County and Pennsylvania history.

ACKNOWLEDGEMENTS

The author gratefully acknowledges the following organizations for their generous help in researching this story of the legendary Fitz Randolph family: City of Philadelphia Historical Commission; Free Library of Philadelphia; Hagley Museum and Library (Delaware); Hidden New Jersey; Historical Society of Pennsylvania; Library Company of Philadelphia; Mid-Atlantic Center for the Arts & Humanities; Middlesex County, New Jersey Division of Arts and History Programs, Office of Arts & History; Minnesota Historical Society; Minnesota State University, Mankato; Pennsylvania Academy of Fine Arts; New Hope Historical Society; Princeton University Firestone Library and Seeley G. Mudd Manuscript Library; Temple University Urban Archives; The Smithsonian Institute (Washington, D C); University of Pennsylvania Archives and Records Center; and the Winterthur Museum (Delaware).

For their invaluable information and guidance throughout this project, the author wishes to thank the following members of the Randolph family: David Story Randolph, Evan Randolph IV, Hanna Randolph Shipley, John Randolph and Leonard Beale Randolph.

SPECIAL ACKNOWLEDGEMENTS

Sue Kaufmann
Michael Moran
Susan P. Neely
Bernard F. Stehle
Charles F. Tarr

ILLUSTRATIONS

1. The Paoli Battlefield
2. The Death of Roland at the Battle of Roncevaux Pass, illuminated manuscript
3. Reliquary of Charlemagne, Aachen Cathedral
4. The Fitz Randolph Coat-of-Arms
5. The *Mayflower*
6. The *Arbella*, Governor Winthrop's Flagship
7. Salem Witch Trials Memorial
8. The Fitz Randolph House in East Jersey Old Town Village
9. The Indian Queen Tavern in East Jersey Old Town Village
10. Holder Hall, Princeton University
11. Fitz Randolph Memorial Plaque, Princeton University
12. The Fitz Randolph Gate at Princeton University
13. Portrait of Benjamin Randolph, water color on ivory by Charles Wilson Peale
14. Declaration of Independence Desk (1775-1778) by Benjamin Randolph
15. The Honorable Theodore Fitz Randolph
16. Justice Randolph Manning
17. Joseph Fitz Randolph Jr.
18. The New Jersey State House, Trenton
19. The Jonathan Singletary Dunham House
20. Millstone from Jonathan Singletary Dunham's grist mill
21. Memorial Stone erected "in memory of Jonathan Singletary Dunham"
22. Band Sampler by Mary Fitz Randolph
23. Friends Meeting House, Randolph, N.J.
24. Independence Hall, Philadelphia

25. Tombstone of Captain Nathaniel Fitz Randolph
26. Captain Edward Randolph
27. The approximate site of the 4th Picket Post commanded by Lieutenant Edward Fitz Randolph
28. The Randolph House at 212 N. 2nd St., Philadelphia
29. Elfreth's Alley, Philadelphia
30. First Bank of the United States, Philadelphia
31. The Arch Street Friends Meeting House
32. Arch Street Bridge, at Front St., by W. L. Breton
33. Julianna Randolph (1794-1876)
34. Typical 18th-century Philadelphia Trinity Houses
35. Numbers 2000, 2002 and 2004 Arch Street in 1879
36. Julianna Randolph Wood (1810-1885)
37. Richard Davis Wood
38. George Bacon Wood
39. The Union Mill Dam, Millville, N.J., in 2018
40. Millville Manufacturing Company, mill buildings and Manatico bleachery, aerial view, Millville, N.J.
41. The David Wood Mansion, Millville, N.J.
42. George Wood
43. Wawa Store, 6th & Chestnut Streets., Philadelphia
44. Jacob Randolph, MD
45. Pennsylvania Hospital, Philadelphia
46. The Physick-Randolph House, Philadelphia
47. Laurel Hill Mansion, Philadelphia
48. Emlen Physick, MD
49. The Emlen Physick House, Cape May, N.J.
50. Dr. Physick's Study, the Emlen Physick House
51. Oliver and Rachel Randolph Parry
52. Townhomes, the 1700 block of Green Street, Philadelphia
53. Townhomes, the 2100 block of Mount Vernon Street, Philadelphia
54. Major Edward Randolph Parry
55. Richard Randolph Parry
56. "The Execution of 38 [Dakota] Sioux Indians by U.S. Authorities…"
57. Parade on Front Street, Mankato, Minnesota
58. The Parry Mansion, New Hope, Pa.
59. Captain Oliver Randolph Parry

60. The Wills, Jones-McEwen Company Dairy
61. Evan Randolph
62. The Susan Jenks Wiggins Farmhouse, Wycombe, Pa.
63. Lake Luxembourg in Core Creek Park, Middletown, Pa.
64. The Bridgetown Mill, Bridgetown, Pa.
65. The Bridgetown Mill House Inn
66. William Pearson Jenks
67. The B&O Railroad Bridge over Main Street, Ellicott City, Md.
68. John Story Jenks, William H. Jenks, and Rachel Story Jenks
69. Frogmore Mills, Philadelphia, Pa.
70. Evan Randolph Jr.
71. Evan Randolph III, with granddaughter Rachel
72. John Randolph
73. A section of Schuylkill River Park at Walnut Street, Philadelphia
74. John Randolph Family in 2000

So live, that when thy summons comes to join
The innumerable caravan, which moves
To that mysterious realm, where each shall take
His chamber in the silent halls of death,
Thou go not, like the quarry-slave at night,
Scourged to his dungeon, but, sustained and soothed
By an unfaltering trust, approach thy grave,
Like one who wraps the drapery of his couch
About him, and lies down to pleasant dreams.

—William Cullen Bryant (1794-1878) from "Thanatopsis"

INTRODUCTION

In the early morning hours of September 21, 1777, Lieutenant Edward Fitz Randolph lay wounded and motionless on the cold, wet, fetid battlefield near Paoli, Pennsylvania, left for dead by the British soldiers under the command of General Charles Grey. A bayonet had gouged out Lieutenant Fitz Randolph's left eye as he fought to protect the 4th picket post outside Brigadier General Anthony Wayne's encampment. The British departed with seventy prisoners, leaving fifty-two men dead and one hundred or so wounded (many of them mortally).

It was a devastating defeat for the Americans, but it set the tone for future battles and taught critically important lessons to General Washington regarding battle strategy. The massacre inspired a strong resolve within the Continental Army to persevere. "Remember Paoli!" became a frequent rallying cry to encourage those fighting in other battles.[1]

The Paoli Battlefield—Author Photograph

Nearly a thousand years earlier, in August 778, as Charlemagne and his army marched toward the Pyrenees Mountains on their way back to France after destroying the great Basque city of Pamplona (its history dating back to 75 BC, named after the Roman general Pompey), his army suffered a surprise attack by the Basques, outraged by the destruction that Charlemagne had inflicted on their city. Charlemagne had ordered that the walls of Pamplona be torn down and the city totally destroyed because he feared that the anti-Frankish population of the town would soon use it to launch an attack against him. The city was dominated by a local Basque faction and by Muslims at the time it was sacked by Charlemagne, who was seeking to expand his kingdom and to extend the dominance of Christianity.

The stunning ambush by the Basque warriors at Roncevaux Pass, a high mountain passage in the Pyrenees between France and Spain, cut off Charlemagne's rearguard, resulting in the Basques capturing the baggage wagons and plundering all of the equipment, including tents, armor and weapons, as well as seizing the gold that Charlemagne had received as appeasement from Husayn, governor of the neighboring city of Zaragoza,.

Under the valiant leadership of Roland, Charlemagne's rearguard bravely fought off the infuriated Basques long enough for the king to regroup and evacuate his army to safety. Having refused to call on the main body of the army for assistance, Roland and all of the soldiers under his command were slaughtered. The Battle of Roncevaux Pass, as it came to be known, was the only significant defeat ever experienced by Charlemagne. "Remember Roland!" became a rallying cry in many future wars.[2]

The Death of Roland at the Battle of Roncevaux Pass, from an illuminated manuscript (c. 1456-1460) — Public Domain

Remarkable in their similarity, the Battle of Paoli and the Battle of Roncevaux Pass demonstrate the bravery and resolve of two separate armies at war in two different millennia. Lieutenant Edward Fitz Randolph was a direct descendant of Charlemagne through his great-great-grandfather, Edward Fitz Randolph Jr. He survived the Battle of Paoli, no doubt strengthened by his unfaltering trust in his God, and by his undying love for his fiancée, Anna Juliana Steele.

William Cullen Bryant, at age seventeen, used the words "unfaltering trust" in his 1811 poem "Thanatopsis," the precocious teenager's philosophical contemplation of death as a natural part of God's plan. Seven decades after the twenty-three-year-old Lieutenant Edward Fitz Randolph lay mortally wounded at Paoli, Bryant's words were summoned for the eulogy of Edward's son, Jacob Randolph, MD, following the doctor's premature death in 1848:

> During his short illness he was collected, and in the full possession of his mind. He prepared for death without fear, doubtless, 'Sustained and soothed by an unfaltering trust' in the principles of the Society in which he had been raised.[3]

The words "unfaltering trust" clearly describe the sustained faith and fortitude characteristic of the Fitz Randolph family and their leadership through the ages. What follows is a story about the Fitz Randolph family's role in the development of America. It begins with the arrival of Edward Fitz Randolph Jr. in Plymouth Colony in 1630, during the Great Migration from England in search of freedom and opportunity. It focuses on nine generations of the family from colonial times to the Revolutionary War, through the Industrial Revolution and the Civil War, to the modern era and into the twenty-first century.

PART ONE

Fitz Randolph Origins

Reliquary of Charlemagne, Aachen Cathedral, Germany

In his 1907 work, *Fitz Randolph Traditions—A Story of a Thousand Years*,[4] Lewis V. F. Randolph (1838-1921), an eighth-generation descendant of Edward Fitz Randolph Jr., tells the story of the first thousand years of his illustrious Fitz Randolph Family.

Early descendants of Charlemagne, the Holy Roman Emperor who united Europe and later descendants of William the Conqueror as well, the Fitz Randolph lineage has been influential in shaping world history for more than a millennium.

Charlemagne (742-814)

Charlemagne (Charles I, Carolus Magnus, Charles the Great), was the son of Pippin III, who, with the approval of the Pope, had seized the Frankish Kingdom in 751 and held power over it until his death in 768. Upon his death, his sons Charles and Carloman inherited his empire. Charles quickly moved to seize complete control by entering into an alliance with the King of the Lombards and marrying the king's daughter, the first of his long line of wives and concubines. When Carloman died in 771, Charles I assumed complete control of the Frankish empire, denying the claims of his brother's heirs. At the age of twenty-five he was king of the Lombards and king of the Franks, and for the last fourteen years of his life, the first king of what would later be known as the Holy Roman Empire. A warrior king who spent most of his nearly four decades in power leading military campaigns, he also sought ways to improve the daily lives of the people throughout his kingdom. He appointed Alcuin, a friend and noted scholar from England, as his minister of education. Alcuin envisioned a system of free education for all boys.[5] Charlemagne's goal was to unite Europe and spread Christianity, vowing that anyone who refused baptism into the Christian faith would be executed. Indeed, in 782, at the controversial Massacre of Verden, Charlemagne is said to have ordered the slaughter of about forty-five hundred Saxons unless they converted to Christianity. This was a far cry from his Fitz Randolph descendants, who, a thousand years later, would struggle to bring freedom from religious persecution and the abolition of slavery to the American colonies.

Despite his unrelenting warfare Charlemagne managed to sire eighteen children with multiple wives and concubines. And he is known to have cherished his extensive family. The preeminent medieval historian Frank Barlow describes him as follows:

> The ideal warrior chief, Charlemagne was an imposing physical presence blessed with extraordinary energy, personal courage and an iron will. He loved the active life—military campaigning, hunting, swimming—but he was no less at home at court, generous with his gifts, a boon companion at the banquet table, and adept at establishing friendships. Never far from mind was his large family … over whose interests he watched carefully….
>
> Charlemagne possessed considerable native intelligence, intellectual curiosity, a willingness to learn from others, and religious sensibility—all attributes which allowed him to comprehend the forces that were reshaping the world around him.[6]

Origin of the Fitz Randolph name

Cicero Pangburn McClure (1847-1925),[7] a descendant of Nathaniel Fitz Randolph of Princeton, New Jersey, has suggested that the origin of the name "Randolph" comes from the Viking *Harulf* (high wolf), *Hraudulf* (red wolf) or *Hroarulf* (fierce wolf); that is, *high, red* or *fierce wolf* and the

Norman Prefix "Fitz" (son of), thereby giving rise to the surname "Fitz Randolph." Centuries later, many descendants would discontinue using the prefix "Fitz" as part of the surname. Others, Like Lewis V. F. Randolph, would abbreviate it, preferring to use "F" simply as middle initial.

In 2019, however, David Story Randolph provided a more plausible explanation of the family name: "The name 'Randolph' is derived from the Norse *rond* ('shield') and *olf* ('wolf'), referring to the circular Viking shields lining the sides of a Viking longboat. So, the name, 'Randolph' would mean 'wolf-shield,' or 'shields like a wolf,' and was probably a nom de guerre before it became a specific family name."

David Randolph claims that the "Fitz" of his family's historic name, Fitz Randolph, is from the French/Norman *fils* or *fis* ("son of"), used to designate descendants of the Danish warriors in Normandy, the "Land of the Northmen," after its colonization by Danes in the ninth century AD.[8] Le Conte Gerard Fis Randolph came to Britain in 1068, a fact later documented in the second volume of the Domesday Book—the comprehensive record of the value, ownership and liabilities of land and properties in England commissioned by William I in 1086 and completed that same year. The Domesday Book was believed to embody the kind of final and undisputed accuracy of accounting that would be required of all men at the end of the world. (The word "Domesday" is commonly thought to refer to "Doomsday," that final day of reckoning before God.)

In the first millennium, the "Fitz Randolph" ancestors were warriors who invaded lands, established empires, forced allegiance to Christianity upon all whom they conquered, and expanded education and culture. Many of them became farmers with extensive land holdings. In the second millennium descendants have included decorated war heroes, noted physicians, industrialists, lawyers, bankers, artisans, farmers, merchants, social activists, judges, a governor, members of Congress, and four presidents (Gerald R. Ford, George H. W. Bush, George W. Bush and Barack Hussein Obama). In his 1907 work, L. V. F. Randolph underscores the importance of the Fitz Randolph alliances with other prominent families throughout the centuries:

> In the ages gone by the Fitz Randolphs were from time to time exceedingly fortunate in their marriages, gathering increase of strength and character and standing—as well as of wealth—from a number of these alliances. It may safely be said, however, that, in no instance of this sort did

greater advantage accrue to him who made the contract than was gained by the young Edward, who in May, 1637, at Scituate, Mass. married Elizabeth, the daughter of Thomas and Anne Blossom.[9]

In 1630, Edward Fitz Randolph Jr. (the "Edward" above, a direct descendant of Charlemagne) left his home in Sutton-in-Ashfield, Nottinghamshire, England on his journey to the New World. Sutton-in-Ashfield was first recorded as "Sutone" in the Domesday Book. The Fitz Randolph family had lived there for centuries, during which they became Lords of Spennithorne, a nearby village located in North Yorkshire, above the Ure River.

The recorded history of Spennithorne begins with Ribald (1050-1121), son of Eudo, Duke of Brittany. Spennithorne and nearby Middleham were gifts to Ribald from his brother Alain, who, after his wife died, became a monk at the Abbey of Saint Mary in York. Eudo was the first cousin, once removed, on his mother's side of William the Conqueror. Middleham was first settled by the Romans around 70 A D. Some of the earthworks from the castle that Alain had built there (and had given to Ribald) can still be seen today. The area is known as "Williams Hill." According to the Church of England, the Anglo-Saxons had been removed in favor of a Norman lord by 1086. By the thirteenth century the Spennithorne Estate had passed to descendants of the Fitz Randolphs, who held the land until the sixteenth century.

The version of the Fitz Randolph Coat-of-Arms pictured below was registered as the ancestral arms of Edward Fitz Randolph Jr., a pilgrim who arrived in America in 1630. It was approved on June 13, 1972 by the Committee of Heraldry, New England Historic Genealogical Society (listed as Number 625 in the Roll of Arms).[10] An earlier publication, Burke's General Armory (1884), notes:

> Fitz Randolf (Langton Hall, Co. Notts, 1614, and Chesterfield Co. Derby, Edward Fitz Randolph, Visit Notts, 1614. Argent. A chief indented as crest—on a chapeau or, turned up azure, a wyvern (a legendary creature with a dragon's head and wings, a reptilian body, two legs, and a tail often ending in a diamond- or arrow-shaped tip) of the last. This gives a description identified with the Fitz Randolphs of Nottinghamshire and Spennithorne.

Ranulf Fitz Robert, 4th Lord of Middleham and Spennithorne, born in 1251, bore the arms of his grandfather Glanville, "argent, a chief indicated azure. Crest, on a chapeau or turned up a wiverne of the last." His second son Ranulf bore the Arms of his grandfather Glanville. Ranulf's descendants in the male line continued at Spennithorne until the 16th century.[11]

The Fitz Randolph Coat-of-Arms—Courtesy of New Hope Historical Society

Spennithorne is perhaps best known in modern times as one of the locations for the popular BBC television series *All Creatures Great and Small*. The St. Michael and All Angels Church shown in the series occupies the site of the original church thought to have been built by Robert Fitz Randolph in the middle of the twelfth century but was completely demolished. The church's existing tower dates back to the fourteenth century. Many of the scenes in the series were also shot in Leyburn, a village located about two miles southeast of Spennithorne. Today, the rustic town of fewer than two hundred inhabitants is a much-sought-after vacation spot for quiet weekend retreats in its centuries-old cozy cottages.

The following two pages show the lineage of Edward Fitz Randolph Jr., Pilgrim, traced back to Charlemagne. The data is derived from L. V. F. Randolph's *Fitz Randolph Traditions—A Story of a Thousand Years*.

Lineage of Edward Fitz Randolph Jr., Pilgrim

Charlemagne (742-814)
▼
Pepin (773-810)
▼
Bernard (797-818)
▼
Pepin of Perrone (817-840)
▼
Herbert I (840-907)
▼
Herbert II (884-942)
▼
Robert of Vermandois (920-967)
▼
Geoffrey I (938-987)
▼
Conan I (950-992)
▼
Geoffrey II (980-1008)
▼
Eudo (999-1079)
▼
Ribald (1050-1121)
▼
Ralph Fitz Ribald (1080-1168)
▼
Robert Fitz Ralph (1110-1185)
▼
Ranulph Fitz Robert (1180-1251)
▼
Ranulph Fitz Ranulph (1220-1294)
▼
Ralph Fitz Ranulph (1250-1316)
▼
Ranulph Fitz Ralph (1300-1343)
▼

John Fitz Randolph (Fitz Ranulph) (1325-1369)
▼
Ranulph (Randall) Fitz John (1345-1388)
▼
John Fitz Ranulph (Fitz Randall) (1374-1405)
▼
Ralph Fitz John (Fitz Randall) (1398-1457)
▼
John Fitz Randolph (1420-1474)
▼
John Fitz Randolph (1460-1514)
▼
Christopher Fitz Randolph (1495-1574)
▼
Christopher Fitz Randolph (1530-1588)
▼
Edward Fitz Randolph (1565-1614)
▼
Edward Fitz Randolph Jr. (1607-1675)

PART TWO
The Fitz Randolph Family Emigrates to America

Edward Fitz Randolph Jr. (1607-1675)

Edward Fitz Randolph Jr., a Pilgrim, was the son of Sir Edward Fitz Randolph, Lord of Sutton and Chesterfield. He departed from his home in Sutton-in-Ashfield, a small town in Nottinghamshire, England, to journey to Plymouth Colony with his widowed mother, Frances, as part of the Great Migration of 1630. They sailed on one of the eleven ships included in the Winthrop Fleet.[12] Edward, then twenty-three years old, was influenced by the religious thought of those with whom he traveled to the New World, and would maintain his association with them for the rest of his life. He joined their separatist non-conformist religious society they established and was considered a dedicated member.

King Charles I, the grandson of Mary, Queen of Scots, married Princess Henrietta Maria, daughter of King Henry IV of France, a Catholic. Therefore, Charles was seen to favor the Catholic religion. Adding to that concern, he had taken increasingly hostile actions against the Puritans and Separatist. Charles preferred a High Anglican form of worship, and his wife's being a Catholic created deep suspicions about him, particularly among the Puritans. Charles dissolved parliament three times, and in 1629 he eliminated parliament entirely, resolving to rule his kingdom without them by divine right. At the same time, the sustained suppression of Separatists led many of them to flee to Holland and then to the American colonies.

The Puritans

Both the Puritan and Separatist groups were Protestants. The Puritan (non-separatists) preferred to remain part of the Church of England, while urging that the Church distance itself from Roman Catholic beliefs. They believed that they should be led not by a king but by the head of the Church of England. Unrest and distrust of Charles I continued to mount until a radical group of Members of Parliament, led by Oliver Cromwell, a leader among the Puritans at the time, revolted. In 1629, a year before Edward Fitz Randolph Jr. left for America, Cromwell entered Parliament and assembled the New Model Army, which eventually defeated the Royalists at the Battle of Naseby in 1645. Cromwell succeeded in having Charles I put on trial for treason. Found guilty, the king was executed in 1649. Twenty years earlier Cromwell had already become known as a profane Puritan who had attacked the bishops. He believed that every Christian could form a relationship with God by direct contact, and that the clergy's chief responsibility was to inspire them. In the words of biographer John Buchan, Cromwell

> "found Christ"—not by any process of reasoning, but by an intense personal experience in which his whole being was caught up into an ecstasy of adoration and love....he was in essence a mystic, and the core of his religion was mystical experience continually renewed.[13]

Cromwell distrusted the hierarchy and the established Church. As Lord Protector of the Commonwealth, he did away with the use of the *Book of Common Prayer* in churches, replacing it with new services focused on extensive sermons and extemporary devotions; he did, however, allow the use of the *Book of Common Prayer* in the privacy of one's home. Marriages in churches were forbidden and many who died during that time were buried without religious ceremonies. Churches were desecrated as Cromwell directed the destruction of altars, statues, and stained glass windows. Bishops were abolished and congregations were allowed to select their own ministers. A general in the civil war against the rule of Charles I, Cromwell led the overthrow of the Stuarts. He declared that Britain was a Republic ("The Commonwealth") and assumed the title Lord Protector, which in essence was the king. Cromwell's son, Richard, failed to win the support of the New Model Army. He was forced to resign and exiled to France. After Cromwell's Protectorate collapsed, Charles II took the throne at the request of the army, and the monarchy was restored.

The Separatists

The Separatists, with whom Edward Fitz Randolph Jr. was affiliated, was a movement that had been created by Robert Browne in the previous century during the reign of Queen Elizabeth I. Browne was the first prominent person known to have become a Separatist, seceding from the Church of England. After graduating from Cambridge University, he could have become a minister, but he declined the post and opposed the Church of England. Browne's radical beliefs—preaching without the Church's required license, creating public disturbances and failing to pay taxes—led to his imprisonment numerous times during his lifetime. (He died in 1633, at age 82, during his final such confinement.)

Browne and some of his followers moved to London after his being released from prison the first time, in 1581, then to Holland, where he wrote a number of pamphlets addressed to his followers, in which he expressed his beliefs and how he envisioned the future of the church. In 1583 a royal proclamation banning the sale of Robert Browne's books in England was issued. He was imprisoned again in 1584.[14]

The Separatist Pilgrim movement (which included Edward and, later, Edward's wife, Elizabeth Blossom) had decided to leave the Church of England and move to America. They became known as "Brownists" because they believed, as did Robert Browne, that God had selected them, so they would therefore be saved. Like the Separatists, many of the Puritan non-separatists left the country to escape the religion established by the state as well as to flee the Catholics in Yorkshire and the Presbyterians in Scotland. Their beliefs have been traced to the 14th century, when they were part of the drive for religious freedom that culminated in the publication of Wycliffe's Bible by the outspoken John Wycliffe. He and his followers believed in private Bible-reading and interpretation as opposed to the extreme papal power and beliefs that were forced upon them from Rome. Wycliffe and several others, including Nicholas of Hereford, John Purvey and John Trevisa, translated the Bible into the vernacular Middle English so that people could better understand and interpret its meaning.

Wycliffe's Bible became the inspiration of the Lollard movement, a pre-Reformation movement that rejected many of the Roman Catholic beliefs. That movement raised the ire of the Church and of the king, who fought hard to suppress it.

The actions of Wycliffe and his followers resulted in the separation of the Church of England from the Catholic Church and, more importantly, in Wycliffe's and his followers' separation from the established Church of England in the sixteenth and seventeenth centuries. As L. V. F. Randolph noted, "The pilgrim, Edward, became very soon a factor of importance. He was a man of substance as well as character."[15]

Edward would later become a leader of that society after the death of Elizabeth's father, Thomas Blossom.

The Puritans and Separatists establish their Colonies in Massachusetts

The Puritans, who continued to adhere to the practices of the Church of England, established the Massachusetts Bay Colony, settling in the Salem and Boston areas. The Separatist Pilgrims settled in the Plymouth Rock area of Massachusetts. Both groups were responsible for initially establishing the colonies in New England. There were fewer separatists and they were poor and less educated than the Puritans. Only half of the passengers who sailed to New England on the first voyage of the *Mayflower* survived the ordeal of that first winter in Massachusetts. Before bearing the Pilgrims on their journey, the *Mayflower* had been a cargo ship transporting fish and lumber. By shipping standards of the day it was a large vessel (eighty feet long and twenty-four feet wide), but for the one hundred and two passengers cramped on board, sailing across the Atlantic Ocean proved to be a harrowing, indeed deadly experience. With no living quarters beyond what accommodated the ship's crew, the pilgrims had to live on the gun deck (an area about feet above the main deck), exposing them to the elements with little-to-no protection. Although blessed with clear and calm weather in the early weeks of their journey, their peace was shattered halfway across by a series of torrential storms that resulted in at least one death among the pilgrims—and cracked the main mast of the ship. (Four years after the last of its historic crossings, the *Mayflower*, in ruins, was sold for scrap.)

While hundreds of Separatists continued to arrive in New England over the following decades, by contrast, ten times as many Puritans landed during the same period. By the time of the American Revolutionary War, nearly fifty thousand Puritans had settled in America, constituting almost three-fourths of the colonial population. Proving the old adage that misery loves company, the Puritans and Separatist eventually found common ground when, in 1689, the king revoked their charters to trade and govern in the New World.

The *Mayflower* (artist unknown)—Public Domain

The Winthrop Fleet arrived in New England in 1630, carrying the first Puritans. Setting sail from Yarmouth in the Isle of Wight, it was comprised of eleven ships, including the flagship *Arbella*. These one thousand or so Puritans had given up all hope for freedom to practice their religion in their country. Prepared never to return, they sailed to the shores of New England in two separate departures, the first in April and the second in May. The first group was led by John Winthrop, a Puritan lawyer who had been elected Governor of the Fleet and head of the New England Company that later became the Massachusetts Bay Company. The Company had obtained a charter from Charles I to participate in trade in New England, and its members planned carefully for the establishment of their new colony. As part of their strategy they recruited a variety of skilled laborers and craftsmen who would be needed to ensure the new colony's success.

The *Arbella*—Gov. Winthrop's Flagship, The Pioneers' Village, Salem, Mass.
The Tichnor Brothers Collection, Boston Public Library—Public Domain

Among the prominent passengers who sailed with Governor Winthrop were Sir Richard Saltonstall, who became a founder of the Connecticut Colony, and Sir Thomas Dudley, who later served several terms as governor of the Massachusetts Bay Colony. He was accompanied by his daughter, Anne Bradstreet (1612-1672), the prestigious poet known for her works on the role of women in society and for her questioning of Puritan beliefs. Her first book of poetry, *The Tenth Muse Lately Sprung Up in America* (1650), was published anonymously in London ("By a Gentlewoman of Those Parts") since it was considered "unwomanly" for a woman to be an author. Indeed, Anne Bradstreet fought this bias all of her life, along with the support of her husband, and governor of the colony, Simon Bradstreet, whereas most men of that time scorned women for such bold literary endeavor.

In 1636, six years after he arrived in the New World, Edward Fitz Randolph built one of the earliest houses in Scituate, Plymouth Colony. The town had been settled by a group from Plymouth around 1627. They were joined by immigrants from Kent County, England, who had initially fled their country to settle in Holland before deciding to journey to America. Scituate is located on the south shore between Plymouth and Boston, its name derived from a Wampanoag term meaning "cold brook," referring to a brook that runs to the inner harbor. The town had originally been governed by the General Council of Plymouth, but on October 5, 1636, Scituate was incorporated as a separate entity.

Edward Fitz Randolph Jr. marries Elizabeth Blossom

On May 10, 1637, Edward married Elizabeth Blossom, the daughter of the Elder, Thomas Blossom, and Ann Heilson. Fleeing religious persecution in England, Ann's family had moved to Leiden, Holland, before crossing the Atlantic on the *Mayflower II* in 1629, following a failed previous crossing attempt on the *Speedwell*.[16] Leiden, a city of nearly fifty thousand inhabitants, was a prosperous community twenty-two miles south of Amsterdam known for its expansive textile industry. Leiden was the birthplace of Rembrandt, in 1606; by the time the Pilgrims were preparing to leave for the New World, the young artist was creating his first paintings there, among them *Three Musicians*, *Stone Operation* and *Unconscious Patient*.

A much smaller vessel than the *Mayflower*, the *Speedwell* had barely traveled three hundred miles offshore when it began taking on water. When the pilgrims were forced to turn back from their anticipated journey, shipbuilders advised them that not only were the vessel's masts far too heavy for the small ship, but also that its hull was dangerously worn thin, no surprise since the forty-three-year-old decommissioned warship they purchased had participated in the Battle of the Spanish Armada. Only about a third of the one hundred and five Pilgrims who survived the *Speedwell* fiasco managed to gain passage on the *Mayflower*, but most were forced to remain in Holland. Those fortunate enough to make the trip ended up resenting the fact that many of their fellow travelers were not pilgrims but, in fact, businessmen seeking fortunes in the New World.

Life grew increasingly more difficult for the Pilgrims who had remained in Leiden. Most of them had been farmers back in England, but they had difficulty finding employment in the city, taking whatever jobs they could find, no matter how menial. Making matters worse for them, they did not blend well with the permissive, urban culture in Holland, which they considered a scandalous environment for their children. Leiden University, known for its tolerance, became a destination for intellectuals attracting scholars and thinkers from all over Europe. It was in Leiden that René Descartes published his *Discourse on the Method* (the treatise in which he famously proclaimed, "I think, therefore I am") in 1637. That was the same year in which Edward Fitz Randolph and Elizabeth Blossom were married. The locals, for their part, saw the Pilgrims as odd outsiders. The growing social pressure eventually led many of them to consider emigrating to America, a choice not easily decided, for they worried about the tortuous crossing of the Atlantic, a journey of more than two months. Adding to their anxiety were the stories from families and friends who had endured the misery and numerous deaths in earlier crossings. Also, having become accustomed to life in Leiden and enjoying some of the comforts of the city, they debated whether they would actually be any better off in the wilds of America than in the more civilized (if increasingly hostile) country of Holland.

When Pastor Robinson died in 1625, Thomas Blossom, one of his most ardent followers, wrote to Governor Bradford, communicating his anguish and that of his followers:

> I commend you to the keeping of the Lord, desiring, if He see it good (and that I might be serviceable unto the business) that I were with you. God hath taken away my son that was with me in the ship, when I came back again; I have only two children, which were born since I left you. Fare thee well.[17]

The governor responded to Blossom's plea by increasing his effort to persuade more of the reluctant Pilgrims remaining in Holland to make the journey to the Colony. "So soon as they [the Pilgrims] were able to arrange payment of their obligations to the organized 'Adventurers' in England and to buy out their interest in the Pilgrim colony in New England, they began to bring over the remainder of the brethren—though at great cost, sacrifice and anxiety," L. V. F. Randolph noted.[18] The "adventurers" were, for the most part, financial speculators empowered by the king. Thomas

Blossom arrived in Plymouth in 1629 and soon became one of the most respected members of the Pilgrim church there. Governor Bradford, who had officiated at the marriage of Thomas and Ann, referred to him as "one of our ancient friends in Holland." Church records describe Thomas Blossom as "an experienced saint and competently established with abilities for his place,"[19] a tribute all the more poignant for the brevity of its promise. His leadership of the Pilgrim church ended with his death in 1633, just four years after his arrival in Plymouth. (Two twentieth-century descendants of Elizabeth's father, Thomas Blossom, and her mother, Ann Heilson—through the 1663 marriage of their son, Peter Blossom, and his wife, Sarah Bodfish—are former presidents of the United States: George H. W. Bush and George W. Bush.)[20]

Governor William Bradford was one of the earliest to have referred to the colonists as "pilgrims":

> And the time being come that they must depart, they were accompanied with most of their brethren out of the city, unto town sundry miles off called Delftshaven where the ship lay ready to receive them. So they left that goodly, and pleasant city which had been their resting place, near twelve years, but they knew they were pilgrims, and looked not much on those things; but lift up their eyes to the heavens, their dearest country; and quieted their spirits.[21]

By the early part of the nineteenth century, the term "pilgrim" was used to describe all of the passengers of the *Mayflower*. And it was also used to describe some of the Plymouth colonists who arrived later.

Puritan religious intolerance intensifies in Massachusetts

In 1639 Edward Fitz Randolph Jr. and Elizabeth moved their family to Barnstable, Massachusetts, a town founded by the Puritan leader Rev. Joseph Hull, who had been expelled from the Church of England. From its beginning, the town was a strong farming community, so it was a good fit for Edward, who had been a farmer all his life. Edward was soon appointed juryman (allowed to serve on juries) and was considered to be "a good man" by Pastor John Lothrop, the esteemed leader of the non-conformist church to which Edward had given his allegiance. The pastor had officiated at the marriage of Edward and Elizabeth, and referred to Edward as "Master Fitz Randolph," recognizing the good reputation of his family.[22] Edward and his family had moved to Barnstable along with Pastor Lothrop and twenty-five other followers. He built his home on an eight-acre plot of land there. His name is included on the 1643 list of men who were allowed to bear arms in New Plymouth. In 1649 Edward sold his house and three other lots and moved to West Barnstable, where he purchased 143 acres and built a new home, residing there for next twenty years. It was during those two decades that the Puritans in Massachusetts Bay Colony became increasingly intolerant of other religions. They believed that it was each person's obligation to live the way he or she thought God had commanded; indeed, John Winthrop, sailing to the New World, had proclaimed to his followers: "[W]e shall be as a City on a Hill. The eyes of all people are upon us."[23]

Continuing its pursuit of greater freedom to practice their religion as they saw fit, the Fitz Randolph family joined Pastor John Lothrop's non-conformist society because they considered the religion and patriotism that was prevalent in New England to be excessively restrictive. The Pastor, a former Anglican clergyman, had left the Church of England because of his strong belief in the separation of church and state. He had previously been incarcerated in England for his independent beliefs, during which time, his wife, Hannah House, died, leaving their six children to beg in the streets. Given his freedom only after agreeing to move to the New World permanently, Pastor Lothrop sailed with some of his followers on the *Griffin*, arriving in Boston in 1634. Soon afterwards, they moved to Scituate, and then on to Barnstable, where the pastor met Edward and Elizabeth Fitz Randolph. Pastor Lothrop later remarried and had five additional children. He died in Barnstable in 1653.

The extreme religious beliefs of the Puritans, who controlled both the church and the state in New England, led them to begin the practice of whipping and branding dissidents, especially the Quakers, who were regarded as intruders posing a danger to the Puritans' religious community. Many Quakers were mutilated and hanged for being infidels.

Thomas Maule becomes an early leader of the Quakers in New England

Thomas Maule, a Quaker who was born in Warwickshire, England, moved from Barbados to Boston in 1668, then to Salem in 1679. Maule was gifted with many talents. He was a well-known tailor who also became a general merchandiser. His skill as a carpenter, too, was widely known, and he was heavily involved in the construction and real estate business. His son, Thomas, also apprenticed as a carpenter. In 1688 the local Quaker community was the recipient of Thomas Maule's skill and generosity when he led the way in building the Meetinghouse in Salem, thought to be the first Quaker Meetinghouse built in America. Maule donated the land and building materials (much of the timber being recycled from other buildings). It is believed that the meetinghouse—now the Peabody Essex Museum—still contains some of the original wood used in its construction more than three centuries ago.

The Quakers were revolutionaries who opposed royalty. The society was formed after its founder, George Fox, heard a "voice from the Lord" in 1647. Decades later, the Quakers continued their protests that the country should turn back to democracy; as a consequence, they were sought out and persecuted by the king. As historian James Walvin notes: "Despite protestations of loyalty, the Quakers were plunged into a spiral of oppression, the scale and depth of which surpassed all previous agonies. By the end of January 1660, jails across the country were filled with them."[24]

The Salem Witch Trials

Shortly after settling in Salem, Thomas Maule began criticizing the Puritan establishment. When he accused Rev. John Higginson, the minister of Salem, of "preaching lies and instructing in the doctrine of devils," a judge ordered that he "be whipped ten stripes well laid on." Fear of the devil, who the Puritans believed was constantly trying to destroy their religion, was rampant. Uneasiness about their situation in a strange land, along with King Charles II's revocation of the Bay Colony charter, created economic worries among the Puritans. All of that, coupled with a smallpox epidemic that ravaged the colonies, convinced the Puritans that the devil was certainly at work—and growing stronger. When several young girls began to exhibit strange contortions of their bodies and started babbling incoherently, the Puritans deemed them to be witches who harbored the devil within them. This led to the mass hysteria that prompted the witch trials.

Although Maule and his wife, Naomi, believed in witches, and even testified against Bridget Bishop, the first person put to death during the Salem Witch Trials of 1692, they soon became alarmed by the frenzied way in which the trials were being conducted. More than two hundred persons were accused of witchcraft, twenty of whom were executed during the ensuing trials. Of the twenty victims, nineteen (sixteen women and three men) were hanged; and an elderly man, Giles Corey, was slowly crushed to death under the incrementally heavier weight of rocks pressed upon his supine body over a three-day period as he remained mute, steadfastly ignoring the repeated efforts by the Puritans to force him to voice a plea of 'guilty' or 'not guilty.' Seventeen additional people who were accused died in prison.

The Salem Witch Trials Memorial, a small park located approximately where the hangings took place, was dedicated in 1992, three hundred years after the trials. The memorial ground is framed by twenty granite benches, each inscribed with the name of the accused and the means and date of execution.

Salem Witch Trials Memorial, Salem, Mass.—Author Photograph

Thomas Maule inspires the creation of the First Amendment to the Constitution

When Maule declared in a pamphlet published in 1695 that God would adversely judge the prosecutors of the witch trials, he was arrested and imprisoned for a year. He was later acquitted of all charges when a Puritan jury concurred with Maule's argument that the Court had no right to suppress his expression of religious belief. This event is considered to be one of the crucial points in the eventual adoption of the First Amendment to the United States Constitution. "Not only did Thomas Maule's acquittal pave the way for the First Amendment, it set a precedent for freedom of the press as well. Lawyers cited it as precedent for the John Peter Zenger trial in 1735 which established the right to print controversial opinions."[25]

In his classic novel *The House of the Seven Gables*, Nathaniel Hawthorne based the character Matthew Maule on Thomas Maule. Indeed, one can easily imagine Thomas prophesizing a curse upon the haughty and usurping Colonel Pyncheon that the fictional Matthew Maule utters just before being hanged: "God will give him blood to drink."[26] Unlike Hawthorne's Matthew Maule, though, Thomas escaped that tragic fate and lived until the age of 79.[27] The actual house upon which Nathaniel Hawthorne's tale is based is located about one block from the site of the Salem Witch Trials. Once owned by Hawthorne's cousin, Susanna Ingersoll, the house where she often entertained the famous author is now a museum. According to biographer Brenda Wineapple, "Its seven-gabled state was known to Hawthorne only through childhood stories from his cousin; at the time of his visits, he would have seen just three gables due to architectural renovations."[28]

In the end, the ensuing shame and disgrace of the witch trials brought upon the Puritans by the mass hysteria of 1692-93 helped to bring an end to the repressive theocracy they had established.

Thomas Maule continued writing and publishing his pamphlets, and devoted his energy to the church he loved until his death in 1724 at the age of seventy-nine. A century later, in 1828, Thomas's third generation grandson, William Maule, would marry Mary Randolph, the third generation granddaughter of Edward Fitz Randolph Jr.

Edward Fitz Randolph moves his family to New Jersey

Edward was aware, no doubt, of the writings of Joseph Glanvill, a British philosopher who defended the reality of witchcraft and ghosts and the preexistence of the soul, and most probably knew of Cotton Mather's preaching that demons were alive and that to deny their existence was to deny God himself, beliefs that had helped drive the fervor leading to the Salem Witch Trials. But Edward had seen enough of the Puritan fanaticism. When he learned that the New Jersey Proprietors, wealthy friends of the king who were given land and colonial charters to govern, promised complete religious freedom to those who would settle in that province, Edward sold his Massachusetts property in 1669 and moved his family nearly three hundred miles to Piscataway, in East Jersey. There he purchased from the Proprietary two hundred and twenty-seven acres of land located near the mouth of the Raritan River, thus becoming a Founding Family of New Jersey. Proprietors were wealthy friends of the king who were given land and colonial charters to govern. Lewis V. F. Randolph describes the situation in New Jersey at that time:

> The augmenting restrictions and extractions of Puritan rule in New England seemed oppressive and unscriptural to a considerable body of excellent men and women who longed for a large liberty of thought. Religious freedom, complete and unstinted, was promised to early settlers by the New Jersey Proprietors, and this constituted the chief lure to the pious pilgrims.[29]

Around the same time, Edward's older sons are also known to have purchased land nearby. Such settlements in East Jersey were founded along the lines of the New England model. Each settler received a house lot, an upland lot, a farm lot along the Raritan River, and a meadow lot. These properties were located throughout Piscataway. The following Fitz Randolph properties are recorded in the New Jersey State Archives:

> Two house lots, consisting of 30 acres located in Piscatawaytown (this was located on what is now Woodbridge Avenue in Edison near what is now the St. James Episcopal Church). There was an upland lot

consisting of 15 acres, likely located in Edison. The River lot, consisting of 112 acres was located along the Raritan River near present-day Hillside Avenue in Piscataway. This lot was sold, however, by 1687 and had never been developed. An upland lot of 50 acres was located in Edison or perhaps the eastern section of Piscataway. Another upland lot of 60 acres was located in the Vineyard, near Dismal Swamp in Edison. There were also two meadowland lots, each consisting of 5 acres located in the Great Raritan Meadows in Edison.[30]

The Territory of Jersey

In 1664 Sir George Carteret and John, Lord Berkeley were given the tract of country east of the Delaware River extending to the Hudson River and to the Atlantic Ocean, by the Duke of York, who was the proprietary of New York. The territory that they were assigned was named "Jersey" in honor of Carteret, who was the Governor of the Isle of Jersey, the largest of the Channel Islands. King Charles II had given part of Jersey through the Duke of York to Governor Carteret as a reward for the governor's help that he had given the king during his exile in the Isle of Jersey in the 1640s.

The Territory of Jersey was divided into East Jersey, with its capitol in Perth Amboy, and West Jersey, its capital in Burlington.

Typical of the era, several of the twelve children of Edward and Elizabeth died at very early ages. Lack of sanitation and frequent infections, as well as the uncontrollable spread of smallpox, influenza and other contagious diseases, claimed the lives of some forty percent of infants and young children in colonial times. Those who observed strict Puritan beliefs accepted such deaths as punishment by God for Original Sin, believing that the agony of childbirth that women suffered was attributable to Eve's role in the Garden of Eden. But for the Fitz Randolph Family, who rejected Puritan beliefs, the early deaths of three of their children—Nathaniel, Mary and John—were ungodly tragedies.

All nine of the remaining Fitz Randolph children eventually married: Hannah (1648) to Jasper Taylor; Mary (1650) to Samuel Hinckley; John (1653) to Sarah Bonham; and Elizabeth (1657) to John Langstaff, after whose death, Elizabeth and Andrew Wooden were married in 1676.

Elizabeth and Andrew both passed away in 1702. Hope married Ezekiel Bloomfield in 1680. Edward's son Thomas married Elizabeth Bathsheba Manning in 1686.

Edward died in 1675 about six years after relocating his family to East Jersey. His widow, Elizabeth, married Captain John Pike in 1685. Pike had moved from Newbury, Massachusetts to East Jersey at the invitation of Governor Carteret twenty years earlier, whereupon he formed a corporation to settle in Woodbridge and was granted three hundred acres. Pike later became "president" of Woodbridge and soon after was appointed to the Governor's Council. He was awarded the title Captain after serving in the New Jersey militia. His descendent Zebulon Montgomery Pike was an explorer and general, after whom the fourteen thousand-foot-high mountain "Pikes Peak" was eventually named. It is thought that Pike, on one of his many expeditions, was the first American to set eyes upon the mountain in 1806, but his attempt to reach its top failed. Concerned about the increasingly dangerous weather conditions and the physical demands on his soldiers, ill-equipped for the task, General Pike decided to descend to the base.

John Pike died in 1688, just three years into his marriage. Elizabeth lived until 1713, reaching the age of ninety-three. She was buried next to Edward in the west corner of the churchyard at St. James Church. Unfortunately, during the American Revolutionary War, when British troops marched over King George's Highway to Woodbridge Avenue, fortifications were built across the plot. After the war, the cemetery was leveled, making it impossible to locate Edward's and Elizabeth's graves.

The East Jersey Old Town Village

Thomas and Elizabeth had seven children. They were members of the Seventh Day Baptist Church. A weaver by trade, Thomas served two years as Deputy to the General Assembly of East Jersey (1693-94). He owned ninety acres of land in Piscataway, New Jersey. Thomas's son David was elected to the office of Freeholder in 1749 and served in a number of government offices, including Overseer of Roads. David is thought to have built the Fitz Randolph House, in 1743. According to the East Jersey Old Town Village, the house is representative of some of the first farmhouses that were small shelters built toward the middle of the eighteenth century on the higher elevations surrounding the Raritan River. The original wood floors and plaster walls remain as do the original hardware on the doors as well as many of the windows (with their panes). The house was occupied by generations of David's family until 1848.

The Fitz Randolph House in East Jersey Old Town Village—Author Photograph

The Fitz Randolph house is now an historic building in the East Jersey Old Town Village. The Village exists today mainly as a result of the efforts of a local physician, Dr. Joseph Kler, of nearby Bound Brook, New Jersey. In 1929, the Wisconsin-born doctor became the first staff physician at Rutgers University, its campus slightly north of the Village. Dr. Kler had a passion for historic preservation during an era that was antithetical to urban renewal. As the Indian Queen Tavern awaited the demolition ball in 1971, Dr. Kler, keenly aware of the historical significance of the inn, assembled a group of dedicated volunteers who obtained permission to move the tavern across River Road.

The Indian Queen Tavern in East Jersey Old
Town Village—Author Photograph

Its name has changed from Drake's Tavern (after James Drake, operator of the ferry between New Brunswick and Highland Park) to the Indian Queen Tavern, but its place in early American history has clearly been established. George Washington once attended a dinner there in his honor. The East Jersey Old Town Village reports that the tavern is believed to have been built originally as a private home in the early 1700s, and later enlarged. By the time of the Revolutionary War it was considered to be a rather upscale establishment. David McCullough, in his Pulitzer Prize-winning book *John Adams*,[31] recounted one of the most humorous tales of the Revolutionary War, and it occurred at the Indian Queen Tavern. McCullough relates that Benjamin Franklin and John Adams had journeyed to Staten Island following Congress's agreement to accept the request of General William Howe, the Commander-in-Chief of the British forces, for a meeting to try to reach an agreement to end the war following the disastrous British defeat in the Battle of Long Island, August 27, 1776.

John Adams and Benjamin Franklin at the Indian Queen Tavern

Benjamin Franklin travelled from Philadelphia to the meeting in a two-wheel chaise accompanied by a servant; John Adams, who had opposed

Howe's proposal from the beginning, rode on horseback, unaccompanied. On their way to Staten Island, the two met and stayed at the overcrowded Indian Queen Tavern, then located in New Brunswick. The tavern being already overbooked, they were forced to share the same room—and its one bed—for the evening. McCullough does not fail to recount the ensuing comical aspects of these two distinguished Founding Fathers—a veritable Revolutionary War "Odd Couple"—forced to spend the night together.[32] While Adams complained that the room was too cold, Franklin kept opening the window wider, insisting that fresh air prevents disease. They debated the scientific considerations of Franklin's argument to no avail. Adams later wrote: "I was so much amused that I soon fell to sleep." In the end, though, it appears that Adams may have won the argument. In his biography of Dr. Benjamin Rush, Stephen Fried quotes the renowned physician on the death of Benjamin Franklin: "As the last word on their long debate about dangerous air, Rush noted that Franklin's 'pleurisy was caught by lying with his windows open.' "[33]

Because of Dr. Kler's leadership and dedication, the historic Indian Queen Tavern became the centerpiece in what later became the East Jersey Old Town Village, where other structures from nearby New Brunswick and Somerset County have been assembled to portray the diverse history of central New Jersey during the Fitz Randolph years. The Fitz Randolph House was moved into the Village from its original location across River Road, which runs alongside the park, at Low's Road, about a quarter of a mile north. The Village is located along the Raritan River in Piscataway, New Jersey.[34] Long before the Dutch and English first traveled on it, the river was famous for transportation and trade by the Naraticongs of the Lenapes and by the Iroquois Nation. The Raritan River was crossed by troops during the Revolutionary War, and a battle raged nearby in 1777. Much later it was a prominent location for mills and factories.

Unfaltering Trust focuses on the lives and descendants of three sons of Edward Fitz Randolph Jr. and Elizabeth Blossom: Benjamin (b. 1663), Joseph (b. 1655) and, primarily, Nathaniel (b. 1642), and their impact on the development of the Unites States of America from colonial times to the twenty-first century.

Descendants of Edward Fitz Randolph Jr. (1607-1675) and Elizabeth Blossom (1620-1713)*

Nathaniel Fitz Randolph (1640-1640)
Nathaniel Fitz Randolph (1642-1713) & Mary Holley (1644-1705)
Mary Fitz Randolph (1644-1649)
Hannah Fitz Randolph (1649-1743) & James Taylor (1648-1719)
Mary Fitz Randolph (1650-1738) & Samuel Hinkley (1642-1727)
John Fitz Randolph (1652-1652)
John Fitz Randolph (1653-1726) & Sarah Bonham (1684-1737)
Joseph Fitz Randolph (1656-1726) & Hannah Conger (1670-1726)
Elizabeth Fitz Randolph (1657-1702) & Andrew Wooden (1662-1702)
Thomas Fitz Randolph (1659-1745) & Elizabeth Manning (1669-1731)
Hope Fitz Randolph (1661-1703) & Ezekiel Bloomfield (1653-?)
Benjamin Fitz Randolph (1663-1746) & Sarah Dennis (1799-1747)

*Note: The genealogy chart presented above, and those throughout the rest of this book, are not intended to show the complete lineage of each Fitz Randolph generation. Genealogy data has been obtained from Ancestry.com, Myheritage.com, and from various Randolph Family records. The charts show the major connections between generations. Names that appear in boldface italics indicate those family members whose stories are included in this book.

PART THREE

Descendants of Benjamin Fitz Randolph (1663-1746) & Sarah Dennis (1709-1747)

▼

Nathaniel Fitz Randolph (1703-1780) & Rebecca Mershon (1710-1789)

Isaac Fitz Randolph (1701-1750) & Rebecca Seabrook (1708-1744)
▼
Benjamin Randolph (1737-1792) & Anna Broomwick (1746-1767)

Nathaniel Fitz Randolph (1703-1780)

Nathaniel Fitz Randolph, great-grandson of Edward Fitz Randolph and Elizabeth Blossom, was the youngest son of Benjamin Fitz Randolph. As his parents had done before him, Benjamin relocated his family from Massachusetts to Piscataway, New Jersey, in 1696. He later moved to Princeton, where he bought about 100 acres of land from Richard Stockton, who had purchased fifty-five hundred acres from William Penn. A portion of Fitz Randolph's land subsequently became part of the original campus of the College of New Jersey, chartered in 1746, and known since 1896 as Princeton University.[35] Richard Stockton's grandson, Richard, was a member of the graduating class of 1748, the college's first; nine years later, at the age of twenty-seven, was elected a trustee of the university. He was the only signer of the Declaration of Independence known to have been imprisoned during the Revolutionary War. He was captured just months after it was signed, following the British invasion of Princeton on November 30, 1776.[36]

Benjamin Fitz Randolph purchased an additional two hundred acres of land in Princeton (which during the Revolutionary War became known as Prospect Farm) and adjacent acreage located on the north side of the town's Main Street between Bayard and Witherspoon Streets. It became known as the Potter Farm in 1824 when John Potter purchased it. Benjamin died in Princeton Township in 1746.

Both Benjamin Fitz Randolph and his wife, Sarah Dennis, whom he married in 1729, were born in Princeton. They were the parents of fourteen children. Nathaniel became a major landowner and respected citizen in Princeton, forever remembered for his efforts in raising funds and donations of land for the trustees to establish the College of New Jersey in Princeton. Nathaniel was the first to donate land, some four and a half acres—now the location of Nassau Hall[37] on the Princeton campus—and funds totaling seventeen hundred pounds (approximately $396,000 in current US dollars). He contributed the first twenty pounds (approximately $4,600). In all, by 1753, owing to Nathaniel's efforts, ten acres of cleared land and two hundred acres of woodland were donated. It is believed that the college would otherwise have been located in New Brunswick, New Jersey had it not been for his initiative. On January 29, 1754 Nathaniel wrote the following note in his personal journal, describing his wholehearted involvement in the establishment of the college:

> When it was first reported that Hamilton, our Deputy Governor, had granted a Charter for a college to be erected in New Jersey and twelve Trustees appointed, I was the first man who proposed to sell subscriptions on foot for this town; also I was the first man that drew a subscription for that purpose and the first man that rode to obtain subscriptions, and did obtain five hundred pounds under the first Charter ... [and] gave a deed to the Trustees for 4 1/2 acres of land for the College.[38]

The College had originally been established by the Presbyterian Synod in Elizabeth, NJ in 1746, where a small group of theological students met in the parlor of the pastor of the Presbyterian Church.

The first roof of the university was raised in November 1755 by the carpenter Robert Smith. In that same year, Nathaniel was present for the laying of the cornerstone of the university. Nathaniel Fitz Randolph's entire plantation was purchased by the College's president, John Witherspoon, from Nathaniel's son-in-law, Thomas Norris.[39] Nathaniel died in 1780 and was interred in the family burial ground. His remains and thirty-two family graves were discovered in 1909 after construction of the university's Holder Hall had begun. Woodrow Wilson, president of Princeton University at that time, directed that the Fitz Randolph family graves be relocated to a new burial site under the eastern arch of Holder Hall. The words on a huge memorial plaque at that location conclude with the following epitaph, in Latin:

> Near this spot lie the remains of Nathaniel Fitz-Randolph the generous giver of the land upon which the original buildings of this university were erected. *In agro jacet nostro immo suo* (Within our field he lies, nay, in his own).

Holder Hall, Princeton University—Author Photograph

Fitz Randolph Memorial Plaque—Author Photograph

Princeton's FitzRandolph Gate dedicated to Nathaniel Fitz Randolph

Augustus Stout Van Wickle, a descendant of Nathaniel Fitz Randolph, bequeathed funds for the construction of the FitzRandolph Gate.

Completed in 1905, it is the main entrance to the Princeton University campus. Because the gate had remained closed after its installation, however, it was considered by many to be a barrier separating the university from the outside community. Indeed, it remained closed for 65 years until, in 1970, that year's graduating class requested that it be opened—and remain so permanently— "as a symbol of the university's openness to the local and worldwide community."

The Fitz Randolph Gate, Princeton University, in 2018—Author Photograph

For many years after its opening, legend had it that if students were to walk through the FitzRandolph Gate on commencement day before services were finished, they would not graduate at all. It has since become a tradition at Princeton that immediately after commencement services the entire graduating class walk out through the FitzRandolph Gate—and into the world.[40] Further honoring the memory of Nathaniel's generosity is the FitzRandolph Observatory, constructed in 1934, providing far greater capacity than the original Halsted Observatory of 1882. Thirty-two years later the university installed a thirty-six-inch reflecting telescope replacing the original that had been in use for over half a century.

Benjamin Randolph (1737-1792)

Charles Wilson Peale, Portrait of Benjamin Randolph, c. 1782, Philadelphia, Pennsylvania, Water Color on ivory, 1 ¼" x 1". Philadelphia Museum of Art, Gift of Mr. & Mrs. Timothy Johnes Westbrook, 1990, 1990-21-1

Benjamin Randolph, the great-grandson of Edward Fitz Randolph Jr. and Elizabeth Blossom, was born in 1737. He was the sixth son of eight children of Isaac Fitz Randolph and Rebecca Seabrook. His father was born and raised in Princeton but moved to Upper Freehold Township in Monmouth County, New Jersey after his marriage to Rebecca. After her death, Isaac married Hanna Dove Lee. They had three children. Isaac died in Upper Freehold Township at forty-nine. By then, Benjamin had moved to Philadelphia, where in 1762 he married Anna Bromwich (Broomwick). She was the daughter of William Broomwick of Princeton, New Jersey. Anna and Benjamin had two daughters.

Benjamin had most probably apprenticed with the Philadelphia cabinetmaker John Jones, from whom Benjamin had rented his first lodging in the city. His wife's inheritance enabled them to purchase property on Chestnut Street, a few blocks from where Independence Hall now stands. Records show that during the French and Indian War, Benjamin was a shrewd investor in privateers (nonmilitary persons who were allowed to engage in war against enemy ships under a commission from the government). The captured ships and cargo were then sold as "prizes of war," a practice authorized under the Prize Law. Proceeds from sales of the items were divided among the privateers, their sponsors, and the American ship-owners including captain and crew. Benjamin was also known as an exporter of lumber to numerous countries. Following Anna's death in 1767, Benjamin married Mary Wilkinson Fenimore.

Profit from his investments enabled Benjamin to expand his cabinetmaking business dramatically by 1764. Purchasing a shop on Chestnut Street, he quickly became known as one of the premier cabinetmakers of the 1760-1780 decades in Philadelphia. He later built a house and larger shop on a lot that been owned by James Hamilton, son of the storied Philadelphia attorney Andrew Hamilton. James had served a one-year term (1745) as mayor of Philadelphia, and for five terms as a member of the Pennsylvania Provincial or General Assembly. He became a member of the Provincial Council in 1746.

A scholarly article in *American Furniture* by Andrew Brunk states that Benjamin Randolph, whose success was rivaled only by Thomas Affleck (with whom his work has often been compared), employed prominent artisans such as Hercules Courtenay, John Pollard, and George Claypoole. While under Benjamin's employ, Brunk tells us, George Claypoole produced many of his most prized works, including eighteen mahogany chairs, two dining tables, two card tables, a breakfast table, a walnut clothes press, a walnut chest of drawers, a mahogany bedstead and cornice, a mahogany sofa, and a mahogany easy chair. He also created the frame for a marble slab for Continental Army General (and delegate to the Continental Congress) Samuel Meredith and his wife, Margaret Cadwalader Meredith. [41] Though not employed by Benjamin Randolph, George's brother Josiah was also among the city's most prominent cabinetmakers.

Benjamin Randolph was most known for his furniture work in the Queen Anne and Philadelphia Chippendale styles. He was called upon by prominent Philadelphians to provide furniture for their new homes, among them, John Cadwalader, an early supporter of the American Revolution who was appointed Brigadier General of the Pennsylvania Militia, commanding troops that crossed the Delaware River with General George Washington on December 25, 1776. Cadwalader commissioned Randolph and Affleck to build the furniture for his new home at 2nd and Spruce Streets, in Philadelphia. One Affleck creation, a mahogany easy chair with its angled knees and hairy paws (1770-71), set a world auction record for a piece of furniture when it sold for $2,750,000 at Sotheby's, New York, in 1987. Nearly a century after his death, Benjamin Randolph's Chippendale chairs were featured in several works by the great Philadelphia artist Thomas Eakins. The bronze plaque (pictured here) is one of those works.

Knitting, by Thomas Eakins (1882-1883, cast 1886), Medium Bronze with brown patina; sand cast in 1886 Size: 20 x 16 1/1 x 5 in. (50.8 x 41.91 x 12, 7 cm) Acc. No. 1887.2.1 Courtesy of the Pennsylvania Academy of Fine the Arts, Philadelphia. Gift of Edward H. Coates

Other prominent Randolph clients included John Dickinson, a Founding Father of the United States and member of the First Continental Congress, and John MacPherson, the Scottish sea captain whose 1760s Georgian-style mansion, "Mount Pleasant" (on which he spared no expense building or furnishing), was described by President John Adams as "the most elegant"[42] of its kind in Pennsylvania. The home was later owned by the infamous Benedict Arnold.

The most famous of Benjamin's clients was Thomas Jefferson, who in 1775 as a delegate to the First Continental Congress (and in the following year at the beginning of the Second Continental Congress), rented residential space from him on Chestnut Street. In May 1776, Jefferson designed a lap desk, commissioning Benjamin Randolph to build it for him. A rectangular box with a small drawer, its two hinged panels on the top, and two retractable legs, can be raised or lowered when reading books or papers. The legs can also be opened and set at an angle for easy use as a writing desk. It was on that very desk—two months after its being commissioned—that Jefferson drafted the Declaration of Independence.

Declaration of Independence Desk (1775-1776), Maker: Benjamin Randolph, Philadelphia, Pennsylvania, Mahogany (Overall Material), Fabric, baiz (Partial Material) Measurements: Overall: 9 ¾ in. x 14 ¾ in. x 3 ¼ in; 24. 765 cm. x 37.465 cm. x 8.255 cm. Unfolded: 19 ¾ in.; x 50.165 cm.—Courtesy of the Smithsonian Institution, National Museum of American History, Washington, DC.

Jefferson counted the lap desk among his favorite possessions, and later he wrote:

> It was made from a drawing of my own, by Ben Randall [sic] a cabinetmaker in whose house I took my first lodgings on my arrival in Philadelphia in May 1776. And I have used it ever since.[43]

Jefferson made use of the desk throughout the Revolutionary War, and afterwards as a diplomat and, ultimately, president of the United States (1797-1801). He presented the desk to his daughter, Eleanor Randolph Coolidge, as a wedding gift in 1825, just months before his death, at age eighty-three. In the November 14 letter accompanying the desk, he boasted, in true Jeffersonian style:

> Mr. Coolidge must do me the favor of accepting this [gift]. Its imaginary value will increase with years, and if he lives to my age, or another half century, he may see it carried in the procession of our nation's birthday, as the relics of the Saints are of those in the Church.[44]

There is no record of any such procession ever taking place. But the desk remained in the Coolidge family until 1880, when they donated it to the Smithsonian Institution.

An outstanding authority on American antiques and on the craftsmen who made them, Thomas Hamilton Ormsbee praised Benjamin Randolph's work as follows:

> Connoisseurs of the Chippendale period of American cabinet making are now agreed that finer chairs were never produced in America. Randolph was a genius in the ability to work in the style of another and yet avoid the copyist's usual crudities and lapses. There is documented proof that he did work for Thomas Jefferson.[45]

Benjamin was reintroduced to the general public in the twentieth century in a 1974 story (published in the Los Angeles Times/Washington Post Service) reporting on preparations for the first major formal dinner for Washington's diplomatic corps to be hosted by Secretary of State Henry Kissinger. The story described the furniture in the room where the dinner was to be held in the State Department's Thomas Jefferson room as follows: "They will find at their service a $50,000 arm chair, plus five matching chairs valued at $20,000 each. The half-dozen chairs are Chippendale walnut attributed to Benjamin Randolph, circa 1765."[46]

Benjamin Randolph continued his cabinetmaking business until he joined the Revolutionary War. He received a colonel's commission. In 1778, as the economy continued its decline, he sold his tools and stock, retiring to New Jersey, where he died in 1791. He is buried in the graveyard of St. Paul's Episcopal Church in Old City Philadelphia.

PART FOUR
Descendants of Joseph Fitz Randolph (1656-1726) & Hannah Conger (1670-1742)

▼

Joseph Fitz Randolph II (1690-1750) & Rebekah Drake (1655-1749)
▼
Ephraim Fitz Randolph (1724-1793) & Rachel Stelle (1720-1791)
▼
Lewis Fitz Randolph (1757-1822) & Rachel Snowden (1758-1822)
▼
James Fitz Randolph (1791-1871) & Sarah Kent (1790-1860)
▼
Theodore Fitz Randolph (1826-1883) & Mary Coleman (1831-1914)
Joseph Fitz Randolph III (1722-1782) & Esther Broderick (1718-1782)
▼
Robert Fitz Randolph (1762-1821) & Anna Campyon (1770-1810)
▼
Joseph Fitz Randolph (1803-1873) & Sarah Ann Cooper (1815-1904)
▼
Joseph Fitz Randolph Jr. (1843-1932) & Hattie Talcott (18846-1891)

Theodore Fitz Randolph (1826-1883)

Theodore Fitz Randolph's father, James, was the great-great-grandson of Joseph Fitz Randolph, the son of Edward Fitz Randolph Jr. and Elizabeth Blossom. Theodore was born in 1826 in Mansfield, Tioga County, Pennsylvania. His mother was Sarah Kent Carman.

James Fitz Randolph and his brother, David, were experienced printers who had received their training while working in Virginia for the *Alexandria Gazette*. They were very active politically in their community.[47] The two brothers established the *Fredonian*, a New Brunswick newspaper, in 1811. James was a United States Collector of Internal Revenue, Clerk of the Court of Common Pleas, and was elected to the New Jersey Assembly in 1823 and 1824. In 1828 he was elected to the 20th United States Congress as an Adams candidate to fill the seat left vacant by the death of Congressman George Holcombe.[48] He was reelected to the 21st and 22nd Congresses as an Anti-Jacksonian, serving until 1833.

The Honorable Theodore Fitz Randolph, Courtesy of the U.S. Senate Historical Office

After John Quincy Adams was defeated by Andrew Jackson in his 1828 reelection bid, his supporters became affiliated with Henry Clay. The Anti-Jackson Party was organized as the National Republican Party in 1825. The Party loathed the "party" politicians for "pandering" to local interests at the expense of the national interest.[49] It was dissolved in 1834, and supporters switched to the Whig Party. Following his political career, James Fitz Randolph was president of a New Brunswick bank. He lived to see his son, Theodore, elected governor of New Jersey in 1869. James died in 1872, the final year of Theodore's term as governor.

Theodore attended public schools in New Brunswick, New Jersey, but before he was sixteen years old he worked for a time as a writer and proofreader for the *Fredonian*, his father's newspaper. When he turned sixteen, Theodore began his work in the coal and iron business. In 1840 he moved to Vicksburg, Mississippi, where he met his wife, Mary Frances Coleman. After twelve years in Vicksburg, they moved to Jersey City,

New Jersey. Theodore's keen interest in mining and transporting iron ore eventually led to his being named president of the Morris and Essex Railroad (M&E), one of the earliest railroads in the United States; Built in 1835, it connected the urban areas of Newark, New Jersey to the more rural towns of Morris County; two years later, under an arrangement with the New Jersey Rail Road (predecessor of the mammoth Pennsylvania Railroad), the M&E extended its service to Jersey City. Originally opened for transporting passengers only, the M&E expanded its service to hauling freight from the iron and coal mines and from the rich agricultural communities.

During Theodore's presidency, the Morris and Essex Rail Road significantly expanded its service to the far western and northern parts of the state. It eventually became part of the famed Delaware, Lackawanna and Western Railroad.[50]

He was also noted for his invention of a stitching machine and a steam-powered typewriter.

In 1859, Theodore was elected to the New Jersey State Assembly, where he served for four years. He became a state senator in 1862, and on February 4, 1863, one month after President Abraham Lincoln's Final Emancipation Proclamation, he delivered what was his most forceful resolution. It had become clear that the war to preserve the Constitution of the United States had become a war for the abolition of slavery. His resolution expressed vehement opposition to the war—reflecting the view of the conservative Democrats of which Theodore was a member. The third point of Senator Fitz Randolph's resolution in the Senate of New Jersey Committee on Federal Relations reads as follows:

> That it is the deliberate sense of the people of this state, that the war power within the limits of the Constitution is ample for any and all emergencies, and that all assumptions of power under whatever plea, beyond that conferred by the Constitution, is without warrant or authority, and, if permitted to continue without remonstrance, will finally encompass the destruction of the liberties of the People and the death of the Republic, and, therefore, to the end that in any event the matured and deliberate sense of the people of New Jersey may be known and declared, we their Representatives, in Senate

and General Assembly convened, do, in their name and in their behalf, make unto the Federal Government this, our solemn protest, against a war waged with the insurgent States for the accomplishment of any unconstitutional or partisan purposes; against a war which has for its object the subjugation of any of the States with a view to their reduction to territorial condition; against proclamations from any source by which, under the plea of "military necessity," persons in States and Territories sustaining the Federal Government, and beyond military lines, are liable to the rigor and severity of Military Law; against the domination of the military over the civil law in States, Territories or Districts not in a state of insurrection; against all arrests without warrant; against the suspension of Habeas Corpus in States and Territories sustaining the Federal Government, "where the public safety does not require it," and against the assumption of power by any person to suspend such writ, except under the express authority of Congress; against the creation of new States by division of existing ones, or in any other manner not clearly authorized by the Constitution, and against the right of Secession as practically admitted by the action of the Congress, in admitting as a new State a portion of the State of Virginia; against the confiscation and seizure of property without judicial process; against the power assumed in the proclamation of the President made January 1, 1863, by which all the slaves in certain states and parts of states are forever set free; and against the expenditure of the public moneys for the emancipation of slaves, or their support at any time under any pretence whatever; against any and every exercise of power upon the part of the Federal Government, that is not clearly given and expressed in the Federal Constitution, "reasserting that the powers not delegated to the United States by the Constitution, nor prohibited by it to the States are reserved to the States respectively, or to the people."[51]

Senator Fitz Randolph's antiwar views expressed the thoughts of New Jersey Governor Joel Parker in his inaugural address. The resolution was adopted by the Senate of New Jersey along party lines within three weeks.

In 1869 Theodore became the twenty-second governor of New Jersey, succeeding Governor Marcus L. Ward. He was the first Democratic governor elected in New Jersey after the Civil War. During his four-year term, the state prison system was restructured, and anti-election bribery laws were passed.

Gov. Fitz Randolph eliminates Camden and Amboy Railroad tax monopoly

One of the Fitz Randolph administration's most notable achievements was the elimination, in 1870, of the railroad monopoly tax, which had given the Camden and Amboy Railroad, the first passenger railroad company in New Jersey history, exclusive rights to transport passengers between the Hudson and Delaware Rivers. In the following year, the Camden and Amboy was also given authority to combine its operations with the Delaware and Raritan Canal Company, thus granting the United New Jersey Railroad and Canal Company exclusive control over both rail and water transportation in the profitable corridor between New York City and Philadelphia. The company had taken advantage of its monopoly by charging outrageous fares for transportation. Two dollars and fifty cents, the price for even a second-class ticket, was more than twice the average weekly wage for a worker in New Jersey at the time. Gradually the company began ignoring needed repairs on the railroad lines, resulting in sometimes fatal accidents.

The most prominent victim of the Camden and Amboy Company's neglect of the line was Cornelius Vanderbilt, who broke one of his legs in a train accident in 1833 on the run between Hightstown, New Jersey and Spotswood. Former President John Quincy Adams was a passenger on that train as well, but he escaped injury. One passenger was killed in the accident—the first recorded death on a train in United States history. (At least one other passenger died of injuries several days after the accident.) It is said that Vanderbilt, who afterwards accumulated his enormous wealth from his railroad operations, vowed after surviving the accident that he would never again travel by train. It was at least one vow that Cornelius Vanderbilt certainly never kept. By the mid-1860s he had become a giant in the railroad industry, counting among his major acquisitions the New York Central Railroad.[52] The Camden and Amboy railroad's monopoly had paid huge dividends to the State of New Jersey, which taxed folks who were traveling through the state, thus negating the need to raise taxes on its residents. New Jersey Almanac.com, published by Joshua Ventures, reports that the corruption that resulted between the "Joint Company" (as the Camden and Amboy was called) and, principally, the Democratic Party in control at the time, was so unscrupulous that it gained the reputation around the country as the "State of Camden and Amboy."

Historian Irving S. Kull described the situation:

> It is not strange that, through the benefits derived by the State from the monopoly, New Jersey could boast that her citizens enjoyed the lowest taxation in the Union, and that her citizens should resent any move which would injure the prosperity of the Joint Companies.[53]

The Establishment of Greystone Park Psychiatric Hospital

In 1870, with Governor Fitz Randolph's leadership and approval, the New Jersey Legislature appropriated 2.6 million dollars for a new mental asylum to be established in Morris Plains, near Morristown. Greystone Park Psychiatric Hospital was completed in 1876,[54] its Second Empire structure designed by the nationally renowned architect Samuel Sloan. It is clear why Sloan had been selected. Six of his previous architectural designs are included in the United States National Historic Landmarks, namely the Fulton Opera House, in Lancaster County, Pennsylvania; the Fayette School, in Philadelphia; the iconic Asa Packer Mansion, in Jim Thorpe, Pennsylvania; Longwood, the Haller Nutt Mansion in Natchez, Mississippi; the Mills Building, at the South Carolina State Hospital; and Leigh Street Baptist Church, in Richmond, Virginia. The construction of Greystone Park Psychiatric Hospital was championed by Dorothea Dix, a nurse and mental health advocate from Massachusetts who had seen firsthand the overcrowded and deplorable conditions that prevailed in the New Jersey's mental hospitals. Dix had toured the jails and almshouses throughout the state, reporting the grim details of her findings to the State Legislature.

Dix implored the legislators to provide "moral treatment" for the mentally ill, emphasizing the extent of the problem by citing the case of a former legislator who in his old age and declining health had been placed in an almshouse. She encountered him in the basement of the facility, where he had no access to any services or comfort. On January 24, 1845, the day after her report was introduced to the New Jersey Senate by Senator Joseph S. Dodd, the resolution to create an asylum passed the legislature. Greystone was built to house about six hundred patients, but by 1911, as the demand for the hospital's services dramatically increased, it was expanded to house more than twenty-six hundred patients, many sleeping on cots placed in long corridors throughout the hospital. In 2019, more than a hundred and forty years after it had originally opened, the hospital provides quality services to the chronically mentally ill in a smaller setting—but with much greater professional care and treatment.

"Mr. Moneybags of Morristown"

Theodore Fitz Randolph's coal company had been one of the largest producers in New York, making him a very wealthy man before he became active in New Jersey public affairs upon moving to Morristown. He was so rich that people in his surroundings commonly referred to him as "Mr. Moneybags of Morristown."[55] When the Republicans took control of both houses of the state legislature in 1871, Theodore became an extremely partisan governor, vetoing most of the legislature's bills. Probably the most notorious of his vetos was brought against the Republicans' effort to restructure the powerful government of Jersey City which was controlled by Theodore's Democrat Party.

As governor, he appointed Henry Kelsey, a newspaper editor from Sussex County, to the office of Secretary of State in 1870. Kelsey went on to serve in that position for seventeen years, being twice reappointed by succeeding Republican governors. He is considered one of the most influential figures in the State House in Trenton in the late nineteenth century.

Gov. Fitz Randolph continued his involvement in politics after completing his term. In 1875 he was elected to the United States Senate, where he served as chairman of the Committee on Military Affairs in the 46th Congress for two years; he also served on a special Senate committee to investigate the disputed election returns from South Carolina during the presidential election of 1876. Senator Fitz Randolph was a frequent critic of President Ulysses S. Grant, but like Grant, he was opposed to government aid to parochial schools. He was an early advocate of the redemption of paper currency. In 1882 having completed his second term in the Senate, Theodore retired to his home in Morristown, New Jersey. He had not been in good health, and died from heart disease at his home in 1883.

Joseph Fitz Randolph (1803-1873)

Joseph's father, the Rev. Robert Fitz Randolph, was the son of Joseph Fitz Randolph III, and the great-grandson of Edward Fitz Randolph Jr. and Elizabeth Blossom. Joseph was born in New York City on March 14, 1803, and grew up in Piscataway, New Jersey, the epicenter of the Fitz Randolph family. He attended private schools there and had several private tutors. Although he had been preparing to enter Rutgers University, Joseph changed his mind and decided to study law. At the age of twenty-two he was admitted to the New Jersey Bar and began his law practice in Freehold, New Jersey. He became a prosecuting attorney for Monmouth County in 1836.

Shortly after becoming prosecutor, Joseph entered politics and was elected Congressman-at-Large to the 25th, 26th and 27th Congresses as a member of the Whig Party. While serving in the 26th Congress he was chairman of the Committee on Revolutionary Claims. After six years (1837-1843) he left Congress, returning to his law practice and moving his residence to New Brunswick. Still very much interested in politics, he became a delegate to the New Jersey State Constitutional Convention in 1844, serving on a committee responsible for revising the statutes of the State of New Jersey.

In 1845 Joseph and his wife, Sarah, relocated again, this time to Trenton, whereupon he was appointed an Associate Justice of the New Jersey Supreme Court, a position which he kept until 1852. As the threat of civil war continued to intensify, he agreed to serve as a member of the Peace Conference of February 1861, held in Washington, DC. The conference was established at the urging of former President John Tyler when, upon Georgia's becoming the fifth state to secede from the Union, civil war appeared to be inevitable. The fifty-eight-year-old Joseph Fitz Randolph was probably the youngest delegate to the group, which was scoffed at by critics as an over-the-hill gang led by the ailing and aging former president. In fact, John Tyler died one year later, at age seventy-two. The Conference received no support from Lincoln, who feared that any further agitation created by the conference could worsen the situation if no compromise could be negotiated. The delegates (representing twenty-one states) met at the Willard Hotel in Washington, DC. After a month of meetings and proposals to achieve a compromise that would keep the slave states in the union, the Peace Conference of 1861 failed. Just weeks later, on April 12, war broke out.

In a report on the delegates and proceedings of the conference, published three years later, L. E. Crittendon wrote:

> Alas, a great many historians will write about the failure of compromise and how the great compromisers of 1850 were no longer on the scene in 1860-1861 to prevent the Civil War. From the speeches by congressional representatives and senators of the slave states, it is quite clear that nothing but a perpetual guarantee of slavery and the acquiescence in all pro-slavery policies would have been sufficient.[56]

The Honorable Joseph Fitz Randolph—lawyer, prosecutor, judge and would-be peacemaker—passed away on March 20, 1873. He was laid to rest in Easton Cemetery, Easton, Pennsylvania.

Justice Randolph Manning (1803-1864)

Justice Randolph Manning by Lewis T. Ives, Courtesy of the Michigan Supreme Court Library

Joseph Fitz Randolph's great-nephew, Justice Randolph Manning, the son of Samuel Manning and Elizabeth Fitz Randolph, shared a devotion to politics and government service similar to that of his great uncle. Born and raised in Plainfield, New Jersey, Randolph studied law in New York City, where he was admitted to the bar in 1832. He moved to the City of Pontiac, in what then was the Michigan Territory, where he established a law practice. When the State of Michigan was formed in 1837, Randolph, twenty-three, was elected to the 5th District of the Michigan State Senate. In the following year he was appointed Secretary of State, a position in which he served for two years, soon afterwards serving as Chancellor of the Michigan State Court of Chancery (1842-46). He also served on the Board of Regents for Michigan State University. Randolph wedded Eliza Carley in 1848, their marriage producing four children: Camilla, Eliza, Randolph Jr. and Isabella. Randolph Manning remained a Democrat until 1854, but his New England ancestry had early on formed his opposition to slavery, resulting in his leaving to join forces with the newly established Republican Party. Randolph Manning was appointed Associate Justice of the Michigan Supreme Court in 1858 and served in that position until his death in Pontiac in 1864.

Joseph Fitz Randolph Jr. (1843-1932)

Joseph's father was a United States Congressman and an Associate Justice of the New Jersey Supreme Court. His cousin, Theodore Fitz Randolph, was a State Senator, Governor of New Jersey, and a United States Senator. What better motivation for a career in government could Joseph Fitz Randolph Jr. have had? After studying at Trenton, Academy, Joseph entered Yale University as a sophomore in 1859, the year his cousin Theodore was elected to the New Jersey State Assembly for his first term. After he graduated from Yale in 1862, Joseph studied at universities in Berlin, Heidelberg and Göttingen, and at the École de Droit, Paris. When he returned to his home in Trenton, he studied law at his father's law office before entering Columbia Law School. He was admitted to the New York Bar in 1866 and to the New Jersey Bar in the following year. He practiced law in New York City for one year and in Jersey City from 1867 until 1911.

Joseph Fitz Randolph, Jr., Photograph, Courtesy of New Hope Historical Society

In 1872, Joseph married Harriet William Talcott in Jersey City. They had no children. Joseph served as Advisory Master in the Court of Chancery of New Jersey from 1885 to 1905, his main responsibility being to preside over equity cases, including property disputes. The court also had jurisdiction over divorce cases and was delegated jurisdiction over "lunacy" cases. Possessing a seemingly boundless energy, Joseph worked as bankruptcy referee in the New Jersey District Court from 1894 to 1898, and served as president of the New York Title and Abstract Company (NYT&C) from 1888 to 1895. Soon after becoming president of NYT&C, he was elected president of the Morristown Board of Education, and Chairman of the Executive Committee of the Morristown Civil Service Association. From 1887 to 1890, he was Trustee of the German Theological Seminary in Bloomfield, New Jersey, which was authorized in 1909 to issue Bachelor of Arts degrees. It changed its name to Bloomfield College in 1961. Joseph was an Elder in the South Street Presbyterian Church in Morristown from 1879 to 1914, and served as manager of the American Bible Society from 1911 to 1916.

After Harriet's death in 1891, Joseph became a partner in two prestigious law firms—Randolph and Talcott; and Randolph, Talcott and Black—while maintaining his own private practice in Morristown. He retired from both law firms in 1905, and from private practice in 1920.

But Joseph had not yet finished with his work on governmental matters. He became an author beginning in 1894 and ending—thirty-four years and seven published books later—in 1929. His works include *Willliams on Executors* (1894); *Randolph on Commercial Paper* in 1901; *Succession Law in New Jersey* (1906); *The Lord's Death* (1909); *New Jersey Transfer Tax Laws* (1913); *The Law of Faith: With a Lawyer's Notes on the Written Law* (1914); *U.S. Inheritance and Transfer Taxes* (1917); *Succession Statutes in New Jersey, New York and Pennsylvania* (1925); and *Beliefs and Bibles* (1929).

In his inspiring book *The Law of Faith*, Joseph summed up his thoughts about the meaning of faith in his life's work:

> Faith then is life's necessity. Is it a duty or an open choice? If man is a workman with tools and powers, must he use them, or may he throw them away? May he elect not to believe what he sees—not to recognize established and visible authority—not to follow tried and acknowledged leaders—not to obey any law but his desire—not to aspire to anything better than he is himself? May he refuse faithfulness and truth and obedience and intelligence and confidence, and yet ask them in all those who are bound to him in ties of love and service? With different powers and opportunities men see things differently and must

always do so. But there are things of the spirit, which are as elementary and plain to all as the heat of fire, the cold of ice, the hardness and the crushing weight of iron. Cannot this be said of much simple truth and duty?[57]

Joseph concluded this work with his understanding of the Quaker belief of the spirit within:

> Within us—our faith is our life, and makes us share, knowingly and unknowingly, in the world's life and in the life of the Life-giver. Outside of and around us 'the Faith' is the whole world's life and being—the universe of fact—the created things of God—the gospel—the whole unsearchable purpose, and the very person of Him who is the Life and Truth.

In addition to his books, Joseph wrote twenty-seven articles and essays in one hundred and three publications. His books were so popular that most of them had multiple printings. Joseph Fitz Randolph Jr. died of pneumonia and myocarditis on February 16, 1932, three years after the publication of his final book.

PART FIVE

Descendants of Nathaniel Fitz Randolph (1642-1713) & Mary Holley (1644-1703)

▼

Samuel Fitz Randolph (1668-1754) & Mary Jones (1672-1760)
▼
Prudence Fitz Randolph (1696-1766) & Shubal Smith (1692-1769)
▼
Mary Smith (1717-1784) & Jonathan Dunham (1709-1748)

Edward Fitz Randolph (1672-1760) & Katherine Hartshorne (1682-1759)
▼
Mary Fitz Randolph (1710-1779) & William Thorne (1684-1735)
Mary Fitz Randolph & James Jackson (1704-1750)

Hartshorne Fitz Randolph (1723-1806) & Ruth Dennis (1727-1770)
Nathaniel Fitz Randolph (1714-1780) & Mary Shotwell (1722-1743)
▼
Captain Nathaniel Fitz Randolph (1747-1773) & Experience Inslee (1750-1813)

Nathaniel Fitz Randolph (1642-1713)

Nathaniel Fitz Randolph, the oldest son of Edward Fitz Randolph Jr. and Elizabeth Blossom, married Mary Holley in Barnstable, Massachusetts in 1662, the daughter of Joseph Holley and Rose Allen of Sandwich,

Massachusetts, both originally of Somerset, England. Holley was appointed one of the committeemen for dividing meadowlands in Sandwich, and he was a landowner there. He was included on the list of freemen in 1675, and as such he was accepted as a member of the church and authorized to own land. Nathaniel, Jr. and Mary had seven children: John, Isaac, Nathaniel, Samuel, Joseph, Edward and Martha.

Gerald R. Ford, the 38th president of the United States, was a direct descendant of Joseph and Rose Allen Holley. Ford, born Leslie Lynch King, Jr.,[58] changed his name to Gerald Rudolph Ford, Jr., taking the name of his stepfather. After an extremely difficult marriage, his mother, Dorothy Ayer Gardner, divorced his biological father six months after Gerald was born. In his autobiography[59] President Ford recalled that he learned about his biological father when he was twelve years old. His mother married Gerald Rudolph Ford, a paint salesman, who adopted Mr. Ford. Dorothy Ayer Gardner was a descendant of Experience Holley, the daughter of Joseph and Rose Holley.

Nathaniel Fitz Randolph was one of the first men in Plymouth Colony to seek religious tolerance for the Quakers. After joining the Quakers in 1677, he and many others suffered persecution from the Plymouth Colony government. They were forbidden to practice their religion and were forced to pay taxes to the proprietors to support the established government and church. Any families who refused to baptize their children were banished. Nathaniel and his family moved out of what is now Barnstable County in the following year, 1678, relocating to Woodbridge, New Jersey, in what was known then as East Jersey.[60]

The Proprietors

Proprietorships were awarded by the king to individuals or groups under a charter as payment for debts that he owed them. The proprietors themselves were appointed by the king and given the full prerogative of establishing a government and distributing land in the colonies. They could establish towns and ports and order the construction of public buildings. They also had the authority to establish churches, make laws and issue decrees. Proprietors recovered their investments in the colonies by collecting yearly land fees, called quitrents, from settlers who purchased land from them. Land was titled in the name of the proprietor, not the king. The proprietary colonies were divided into eastern and western divisions, with the East Jersey division associated with New York and New England, while West Jersey was affiliated with William Penn and his Noble Experiment in Pennsylvania.

Nathaniel was appointed Associate Justice of East Jersey in 1688, at a time when tensions between the new king, Charles II, and the proprietors of East Jersey had been rising dramatically. The successors of Sir George Carteret and John, Lord Berkeley became corporate Proprietors of East Jersey and West Jersey respectively.

The Eastern Proprietors demanded more freedom in the administration of their governance. But it had become clear that not only did the new king, James II, have no intention of granting greater independence, he had in fact, decided to strengthen his hold over them. The proprietors' fears were realized when they learned that the king had decided to replace Thomas Dongan, the popular then-governor, with Sir Edmund Andros. However, it soon became apparent to the king that Andros, who had been quite successful in Boston, was so preoccupied with his duties there that he could pay little if any attention to activities in the Province of East Jersey. Tensions were finally eased when William III and Mary, who succeeded James II, expelled Andros. So the proposed changes never occurred in East Jersey, and peace prevailed. Historian Irving S. Kull describes the situation at that time as follows:

> The outburst which greeted the English Revolution in New England and New York had no counterpart in New Jersey. It was assumed that the proprietary authority would be restored. Accordingly, Andrew Hamilton, who had not declared himself for either James II or William of Orange, was the logical person for Governor. He found it necessary to return immediately to England for instructions; but in so doing was captured by the French. There was no legitimate authority left in the province.... From June, 1689 to August, 1692, East Jersey had no government whatsoever. [61]

Such was the tumultuous period of time in which Nathaniel Fitz Randolph was an associate justice serving the needs of the province, helping to provide justice, and keeping local order. In March 1692, Colonel Andrew Hamilton returned to the provinces and was accepted by the English proprietors in East Jersey and West Jersey. Nathaniel was appointed to represent Woodbridge, Middlesex County, in the Provincial Assembly when the East Jersey counties were divided into townships for the administration of local government.

Establishment of the New Jersey State Legislature

Governor Hamilton quickly decided to enforce the payment of quitrents (land taxes, in essence) to support the government. Since the tax had not been collected for thirty years, the decision created considerable agitation among the colonists. Coupled with the king's attempts to recruit soldiers for the war against the French, the proprietors unyielding insistence on their right to collect quitrents drove the governor and the Quaker colonists further apart. Hamilton was removed in 1697 after the East Jersey Assembly used a controversial interpretation of the 1696 Navigation Act to remove him because he had been born in Scotland. His successor, Jeremiah Basse, was so ineffective as governor that Hamilton was reappointed two years later. Despite all of the chaos, Governor Hamilton achieved some notable successes, including the establishment of the first patented postal service. He was also able to remain on good terms with the Quakers. The unusual coupling of the Scotsman and the Quakers enabled him to pass a number of significant laws. Soon, however, he found himself in the same predicament faced by his predecessor with regard to the imposed taxation. Rioting broke out just a few months after Hamilton returned, and he delegated his authority to Lewis Morris in Perth Amboy, the capital of East Jersey, appointing him Chief Justice. Hamilton returned to his home in Burlington, the capital of West Jersey. Irving S. Hull describes the situation: "So systematic was the interference with the course of government that this bears in New Jersey history the name of 'Revolution.' "[62]

East Jersey Proprietors sided with Morris, the West Jersey Proprietors with Andrew Hamilton. Morris, who was born in New York, had distinguished himself for his service in politics for more than half a century. His father had served as a soldier under Oliver Cromwell and been self-exiled. The proprietors of East and West Jersey attempted to settle the dispute over governance by proposing to surrender if King William III would reserve their rights regarding free trade.

But Princess Anne, sister-in-law and cousin of William (who had no children), succeeded him on March 8, 1702, after the king's death from complications of a fall from his horse a month earlier. She accepted the Proprietors' agreement on April 17, and consolidated the two colonies of East Jersey and West Jersey into the Province of New Jersey, making it a royal colony. The queen created a new system of government that by the end of the century led to the establishment of the New Jersey Legislature.

Lewis Morris is appointed first "Separate" Governor of New Jersey

Although the two provinces were united, Edward Hyde, Lord Cornbury, who was the Governor of New York, became the Governor of New Jersey as well when Andrew Hamilton died in 1703. As a result, the two colonies were then governed by one governor, Lord Cornbury, the cousin of the newly crowned Queen Anne. Five years later, Lord Cornbury was removed from the position of governor of New York and New Jersey. Several governors succeeded him until finally, in 1738; Lewis Morris became the first separate governor of New Jersey. With his solid connections among the proprietors both in England and in America, Morris had been influential in the decision of the proprietors to acquiesce to the Queen's decision to unite East and West Jersey as one province. Upon Morris's death, the new governor was faced with the task of dealing with a government in which nine out of the twelve Council seats that had been appointed by Morris were held by proprietors. The remaining three council members were sympathetic to the proprietary cause. The reputation that Governor Morris had earned for his many years of distinguished service in government quickly evaporated, though, after he had taken office. Kull describes the situation:

> With Advancing age ... his egotism led him to believe that his worth was not appreciated, and his administration, instead of being a popular one, was a disappointment to the people, who soon learned by experience that the new governor assumed a different attitude from that which he had previously taken.[63]

Governor Morris's "air of superiority" led him to dissolve three Assemblies in 1744 and 1745. After Morris's death, New Jersey was ruled by a succession of four governors, each of whom possessed a similar type of authoritarian superiority and resulting unpopularity. Nevertheless, both Morris County and Morristown, New Jersey were named for Governor Lewis Morris.

William Franklin, the last to serve as the Royal Governor before the Revolutionary War, was appointed Governor of New Jersey in 1762, his term ending in 1776. The son of Benjamin Franklin, William had learned much from his travels to England with his illustrious father, and had made many friends there. Later, as governor, when it appeared to the English government that William had become lax in enforcing the collection of taxes, William, a fierce Loyalist, replied, "No force on earth is sufficient to make the assemblies acknowledge that the Parliament has the right to impose taxes on America."[64]

William Livingston was a member of the Continental Congress in 1774 and Commander-in-Chief of the New Jersey Militia in 1776, the same year he was elected as the first governor of New Jersey during the Revolutionary War. He was admired not only for his decisive actions on the battlefield, but also for his powerful journalistic skills. He printed numerous pamphlets, writing in favor of the colonists. He was continually reelected to office and served as governor of New Jersey until his death in 1790. Trenton became the capital of New Jersey that same year.

The New Jersey State House, Trenton, shown under restoration in 2019—Author Photograph

Following its move from the eastern capital of Perth Amboy to Trenton, the state purchased land on which to build their new state house capitol. The cost of the purchase was two hundred and fifty pounds, five shillings.

The state's capitol was completed in 1792. Noted Philadelphia-based architect Jonathan Duane designed the original stucco-covered American Renaissance-style structure, locating the Senate and House chambers in opposite wings. The governor's office was located on the second floor. As New Jersey continued to grow, the state house was expanded several times in the nineteenth century by renowned architects John Norman and Samuel Sloan. A fire in 1885 destroyed a large portion of the building, but the governor's office and Senate and Assembly chambers survived. More than two centuries later it remains as the third oldest state house in continuous use. Only the Maryland State Capitol, in Annapolis, and the Virginia State Capitol, in Richmond, are older.

In 1798, the year before he was hired to build New Jersey's first state prison, in Trenton, Sloan built his home at nearby 508 Federal St.

The Termination of the East Jersey Proprietor Corporation

More than three centuries passed before the East Jersey Proprietors finally dissolved their corporation. In 1998 they sold the rights to all their land to the New Jersey Green Acres Program, which had been established in 1951 to help meet New Jersey's increasing need for conservation and recreation space. Two-thirds of New Jersey voters approved a referendum in 1998 that would ensure funding for the Green Acres Program under the Garden State Preservation Trust. By 2011 nearly one and a half million acres of land had been preserved throughout New Jersey.

Even more surprising than the long duration of the East Jersey Proprietors is the fact that the Western Proprietorship—based in Burlington, New Jersey, the original capital of West Jersey—continues to be an active corporation to this day. In 1998 journalist Jerry Schwartz reported a story about the demise of the East Jersey Proprietors:

> There were 12 men, most of them from London. Most would never set foot in the New World. But they owned half of what would become New Jersey... 1.1 million acres of verdant field and forest and pristine shoreline. All but a smattering of those lands were sold off long ago, but the corporation survived, its shares handed down

from generation to generation .... The board has fallen victim to a very modern malady: its shareholders, most of them elderly, are afraid they may face legal liability for environmental and other problems on land the board owns and the increasing amount of taxes.[65]

Rising expenses, including increasing insurance costs, caused the descendants of the proprietors, the most famous of whom was William Penn, to agree to sell the small amount of land that remained. Richard Hartshorne, one of the original East Jersey proprietors, netted $3,000 in the sale.

An amusing account of the present-day activity of the still-lingering West Jersey Proprietors group appeared in the *Hidden New Jersey* blog on July 31, 2013.

As you can guess, the whole shebang became a bit of an anachronism over time, given that virtually all the land in the state is deeded to someone by now. In fact, well over 100 years ago, newspapers including *The New York Times* were writing about the ongoing meetings as a curiosity of the past. The former East Jersey seems to have done just fine over the past 15 years without the Proprietors to settle land disputes, but the West Jersey Proprietors continue to meet at the small Surveyor General's office on West Broad Street in Burlington City. Why, then, is there a meeting place in Gloucester? In the late 17th century, the 21-mile distance to Burlington was deemed to be too far for the area's proprietors to travel for an election. Now it's just a matter of keeping up a 325-year old tradition, maybe mixed with a desire to avoid rush-hour traffic on Route 130. Admittedly, there's not much going on with the proprietors these days— the job is largely symbolic—so the Gloucester bunch are basically getting together to vote on who would have to make the schlep if, indeed, there were any business to be done in Burlington. There's not much prestige to being a proprietor, except, I guess, among history enthusiasts, but the ones in Gloucester at least have a park named for them.[66]

Jonathan Singletary Dunham (1640-1724)

Nathaniel's wife, Mary Holley Fitz Randolph, died in 1702. Four years later Nathaniel married Jane Curtis, of Haddonfield, New Jersey. They had one son, Samuel. During the struggle that involved the contention between the Quakers and Scotsmen, Nathaniel's devotion to Quaker beliefs became so intense that when the Woodbridge Monthly Meeting of Friends was established in 1706, the Meeting was held in his home until the construction of the meetinghouse was completed in 1713, the very year of his death. He was buried at the Friends Meeting House burial ground in Shrewsbury, New Jersey.

Nathaniel's granddaughter, Prudence Fitz Randolph, was the wife of Shubal Smith. Their daughter Mary married Jonathan Dunham, the grandson of Jonathan Singletary Dunham, a prominent (albeit controversial) figure in early colonial New Jersey. Jonathan's grandfather had used the surname "Dunham." The debate over the reason why continues to this day. Although his father was Richard Singletary, did Jonathan use the name "Dunham" because, as some argue, he was the son of Richard's previous wife thought to be named Dunham? Or, as others suggest, did he use "Dunham" because he was expecting an inheritance from the Dunham family in England?

Jonathan Singeltary Dunham House, Woodbridge, N. J.—Author Photograph

The ancestors of President Barack Hussein Obama

Jonathan Dunham, also known as Jonathan Singletary (and Jonathan Singletary Dunham), was born in Salisbury, Massachusetts, in 1640. Jonathan's father was Richard Singletary, but the identity of his mother is uncertain. She is thought to have been Susan Cooke, but his mother could also have been his father's previous wife, who died about two years after Jonathan was born. While her surname is thought to have been Dunham, her first name remains unknown.[67]

Jonathan left Massachusetts because, like the others of his faith, he was persecuted by the Puritans, whereas the proprietors in New Jersey guaranteed total religious freedom to all who settled there. He married Mary Bloomfield and moved from New England to New Jersey, where the governor granted him two hundred and thirteen acres of land in Woodbridge Township.

Jonathan will always occupy a prominent place in New Jersey history as the man who, in 1670, built the state's first grist mill. Located on Port Reading Road at the Woodbridge River, it had been in continuous use for nearly two hundred years. Along with the mill, he built his house, which is the oldest building in Woodbridge Township (and one of the oldest in Middlesex County). Originally a two-story structure, additions a century later doubled the square footage of the house. In 1873, the house was given to the adjacent Trinity Episcopal Church, which has used it as their rectory since that time. During the 1680s, East Jersey (where Woodbridge was located) and New York were known widely as the "Granary of the West Indies" because of their large volume of grain exports to that region.

Millstone from Jonathan Singletary Dunham's grist mill—Author Photograph

In addition to his work as a miller, Jonathan became involved in the politics and government of Woodbridge Township, serving as its court clerk and overseer of highways. He was elected to the New Jersey Provincial Council in 1673, the year that the Jersey Blues, the oldest military militia in the state, was created to monitor the Native Americans who were coming from New York and Pennsylvania to hunt and fish.

Memorial Stone erected "in memory of Jonathan Dunham"—Author Photograph

Jonathan died in Woodbridge in 1724. Historian Joseph W. Dally describes the character of Jonathan Singletary Dunham in his book *Woodbridge and Vicinity*:

> Dunham was a man of great energy. When he determined upon an enterprise he pushed it forward to success with indomitable perseverance. So many of his relatives settled in the north of the Kirk Green that the neighborhood was known as Dunhamtown for many years.[68]

President Barack Hussein Obama is a direct descendant of Nathaniel Fitz Randolph and Mary Holley through their son Samuel Fitz Randolph and his wife, Mary (nee Jones). Their daughter, Prudence Fitz Randolph, married Shubal Smith, who was very active with the Woodbridge Friends Meeting House and had been given the responsibility to manage the Friends burial ground. Their daughter, Mary Smith, married Jonathan Dunham, the grandson of Jonathan Singletary Dunham. S. Ann Dunham, President Obama's mother, was the eighth cousin, once removed, from Nathaniel Fitz Randolph.[69] (See the Appendix for the genealogy of Barack Hussein Obama.)

Mary Fitz Randolph (1710-c. 1779)

Band Sampler, Maker: Mary Fitz Randolph, ca. 1726. Materials: Linen and Silk, Embroidered, Woven (Plain), Museum purchase with funds provided by the Centenary Fund. Winterthur Museum

Mary Fitz Randolph was the older of two daughters of Edward Fitz Randolph and Katherine Hartshorne. Their younger daughter, Margaret, died before she was two years old. Even if it were true that Mary, as some writers suggest, was married five times, she would still have been no match for her remote ancestor, Charlemagne, whose wives and concubines totaled at least ten. Mary's first husband was William Thorne (1704-1750) of Flushing, Long Island. They were married on April 17, 1729 at the Plainfield Monthly Meeting. He died in 1750, when Mary was pregnant with their fifth child.

A year later, Mary, a twenty-five-year-old widow with five children to feed and nourish, married James Jackson, her first husband's brother-in-law, a recent widower, having lost his wife, Sarah Thorne.[70] Mary gave birth to five more children before her husband's untimely death at age forty-six. These two are the only marriages of Mary Fitz Randolph for which there is any evidence. A report of a marriage to Joseph Fitz Randolph, a cousin, cites no supporting documentation for it. The report of a third marriage of a "Mary Fitz Patrick, Spinster, to Marmaduke Horseman" (who was believed to be over eighty years old), has not been documented. The "Jacksons plus Relatives and Neighbors Report" in Ancestry.com (updated on October 30, 2017) notes that it is "unknown why researchers have decided that this spinster named Mary Fitz Patrick was Mary Fitz Randolph-Thorne-Fitz Randolph. She wasn't a spinster."

There was thought to have been a fifth marriage, purportedly to another cousin, Jacob Fitz Randolph, who mentions his wife's name ("Mary") in his will, but whether she is the "Mary Fitz Randolph" born in 1710 has yet to be decided. The Morven Museum's biographical outline of Mary Fitz Randolph appears to clear up the entire confusion over her marriages. It points out that she had a cousin and a niece, both of whom were named "Mary Fitz Randolf" [sic]. This coincidence may be the basis for claims by some researchers that Mary was married five times. Mary is thought to have spent her entire life in Woodbridge, New Jersey. She was married only two times, both husbands dying at early ages.[71]

Before any of her marriages, Mary, at the age of sixteen, created a "sampler," the earliest one known to have been made in New Jersey. Samplers date back to Peru three hundred years BC. The earliest work was done in cotton and wool pattern darning on a woven cotton ground. By Mary's time, in the early eighteenth century, they were embroidered textiles used as school exercises and to teach stitchery. Alphabets and verses of poems were added, as well as maps, calendars and multiplication tables: all as part of a young girl's education. Each sampler is the record of a girl's training and confirmation of their cultural standing. For poorer girls the sampler was a way to teach the useful trade of sewing skills for future employment. Samplers were also used to teach religion, family responsibilities and civic duties.

Mary's sampler (recently purchased for its collection by Delaware's Winterthur Museum) is inscribed "MARY FITZ/RANDOLPHH/ AGED 16 YEARS/ MAY 24, 1726," the date of her sixteenth birthday. Winterthur describes Mary's sampler—with its seventy-four figures of birds, plants and mythological beings—as follows:

> This is a linen band sampler worked in 1726 with silk threads by Mary Fitz Randolph of Woodbridge, Middlesex County, New Jersey. Mary's sampler is worked in a style more characteristic of the late 17th century. It is long and narrow, and contains ten bands of various geometric, vine and floral motifs worked in polychrome silk." The dimensions are 22.75" x 6.75".[72]

Henry Francis du Pont, horticulturalist and founder of the Winterthur Museum, is known to have had a love for textiles and needlework. His father, Henry Algernon du Pont, was a West Point graduate and Civil

War hero (earning a Medal of Honor and the rank of colonel). After the war he was elected United States Senator from Delaware. His son's life trajectory was entirely different. As the only one of six children to survive early childhood, Henry Francis was under the constantly watchful eye of his mother. Although a poor student who originally had a low opinion of his own intelligence and ability to learn, Henry managed to graduate from Harvard University. In his early 40s, Henry became interested in American decorative arts and furniture, and was soon preserving the furnishings of old houses scheduled for demolition. His enthusiasm for sharing the knowledge and pursuit of his collections dramatically helped alleviate his well-known shyness, and he became a respected authority on American decorative arts. So respected in his field was he that when Jacqueline Kennedy formed a committee to oversee the White House Restoration, the First Lady designated Henry as chair of the twelve-member panel.[73]

Winterthur is the legacy of Henry Francis du Pont, the great-grandson of the French-American chemist Eleuthere Irenee du Pont, who in 1802 founded E. I. du Pont and Company, the largest manufacturer of gunpowder in the United States. His heirs continued to expand the company, making it the second largest chemical company in the world. But Winterthur was the culmination of Henry's dream to create a place to preserve the best of American furniture and craftsmanship. Winterthur opened its doors to the public as a museum in the autumn of 1951. Outstanding among its famed needlework collection of over seven hundred pieces is the early eighteenth-century sampler of the young Mary Fitz Randolph.

Hartshorne Fitz Randolph (1723-1806)

Hartshorne Fitz Randolph was the son of Edward Fitz Randolph and Katherine Hartshorne, and the great-grandson of Edward Fitz Randolph Jr. and Elizabeth Blossom. His maternal grandfather, Richard Hartshorne, born in 1641, emigrated from Hathhearne, Leicester, England in 1669, and settled in Weikec, Monmouth County, New Jersey, along Raritan Bay. Richard was a lawyer who, after four terms as a Member of Council, became a member of the Provincial Assembly of New Jersey, serving in that position from 1682 to 1704. He was also the Speaker of the Assembly four times. In 1670 he bartered for 2,320 acres of land from the Lenape Indians in exchange for trinkets, alcohol and firearms. His holdings in Middletown Township included all of Sandy Hook. He later built a house on Navesink Highlands (at the time, known as "Portland Poynt"), becoming the first permanent settler in the area. In acquiring the vast amount of land, Richard Hartshorne agreed to allow the Lenape to continue hunting, fishing and harvesting beach plums whenever they wanted. The "Guide to the Hartshorne Family Papers," published by the New Jersey Historical Society, notes the following:

> It is a tribute to Richard Hartshorne and other early settlers of the Bayshore area that in settling here they spilled not a drop of Indian blood in battle, nor did they take an acre of land without the consent of the Indians.[74]

Richard later moved to Middletown Township, where he resided until his death in 1722. He and his brother, Hugh, a Londoner, and a skinner by trade, were confirmed as New Jersey Proprietors in 1682. Richard's influence as a community activist was so powerful that when William Penn and his trustees were assigned the deed to West Jersey Province, they first wrote to Richard Hartshorne, who was already in the province, requesting his consent to be joined with James Wasse and Richard Guy, whom they had authorized to act on their behalf in the public affairs of the colony. Their letter to Richard Hartshorne sets out the details of their proposal:

> There we lay a foundation for after ages to understand their liberty as men and Christians, that they may not be brought in bondage, but by their own consent; for we put the power in the people, that is to say, they to meet and choose one honest man for each propriety who hath subscribed the concessions; all these men to meet as an assembly, there to make and repeal laws, to choose a governor, or a commissioner, and twelve assistants to execute the laws during their pleasure; so every man is capable to choose or be chosen. No man to be arrested, condemned, imprisoned, or molested in his estate or liberty but by twelve men of the neighbourhood; no man to lie in prison for debt, but that his estate satisfy as far as it will go, and be set at liberty to work; no person to be called in question or molested for his conscience, or for worshipping according to his conscience; with many more things mentioned in the said concessions.[75]

Richard agreed to adopt Penn's proposal, thus opening West Jersey for colonization. In the following two years five ships brought eight hundred emigrants, most of them Quakers, to West Jersey. Two companies of Friends, from Yorkshire and from London, were the first purchasers of large tracts of land. Soon the proprietors authorized these groups (and others) to purchase land from the Natives. These settlers were followed by two hundred and thirty emigrants from Kent. The colony of West Jersey prospered under the guidance of William Penn.

In 2019, Richard Hartshorne's land is known as Hartshorne Woods Park. It comprises seven hundred and thirty-eight acres in New Jersey's Bayshore Region of Monmouth County, encompassing sixteen miles of trails, a small beach and a fishing pier. Its southern borders are Hartshorne Road and the Navesink River.[76]

Hartshorne follows his grandfather's role as a community leader

The same kind of moral character and resolve possessed by Richard was certainly passed on to his grandson, Hartshorne Fitz Randolph, who became a leader of his community and fought for the rights of the downtrodden and enslaved. Hartshorne married Ruth Dennis in 1745. They were Quakers and met for worship in the home of William Schooley. They had seven children: Anna, Phineas, Mary, Katherine, Elizabeth, Edward and Richard. In 1758 the Quakers obtained permission from the Woodbridge Monthly Meeting to buy property and build a meetinghouse and plots to bury their dead. After receiving the approval, they raised seventy-three pounds (approximately $13,600 in 2019 US currency) to construct a meetinghouse. Built in Mendham Township, Morris County, it was named the Mendham Meeting. In 1973 the meetinghouse was listed on the New Jersey Register of Historic Places (and on the National Register of Historic Places) as the "finest example of a rural meeting house interior" in the nation.

Friends Meeting House, Randolph, New Jersey in 2018—Author Photograph

In 1753 Hartshorne Fitz Randolph purchased at sheriff's sale a property in the Mine Hill area of Morris County (later Randolph Township)[77] because of its proximity to the meetinghouse. One of the pioneer settlers of the area, Hartshorne built his home on the property—formerly owned by John Jackson, proprietor of a local forge—on what is now Randolph Avenue. He gradually expanded his land holdings by hundreds of acres to build to a farm.

Hartshorne's home was destroyed by fire in 1786, but the meetinghouse still stands today on Quaker Church Road. A magnificent residential community now occupies the vast acreage of land that encompassed Hartshorne's farm in the eighteenth century.

The iconic Singer Sewing Machine Company operated a mine in the Mine Hill area. Isaac Merritt Singer obtained the first patent ever for a machine that drilled through rock. The company sent the ore that it dug from those hills to the Stanhope Furnace for processing. The furnace had been producing iron since 1794; its location on the Musconetcong River, and proximity to the great abundance of iron ore deposits located in the area's twenty-two mines, made it an ideal place for production. Singer had introduced his first Singer Sewing Machine in 1851. Three years later, Elias Howe, who had accused him of stealing his design for the machine, won a patent suit against Singer, and was paid a royalty for every future Singer Sewing Machine sold. His production facilities in New York City and in Elizabeth, New Jersey, produced a total of sixteen thousand sewing machines by 1860. Singer, however, went on to create numerous patents, dying a multi-millionaire in 1875 in England.

It was in Mine Hill where John Jackson's forge produced iron bars that were purchased by manufacturers as far away as Paterson, New Jersey. Jackson declared bankruptcy, however, mostly due to the financial problems he encountered after the British Parliament passed the Iron Act in 1750, which placed strict limitations on manufacturing products in the colonies. Parliament had wanted it both ways. Even as the British encouraged the colonies to produce raw iron ore, they feared competition with manufacturers in England. The Act prohibited the construction of any kind of mills that would enable the mine owners to refine the iron for the purpose of producing marketable products, imposing a fine of two hundred pounds for each offense.

An advocate of the antislavery movement, Hartshorne in 1793 joined with fellow Quakers Isaac Hance and Henry Moore to establish The New Jersey Society for Promoting the Abolition of Slavery, the first antislavery society in New Jersey. The West Jersey Quakers were aligned with antislavery movements in Philadelphia, where the first antislavery protest in the colonies had occurred over a century earlier (in 1688) in the Germantown section of the city. The Pennsylvania Abolitionist Society was established in 1775. Five years later at the Pennsylvania State House (Independence Hall), the Pennsylvania Assembly passed the first state law in the country mandating the "gradual abolition of slavery."

Independence Hall, Philadelphia—Author Photograph

The New Jersey Society protested slavery in a peaceful way by refusing to purchase any goods produced by slave labor. Most Quakers in East Jersey, however, opposed the abolitionist movement, primarily because of their heavy dependence on slaves for working their large plantations and farms. Slave labor had also been crucial to the success of Quakers' businesses in England, even to the extent of their owning a Quaker slave ship, *Society*, which was used in the operation of their lucrative cocoa production business. The Quakers gained control of the confectionery market by Victorian times, eventually leading to their ownership of the three major manufacturers of chocolate in Great Britain: Cadbury, Fry and Rowntree. In America, slave labor was critically important for work on docks and ports. The dependency on slaves in New Jersey's Bergen and Monmouth counties was greater than anywhere else in the state. Support for The New Jersey Society for Promoting the Abolition of Slavery faded after enactment of the state's Gradual Abolition Act of 1804. The law required that every child born of a slave after July 4, 1804 "shall be free; but shall remain the servant of the owner of his or her mother, …and shall continue in such service, if a male, until the age of twenty five years; and if a female until the age of twenty one years." The Society was officially dissolved in 1817.

Hartshorne Fitz Randolph was elected Freeholder of Morris County for Mendham Township in 1757, serving in that capacity for twenty years. He was forced to appear before the Council of Safety in 1777 because of his pacifist beliefs and his reluctance to support the Continental Army. Hartshorne was released, however, when he convinced authorities that neither he nor members of the Quaker Meeting were at all disloyal to the government. Nevertheless, the Whigs confiscated the Quakers' cattle, crops and clothing, and fined them for failure to pay war taxes. Refusing to collect taxes he resigned his position as tax assessor in 1777. Historian Richard T. Irwin notes that Hartshorne "held the additional posts of assessor and moderator, of which the latter was similar to our mayor. This pattern of leadership in local affairs was interrupted by the crisis of the American Revolution.... and began a political exile that was to last for a decade.[78]

Although Hartshorne maintained his Quaker pacifist views, his son, Phineas Fitz Randolph, served in the Morris County Militia as a private, assigned to guard properties in Succasunna and Elizabethtown, New Jersey.

When membership declined after the war, the Mendham Meeting joined with the Hardwick Meeting, creating the Hardwick-Mendham Monthly Meeting. In the following year the population of the northern part of Mendham had grown so large that it was decided to create a new township. The citizens named it Randolph Township in honor of the first-generation Quaker leader, Hartshorne Fitz Randolph. Hartshorne died in 1805. Hardwick-Mendham Meeting changed its name to the Hardwick-Randolph Meeting in 1811, paying further tribute to the popular Quaker leader. Hartshorne Fitz Randolph is buried in an unmarked grave, as he had instructed, in the cemetery at the Randolph Friends Meeting House.

Captain Nathaniel Fitz Randolph (1747-1780)

Nathaniel Fitz Randolph was the first son of Nathaniel Fitz Randolph and his second wife, Mary Shotwell. In 1772 he married Experience Inslee, the daughter of Jonathan Inslee, Jr. and Grace Moores. Her father served in the Revolutionary War, dying in battle on February 4, 1777. Nathaniel and Experience's son was born in 1773 but died in infancy. The couple's only other child, Nancy Agnes, lived to be ninety, passing away on April 15, 1865.

Unlike his uncle, Hartshorne Fitz Randolph, who strictly adhered to his Quaker pacifist beliefs as he settled in what is now Randolph, New Jersey, Nathaniel Fitz Randolph served with the New Jersey Militia, distinguishing himself for his outstanding bravery in the Revolutionary War.

Militias were strike forces that moved in small groups to disrupt British food supplies and stop raids on local farmers; they were also charged with the responsibility for keeping roads open and guarding prisoners who were being transported to trial. Viewed as a vital part of the war effort by General Washington, the New Jersey Militia assisted his troops in the Battles of Long Island, Staten Island, and Springfield.

While widely respected for his military expertise and daring exploits in all of those battles, Captain Fitz Randolph was also respected for his character. One example of many is that he did not allow his men to torture prisoners or rob them of their possessions—a common practice on both sides.

The heroic exploits of Captain "Natty"

Captain Fitz Randolph's greatest contributions to the militia effort were his brave leadership, rugged stamina and sharpshooter expertise. The militia was able to move quickly to cover territory that needed to be defended. Attacking outposts, they hassled the British troops denying them food and rest, constantly harassing them until the British felt safe only when gathered in large numbers. So successful were the militia's maneuvers that they prompted Hessian Officer Johann Ewald to record in his journal:

> What can you not achieve with such small bands who have learned to fight dispersed, who know how to use every molehill for their defense, and who retreat as quickly when attacked as they advance again, and who will always find a space to hide.

Officer Ewald singles out the New Jersey Militia for its outstanding performance:

> Never have I seen these maneuvers performed better than by the American Militia, especially that of the Province of New Jersey. If you were forced to retreat against these

people you could certainly count on constantly having them around you.⁷⁹

The Battle of Long Island (1776)

The Battle of Long Island was the first major battle and British victory of the American Revolutionary War. It broke out in August 1776, just weeks after the colonies declared their independence. The scope of this battle pitted twenty thousand British troops against ten thousand of Washington's Continental Army. More than a thousand of Washington's troops—eight hundred of them wounded, including Nathaniel Fitz Randolph—were captured and thrown into three hellish prisons. The Bridewell Municipal Prison, named for a London jail, was located at what is now City Hall Park in Manhattan. Construction on Bridewell was halted when the Declaration of Independence was signed, leaving it without a roof or windows. The Middle Dutch Church was a make-shift prison. Constructed in 1726, the Middle Dutch Church was probably the first church that was built in New Amsterdam. The church's original worshipers could never have imagined its being converted into one of the most notoriously brutal prisons in American history. Of conditions in the Church, the *New York Times* writes:

> The diseases that broke out among them in consequence of the food and crowded quarters were so fearful that the reality, as described by eyewitnesses, exceeds the imaginative horrors of the Bolgias [part of the eighth Circle of Hell] in *Dante's Inferno*. No provisions were made for the offices of nature, and the whole floor of the Church was one cake mass of dead, dying, excrement and vermin…. Men of iron nerves who went in there, came out almost idiots, and, to the last days of their lives would dream that they were back in the hideous den.⁸⁰

Adjacent to the Church complex, the red brick Rhinelander Sugar House warehouse was built in 1763 to store sugar and molasses imported from the West Indies. William Cunningham, the infamous provost marshall of the warehouse-turned-prison, is known to have stolen food meant for the prisoners, selling it for personal profit. Starving prisoners shouted out from the windows, begging passers-by for food. Anyone trying to assist them would be turned away at gunpoint.

Old Sugar House and Middle Dutch Church—"Our Firemen" (1887) by Augustine E. Costello

In 1892, the storage building (by that time known as the Old Sugar House) was demolished and replaced by the Rhinelander Building. In 1968, it too was torn down, replaced by a police headquarters building at the southwest corner of Rose and Duane Streets in New York City. The sole evidence of the hell that existed there is a monument in the area of the police headquarters that features a "Prisoner of War" window from the Sugar House, although it had probably not been part of the prison itself. (Later in the war, when the British could find no more buildings to incarcerate prisoners, they turned to their ships as a last resort. Thousands died in the hulls of the "prison ships" in the harbor.)

A report about Nathaniel having gone home unexpectedly one evening during the war as the British were searching for him provides an example Fitz Randolph's legendary courage. His mother had seen three British soldiers near the house during the day. When Nathaniel showed up unexpectedly, she was horrified. "Why did you come home, Natty? You know the Tories are determined to take you, and three of them have been prowling around the house today." Pointing to his sword and pistol, Nathaniel replied, "Ah, no three men can take Natty alive." But, as the family settled before the fireplace after dinner, a sharp rap on the door alarmed all but Nathaniel. Historian Joseph W. Dally recounts the scene:

Releasing his sword from the bracket on the wall, the soldier replied: "They shall never take Natty alive!" Loud calls from without for the surrender of the sturdy patriot were responded to by the Captain himself, who, flinging open the bolted door, stood upon the threshold with his drawn weapon in his hand. "I am Natty Randolph," he said, pointing a pistol at the group, "and no three men can take Natty alive! The first who dares to stir is a dead man." ... [H]he ordered the men off the property. The melancholy trio rode down the lane, followed by the eagle eye of the American. They knew that two deadly weapons in experienced hands covered them as they departed. They were, therefore, very circumspect in their deportment until they were out of range, when they struck spurs into their horses and scampered away towards Staten Island.[81]

Among the three hundred Americans killed in the Battle of Long Island was Lieutenant Colonel Caleb Parry, the son of Captain David Parry and Elizabeth Humphrey of Chester County, Pennsylvania. They were Welsh Quaker descendants of Thomas Parry, who had settled in Upper Moreland Township, Pennsylvania (then part of Philadelphia) in the latter part of the seventeenth century. Lieutenant Colonel Caleb Parry was the cousin of John Parry, the father of Benjamin Parry of New Hope, Pennsylvania. It was Benjamin's son, Oliver Parry, who in 1827 married Rachel Randolph, the daughter of another Revolutionary War hero, Captain Edward Randolph.

Caleb Parry's death on the battlefield was summarized by the renowned lawyer and author Samuel W. Pennypacker:

> Before light on the fatal morning of the 27th of August ... Atlee was sent forward to check the enemy at a morass, and he sustained a severe artillery fire until a brigade formed on a height.... Within fifty yards of the summit he was, however, received by a heavy fire from the enemy, who had anticipated him.... At first his detachment, consisting of his own battalion and two companies of Delaware troops wavered, but they soon recovered and charged with so much resolution that the British were compelled to retire from the hill, with a loss of fourteen killed and seven wounded. The

men, flushed with their advantage, were eager to pursue, but Atlee, perceiving a stone fence lined with wood about sixty yards to the front, and thinking it might prove to be an ambuscade, ordered a halt. His conjecture proved to be correct. A hot fire was poured into them from behind the fence, but was returned with so much vigor that the enemy retreated. In his engagement, lasting for fifteen minutes, the brave Parry, long lamented as the first Pennsylvanian of distinction to lose his life for the Revolutionary War, was struck on the forehead by a ball and instantly killed.[82]

Lieutenant Colonel Caleb Parry was buried in Greenwood Cemetery, Long Island, leaving behind his young widow, Elizabeth Jacob Parry, and six children. Colonel Atlee's son, William R. Atlee, married Margretta Wayne, the daughter of General Anthony Wayne, who commanded the troops at the disastrous Battle of Paoli—during which Captain Edward Randolph was severely wounded and left for dead by the British. Prior to his service in the war, Caleb Parry had been proprietor of an inn near Paoli. It was from this Admiral Warren Inn on Lancaster Pike that the British under the command of Captain Charles Grey staged the attack on General Wayne's troops at the Battle of Paoli eleven years later.

The Battle of Staten Island (1777)

In the Battle of Staten Island the following year, Nathaniel Fitz Randolph and the New Jersey Militia fought alongside the Maryland Militia and Canadian troops, a thousand men in all, under the leadership of the American Major General John Sullivan. A strategic British outpost throughout the war, Staten Island was the first place where the British troops landed at the start of the war. The battle was totally unsuccessful for Sullivan. Ten of his men were killed, twenty wounded and about two hundred and fifty captured by the British. Fitz Randolph survived the battle but was later captured by the British, spending many months in prison on Manhattan Island, most probably at Bridewell, the most deadly of the prisons. Bridewell had no roof and no glass in its windows, only openings with iron bars. Winter winds took the lives of hundreds of the exposed and ill-fed patriots. Historian Edwin G. Burrows describes Fitz Randolph's condition: "In mid-March, 1777, Captain Nathaniel Fitz Randolph of Woodbridge, New Jersey, got a letter out to his wife with some decidedly mixed news: his wounds were beginning to heal and he was now 'in pretty good health,' but his comrades were suffering dreadfully."[83] One week after being released from that heinous prison, Nathaniel Fitz Randolph gathered his men together and again marched off to battle.

One subsequent, audacious example of Captain Natty's military tactics has become legendary. While alone one night returning on horseback to a fort he had been assigned to, he is said to have spotted an enemy supply train heading toward it. Resolved to thwart their attack by himself, Nathaniel shouted at the top of his voice for his non-existent troops to attack. Fearing that they were actually surrounded, the British troops fled, abandoning their cargo for Fitz Randolph to claim.

On December 12, 1778 Nathaniel was elected Naval Officer of the Eastern District of New Jersey. (On the previous day, the Town Council of Woodbridge ordered that a sword should be purchased for him as a fitting tribute to his patriotism. This was later presented to him.[84])

In January 1779, after several raids on the British in Staten Island, Captain Fitz Randolph went to the home of Charles Jackson in Woodbridge, where he rested for the evening, laying aside his weapons. During the night he was captured by Captain Ryerson and twelve men from Buskirk's regiment who had been pursuing him. Captain Randolph was again imprisoned in New York, this time enduring two years of tortuous treatment at the hands of the notorious and ruthless provost, who deprived all prisoners there of food and water in a building that lacked a roof and window panes, brutally exposing them to the fierce elements of deadly eighteenth-century winters.

Washington's letter addressing Captain Fitz Randolph's capture

Learning of Nathaniel's imprisonment, and well aware of Fitz Randolph's courageous service, Governor William Livingston wrote to General George Washington, requesting that the general consider an exchange of prisoners in order to secure Fitz Randolph's release. Already having heard of Captain Fitz Randolph's bravery during the war, General Washington responded:

To GOVERNOR WILLIAM LIVINGSTON
Head Quarters, Morristown, March 16, 1780
D. Sir: I have received your Excellencys letter of the 8th of this month in favor of Capn. Fitzrandolph. The Capns. known zeal and usefulness entitle him to consideration and I shall be very well pleased if we can effect any thing towards his relief or releasement. At present commissioners from the enemy, and on our part are sitting at Amboy for the purpose of an exchange of prisoners. Should the parties be happy enough to agree upon terms of a general cartel, your Excellency may be assured that in carrying it into effect, I shall give directions that his exchange be made an object.

As much as he may have wanted to release Fitz Randolph immediately, Washington was constrained by his having to treat all of his men equitably:

But if no agreement of this kind takes place, I cannot promise an exclusive or partial exchange for the Captn. The length of confinement of many of our officers, some of whom have been prisoners since the affair of Long Island, has alone made them extremely sensible of any exchange, which has the least appearance of partiality. This, besides infringing the order for carrying on partial exchanges, which gives the preference to the oldest officer in captivity will put it out of my power to do anything in this line; especially under the present state and circumstances of our prisoners. With the most perfect regard etc.[85]

On May 26, 1780, Nathaniel was released in exchange for a British officer of equal rank (a "Captain Jones") who had been captured by Fitz Randolph's men for the specific purpose of exchanging him for their captain's release. As soon as he was released, Fitz Randolph once again returned to battle, whereupon, less than a month later, he was seriously wounded—this time while pursuing the British in retreat from their defeat in the Battle of Springfield. It is said that a musket ball penetrated his left arm below the left shoulder and exited his right breast. Nathaniel was carried off the battlefield by his cousin, Captain Asher Fitz Randolph. He died from his wounds on July 23, 1780.[86]

Undoubtedly one of the most courageous, skillful and dedicated soldiers to fight in the American Revolutionary War, Captain Nathaniel Fitz Randolph was laid to rest at the First Presbyterian Church cemetery in his hometown of Woodbridge, New Jersey (the graveyard where his father-in-law, Jonathan Inslee, had been buried three years earlier). But the British had yet still not finished with Captain Fitz Randolph. Local legend has it that, in a final act of hatred for their brave rival, they used his gravestone for target practice, riddling it with numerous musket balls, some of which remain imbedded in the stone to this day. His desecrated tombstone bears the following epitaph:

Tombstone of Captain Nathaniel Fitz Randolph, First Presbyterian Church Cemetery, Woodbridge, N. J.—Author Photograph

SACRED
to the Memory of
Cap'n Nathaniel Fitz
Randolph, who died
July Ye 23d A.D. 1780
in the XXIII Year of
his Age
Here lies beneath this stone, repos'd
Patriot Merit hous'd;
His Country called, he lent an Ear
Their Battles fought, & rested here.
                              E. Price

PART SIX

Descendants of Capt. Edward Randolph (1754-1837) & Anna Julianna Steele (1761-1810)

▼

Edward Randolph (1784-1834) & Mary Taylor (1789-1867)
▼
Julianna Randolph Wood (1810-1885) & Richard Davis Wood (1799-1869)
Jacob Randolph, MD (1796-1848) & Sarah Emlen Physick (1801-1873)
Rachel Randolph Parry (1804-1866) & Oliver Parry (1794-1874)
▼
Edward Randolph Parry (1832-1874) & Frances Dimick (1845-1914)
Richard Randolph Parry (1835-1928) & Ellen Read (1846-1916)
▼
Captain Oliver Randolph Parry (1873-1958)
William Randolph (1788-1832) & Ann Evans (1795-1874)
▼
Evan Randolph (1822-1887) & Rachel Story Jenks (1845-1924)
▼
Evan Randolph Jr. (1880-1962) & Hope Carson (1885-1980)
▼
Hope Randolph (1908-2002) & William Platt Hacker (1904-2002)
Evan Randolph III (1909-1997) & Frances Lewis Beale (1912-2004)
▼

Evan Randolph IV (b. 1935) & Penelope H. Dixon (b. 1941)
Leonard Beal Randolph (b. 1937) & Sally Ann Schoettle (b. 1940)
John Randolph (b. 1947) & Alice Moffat (b. 1947)
Francis Lewis Randolph (1951-1974)
Hampton Carson Randolph (1911-1998) & Barbara Reeves (1917-1969)
Rachel Randolph (b. 1915) & Arthur Doucette (1907-1995)
David Story Randolph (1922-1972) & Hannah Wright Sullivan (b. 1923)

Captain Edward Randolph—Oil Painting by Robert Street,
Photograph, Courtesy of the Historical Society of Pennsylvania

Captain Edward Randolph (1754-1837)

Captain Edward Fitz Randolph was the son of Richard Fitz Randolph and Elizabeth Corlies. Richard was a carpenter whose father, Edward Fitz Randolph, was known as "the Quaker financier of Woodbridge," a distinction earned when an appeal was made to the Shrewsbury, New Jersey Friends to contribute funds for the building of a Quaker Meeting House in Woodbridge, Edward responding immediately by contributing four pounds, fifteen shillings and ten pence (about eight hundred dollars in value today).

Elizabeth was the daughter of John Corlies, who in 1676 served under the command of Lieutenant Benjamin Swett in King Philip's War (the First Indian War) of 1675-77. On June 29 of the following year Swett, having only days before been promoted to the rank of captain, was brutally slaughtered as he attempted to defend his men at the Battle of Moore's Brook in Scarborough, Maine.[87]

> Captain Swett ... wounded in twenty places, and exhausted by loss of blood and by fatigue, was grappled, thrown to the ground, and barbarously cut in pieces at the gates of the garrison. ...He [had been] a Captain for seven days.[88]

King Philip's War was the final struggle of the Native Americans to rid their land of the colonists, an effort that ended in catastrophic failure. The total number of people killed during the war—some seven percent of the population of the country at the time—makes it, in consideration of the percent of the population killed, the most disastrous war in American history. According to George Ellis and John Morris in their 1906 study, more than fifty English towns were attacked, a dozen of them totally destroyed. Some twenty-five hundred colonists perished, and more than five thousand Native Americans were slaughtered or died from starvation and disease.[89]

> The winter provisions of the Indians had been destroyed, their shelters burnt and themselves driven out into the woods in the dead of winter to face famine. The hornet's nest had indeed been scorched, but the hornets were loose and the plight of the troops, without shelter or provisions, exhausted and exposed to the fury of the elements, was little better than that of the Indians, and only the fortunate

arrival of Captain Richard Goodale of Boston with a sloop load of provisions, at Smith's Landing the same night, saved them from terrible suffering.[90]

After the war, Richard and Elizabeth settled on a farm in Shrewsbury, New Jersey and lived there for the rest of their lives. Richard was one of seven children and is known to have owned one slave. Richard and Elizabeth both died in 1754, the year in which their son, Edward, the youngest of their eight children, was born.

Edward Fitz Randolph (1754-1837) at the Battle of Paoli

The approximate site of the 4th Picket Post commanded by Lieutenant Edward Fitz Randolph—Author Photograph

In 1777, Richard and Elizabeth Corlies Fitz Randolph's son, Edward, who had moved to Philadelphia when he was twenty years old, was appointed to the Council of Safety, the state's primary organ for "expediting laws" to promote the patriot cause and for suppressing treasonous activity against the newly established state government. Edward was believed by the Council to have been warmly disposed to the cause of American independence. On January 3, 1777 he was an ensign attached to the 4th Pennsylvania Regiment. The regiment (initially known as the 3rd Regiment) was raised in Philadelphia in 1775, and was assigned to Thomas Mifflin's brigade in the Continental Army in 1776. He fought in the Battles of Princeton and Trenton. Edward Fitz Randolph went on to fight in all of its battles, including Brandywine, Paoli, Germantown and Monmouth.[91] The regiment was furloughed in 1781 and disbanded two years later.

In 1777, Edward Fitz Randolph, at twenty-three, was promoted to first lieutenant in Captain Benjamin Fishbourne's Company. He was assigned to command the 4th picket post at the infamous Battle of Paoli, all of the men under his command being from Colonel John McGowan's Company of the 4th Pennsylvania. As a picket commander, Lieutenant Fitz Randolph's specific orders were to remain on duty day and night, always on the alert. Fatigue was obviously the most common condition afflicting picket guards.

General Wayne ordered six picket posts to be set up the evening of September 20, 1777, each with a lieutenant, a sergeant, a corporal and sixteen privates. The 4th picket post was the first one that British troops encountered in the pre-dawn hours the next morning on their way to attack General Wayne's headquarters. Under the command of General Charles Grey, the British had been directed there by a local blacksmith, who, coerced into cooperating, directed Grey's forces eastward on the Lancaster Road toward the Warren Pass in the South Valley Hill. Posted just inside the Warren Pass was the 4th Picket.[92]

Although Lieutenant Fitz Randolph and the surprised soldiers under his command were able to fire on the British troops, they were soon overcome, most of them hacked to pieces by sword and bayonet, others captured. General Grey had ordered his troops not to load their muskets in order that no gunshots alert the enemy.

Lying on the battlefield, his left eye gouged out by a British bayonet, Lieutenant Fitz Randolph was left for dead by the British soldiers. The gunshots from Fitz Randolph's picket alerted General Wayne that he was under attack, but his entire command could have been decimated had the British troops taken a different road toward the battlefield. It is uncertain if the blacksmith had deliberately directed the British to use the more difficult route so as to slow them down, or if he had been unaware of the critical differences of his choice of path to the battle entailed. In Thomas J. McGuire's acclaimed book *Battle of Paoli*, appears this grave summary:

> Lieutenant Fitz Randolph and his eighteen pickets valiantly attempted to make a stand, only to be cut to pieces by the British advance guard. The grisly work of bayonets and sabers cost Randolph an eye and nearly his life; the trauma of that night never left him.[93]

General Wayne's command was dispersed and fled west toward Philadelphia. The British army returned to their camp, but only after stopping at the graveyard of Old St. Peter's Episcopal Church in the Great Valley to bury the bodies of Captain William Wolfe and two others killed at Paoli. Fifty-two of Wayne's troops were killed, about one hundred captured, and some seventy others reported missing. Some of those missing are believed to have died after the battle and been buried by the British along with their own casualties at Old St. Peter's Church.

Later in the morning of the massacre, two neighboring Quaker families gathered the fifty-two bodies that lay scattered on the battlefield and buried them in a mass grave; the gravesite of those brave men is today a memorial that honors their valiant battle.

With the same kind of courage with which his cousin, Captain Nathaniel Fitz Randolph, had fought, Edward was not deterred by his life-threatening injuries. His dedication to battle continued. Surviving the brutal winter of 1777 at Valley Forge, he was promoted to the rank of Captain and joined General Washington's Continental Army in its march from Valley Forge to the Battle of Monmouth in June 1778. Many years later, Edward Fitz Randolph's granddaughter, Julianna Randolph Wood, wrote about her grandfather's ordeal and "narrow escape with his life" at Paoli:

> He had been on picket duty and with his comrades was swept away before the overwhelming numbers of the British, who in the darkness of the night came down upon them; he made a narrow escape with his life. While Edward was lying on the ground, dangerously wounded, two English soldiers [dragoons] rode by, and looking toward him, one observed to the other. "There is a head that looks like it has some life in it," and was preparing to shoot when their officer coming up commanded them to desist and save their ammunition—of which they had none too much—for *live rebels*, instead of those who were already dead.[94]

After the Battles of Brandywine and Paoli, the British seized Philadelphia, and General Howe moved most of his troops to Germantown. Based on the similar battle plan he had used so successfully at Trenton, Washington's plan to deploy four columns to converge on the British troops in Germantown failed miserably. A heavy blanket of fog descended on Germantown, creating massive confusion among Washington's advancing columns. General Wayne's forces collided with General Greene's troops, mistaking them for the enemy in the fog of night. Edward Fitz Randolph was one of the five hundred and twenty-one troops wounded in the battle. The British killed one hundred and fifty two men and captured four hundred and thirty-eight. In the following year, Edward, still recovering from his wounds, wrote from Greenwich, Connecticut to his fiancée, Anna Julianna Steele in Philadelphia, the following passage in which he conveys the bad news that his regiment had been ordered to march hundreds of miles to western Pennsylvania to fight the Indians who "were killing women and children and destroying all that comes in their way."

> But I shall not linger on a subject which I imagine to be disagreeable to you—but recommend you to the care and protection of an all sufficient God and until I shall be so happy as to see you again, believe me to be with the greatest esteem and affection.
> Your unhappy tho compliant lover,
> Edward[95]

Greenwich was no respite for Edward after suffering near-fatal wounds at Paoli and Germantown. Since the beginning of the war Greenwich had been torn apart by loyalists (called "Cowboys" by the patriots) and patriots (called "Skinners" by the loyalists)—each battling the other in a bizarre civil war within the Revolutionary War. (Those locals not aligned with either group referred to both sides as "bandits" and "death squads.") Homes were destroyed and fellow-citizens were killed, while many others fled. That was the hostile environment in which Edward Randolph found himself as he prepared to march farther inland to fight the Indians. Less than a year later, on February 26, 1779, General William Tryon led a total of fifteen hundred British soldiers, Hessian mercenaries and loyalist "cowboys" in a full-scale attack on Greenwich, plundering the town, seizing whatever food or livestock they could find, and destroying the nearby salt works.

Edward's Cousin recruited directly by General George Washington

Captain Edward Fitz Randolph's cousin, also named Edward Fitz Randolph, is said to have been recruited personally by General Washington to find the highest point in the area to monitor British troop movements. G. W. Fitz Randolph provides the following account of the story:

In the year 1777 or '78 Washington, with 6,000 men was encamped on the Ridge of Middlebrook near and west of Bound Brook. The British Army was encamped at New Brunswick, Rahway and Perth Amboy, making incursions into the surrounding country. Doubtless, with intent of guarding against a serious incursion of surprise, Washington was on his way to the top of the mountain back of Green Brook. Be that as it may, he, with an aide-de-camp, mounted, rode in the gateway and up to a group of men standing between the house and the barn on the farm, now known as the Jonah Vail farm. Washington said, 'Can any of you gentlemen guide me to some spot on the mountain from whence a good view of the plain below can be obtained?' Edward Fitz Randolph, one of the group, said, 'I know the best point on the mountains for that purpose,' and added that, if he had his horse, he would take him to it. Thereupon the General requested his aide to dismount and await his return. Fitz Randolph mounted upon the aide's horse, piloted the General to the rock, which today bears the historic name of 'Washington's Rock.' I have given the above nearly word for word as given to me by Ephraim Vail, who died a few years since aged 90 and over, on the farm where he was born and raised. Josiah Vail gave me the same version of the incident; indeed any of the old residents of Green Brook would corroborate the same, were they alive. All these Vails were Quakers, owning adjoining farms, and their word is reliable.[96]

Edward Fitz Randolph marries Anna Julianna Steele

Following his two years of heroic service—during which he lost his left eye at the Battle of Paoli, was wounded at the Battle of Germantown and had fought the Indians in western Pennsylvania—Captain Edward Randolph retired from the military in 1779. Longing to be with his fiancée, Anna Julianna Steele, he returned to Philadelphia, where they were married on May 24th of that year. Anna was the daughter of Henry Steele, a German immigrant who had emigrated to America from Berne, Switzerland, and Anna Margaret Ebright Steele. They lived in the Germantown section of the city after moving from Plainfield, New Jersey. It was during that time that he discontinued using the name "Fitz" as part of his surname (as many of the family would eventually do), referring to himself thereafter as Edward Randolph ("as a matter of convenience").[97]

Impact of de Longchamps case on the Constitution's "Law of Nations" clause

Edward and Anna settled into their home at 212 N. 2nd St., just one block north of his place of business at 126 N. 2nd St. They had purchased the house in 1786 from Charles Julien de Longchamps, a former French soldier who, two years earlier, had created an international incident. He was accused of assaulting Francis Barbe-Marbois, the Consul General of France to the United States, on May 17, 1784 after de Longchamps' request to obtain official documents that would verify his commission in the French army was refused by the French Minister at the time, Chevalier de Luzerne, in the house of the French Minister in Philadelphia. (In an outburst of anger, de Longchamps had shoved Barbe de Marbois.) When de Longchamps encountered de Marbois in a local coffee shop a couple of days later, he confronted him and started a fight, beating the consul with his cane so viciously that customers in the shop had to separate them. When de Luzerne called on the United States Congress to extradite de Longchamps, the Pennsylvania Supreme Court ruled that under the Articles of Confederation the State of Pennsylvania lacked the power to turn him over to the French government. Monsieur de Longchamps instead was fined two hundred dollars and sentenced to prison for two years.

Constitutional scholar Richard Tuck has concluded that the de Longchamps case was a driving force for including the "Law of Nations Clause" in the United States Constitution. In 1787, the federal government was given the power "to define and punish ... Offenses against the Law of Nations" (Article I, Paragraph 8, cl. 10). So, although the Court determined that Pennsylvania had handled the matter appropriately, the Court feared that other states could not be trusted to act in the same manner, thus giving the power in such cases to the federal government.[98]

The sturdy old mansion on 2nd Street stood until the mid-1920s, when it was razed because of its being in the line of construction for the newly proposed suspension bridge over the Delaware River.

In 1790, Philadelphia was America's greatest city. It had once again become the capital of the nation. With its solid brick houses, cobblestone streets, brick sidewalks and comfortable public squares, Philadelphia rivaled many of Europe's finest cities. Indeed, Francois Alexandre Frederic La Rochefoucauld-Liancourt referred to Philadelphia as "one of the most beautiful cities in the world."[99] The market on what was originally called High Street (Market Street by 1750) was one of the finest in the nation. By 1792 Philadelphia's imports and exports exceeded those of the former capital, New York City.

Edward and Anna owned a country home in the area around 11th and Master Sts. in Philadelphia. In 2019 that location now lies at the edge of the sprawling Temple University campus, but in the middle of the nineteenth century it was mostly farmland—far removed from the cramped, bustling commercial section of the city near the Delaware River where Edward's city home was located.

The Randolph House at 212 N. 2nd St., Philadelphia, Drawing by Frank H. Taylor, 1923, Courtesy of New Hope Historical Society

Shortly after Edward established his business in the city, the nation's first financial crisis—the Panic of 1791—broke out. On August 12th of that year the market collapsed; shares in the Bank of the United States had fallen by fifty percent, sending the city into a frenzy.[100] But the Panic had little effect on Edward. The grocery business he had opened just north of the expansive commercial market on Market Street was thriving. It was located in a building at 126 N. 2nd St., constructed on land that was owned by Thomas Coates in the days of William Penn, just a few feet from the western end of Elfreth's Alley, the oldest continuously-used residential street in the United States. The small alley (running just over two blocks from 2nd Street east to the Delaware River) is lined with Georgian-style houses built in the early part of the eighteenth century and originally occupied by tradesmen and merchants of all types, whose shops were located on the ground floor and their residences on the upper floor. The alley was named for one such tradesman: Jeremiah Elfreth, a renowned silversmith in early Philadelphia.

Elfreth's Alley, Philadelphia—Author Photograph

By 1793 Edward had formed a private shipping business in partnership with Josiah Langdale Coates, another well-respected merchant. Josiah's father, Samuel Coates, inherited property from his father, who was prominent in the city and a founding member of the Library Company of Philadelphia, the first library in the country, founded by Benjamin Franklin. Josiah's mother, Mary Langdale, was the daughter of the popular Quaker preachers Josiah and Margaret Langdale, who had been ministers and missionaries in England and continental Europe before coming to Philadelphia. Although it appeared that Samuel and Mary Coates were destined for success, both of their lives were cut short, Samuel dying at thirty-seven and Mary at fifty-seven years old. Following his parents' early deaths, Josiah Coates and his siblings—Thomas, Samuel, Jr., and Alice—were adopted by their aunt and uncle, Mary Coates Reynell and John Reynell,[101] all of whose own children had died in infancy. John was a successful purveyor of products imported from England and the West Indies.

Josiah and his brother Samuel established their own business in the shipping industry. After John Reynell's death, Samuel took over as head of Reynell's company, relocating the shipping business from overseas to the eastern coast of the United States. Stephen Girard was one of their most prominent clients.

In 1797 Josiah formed a partnership with his good friend Edward Randolph. Their friendship and partnership were so close that when Edward's seventh son was born that year he named him Josiah Coates

Randolph. Their business partnership flourished for twelve years, ending only with Josiah's death in 1809. Josiah's only son, George Morrison Coates, worked for Benjamin Hornor, a hardware merchant, later establishing his own hardware business. He married his employer's daughter, Rebecca, and they had six children.

Edward operated the grocery business for nearly three decades at the same location. His business, as well as those of other merchants on 2nd Street, was buoyed by the large number of workers in the city who were employed in the vast building boom that unfolded during the 1830s. The friendship between the Randolph and Coates families endured for four generations.

Edward Randolph was elected to the Philadelphia City Council in 1794.[102] He was one of the first investors in the Philadelphia Bank (1803), later named the Philadelphia National Bank, Prior to its founding, only three banks served the city. The oldest one, the Bank of North America (1782), restricted most of its business to a select circle of associates. Later, the Bank of Pennsylvania—originally founded in 1780 to provide funds for the Continental Army—was reestablished in 1793 upon receiving its charter from the Commonwealth of Pennsylvania. Its business dealings, however, were under the control of only a handful of men who refused to make loans to any members of the Jeffersonian Party. Both institutions were politically oppressive. The founding of the First Bank of the United States (1791) was the result of the efforts of Alexander Hamilton, Secretary of the Treasury, who was known to have confined most of the bank's services to English clients, since nearly all of its stock was owned by Englishmen.

First Bank of the United States, Philadelphia—Author Photograph

The Philadelphia Bank was formed in order to serve the needs of those merchants who, like Edward Randolph, were unable to access funds from the other banks in the city. The country was growing rapidly, creating a serious need for commercial lending for the new generation of ambitious entrepreneurs. Nearly a hundred and forty years later, Evan Randolph Jr., the great-grandson of Edward, would become president of the Philadelphia National Bank.

In 1805 Philadelphia opened the first permanent bridge over the Schuylkill River. The new span was built by Timothy Palmer, at the time probably the country's most well-known designer of wooden bridges. It linked Market Street with the Lancaster Turnpike on the western side of the city, significantly expanding trade and commerce between Philadelphia and Lancaster, located more than sixty miles west of the city. The bridge was later covered to increase its lifespan, making it the first "covered bridge" in the nation. (During the Revolutionary War, the Continental Army had crossed the Schuylkill River on pontoons made of floating logs tied together with rope. As the army left Philadelphia, they destroyed these temporary bridges to prevent the British Army from using them.)

The Lancaster Turnpike began at 34th Street, about five blocks from the river on the west side. The road was eventually extended to the Susquehanna River, in Columbia, Pennsylvania. Quakers were avid bidders on stocks that were sold to build the privately-owned and operated turnpike, the first engineered road in the country. Edward continued to expand his business in the city. Like so many other businessmen, he had prospered in tandem with the city's on-going growth. While he and other entrepreneurs were successful, resulting in many thousands of Philadelphians finding employment, most of the city's untrained workers (as well as its sick and elderly populations) suffered extreme poverty. In *The Lives of Eminent Philadelphians*, Edward's success is described as follows:

> After leaving the army, Mr. Randolph came to Philadelphia, and entered into business at first upon a very small scale. By help of industry, economy, and the reputation for integrity, which he soon established, he gradually increased his means, and extended his business until he became one of the largest East India merchants in the city.[103]

Arch Street Bridge, at Front Street, by W. L. Breton—
Courtesy of The Library Company of Philadelphia

Edward's wife, Anna Julianna, and their daughter Julianna, worked with local agencies in providing assistance to the growing number of poor in the city. The Female Society for the Relief and Employment of the Poor was associated with the Friends Meeting, to which Anna and Edward belonged. The organization was established by Ann Parrish shortly after the tragic 1793 outbreak of Yellow Fever in Philadelphia. The House of Industry, located at 2nd and Arch Streets, in Philadelphia, often provided work to as many as fifty women at a time. Its other purpose was to distribute food and clothing to sick and infirm persons over sixty years of age who were not under the official care of the "Standing Committee" (the charitable arm of the Friends Meeting).

Arch Street was an early enclave of Quakers who settled in Philadelphia

The Arch Street Friends Meeting House—Author Photograph

Arch Street in Philadelphia extended across the city from east to west, 2nd Street to 23rd Street, virtually from the Delaware River to the Schuylkill River. Arch Street became the major area in the city where Quaker families settled. Originally "Holmes Street" (in honor of William Penn's surveyor, Thomas Holmes), Penn later changed the name to Mulberry Street because of the numerous mulberry trees lining both sides of the thoroughfare.

As the city grew and commerce expanded, Penn's son Thomas and other influential merchants sought to have Mulberry Street extended to the Delaware River wharf. But the large embankment— over which Front Street ran—blocked access to the river. Cutting through the blockage divided Front Street of course. So the city built a huge stone arch, stretching sixty feet long over Mulberry Street connecting the two ends of Front Street that had been cut through to extend Mulberry Street to the wharf. The arch was considered one of the greatest engineering feats of its time. Philadelphians began referring to Mulberry Street as "the arch street," the phrase becoming so common that, even after the arch was demolished in the early 18th century, the name stuck. Finally, in 1853, the city officially renamed Mulberry Street "Arch Street."[104] Ironically, it is today once again impossible to reach the riverfront by way of Arch Street. Constructing Interstate Highway 95 in the1960s required building a twenty-five-foot-high retaining wall across Arch Street on the east side of Front Street—near the site where the embankment had originally blocked passage to the river.

An early entry in the records of the Female Society, located on Arch Street, reads as follows:

"Julianna Randolph gave to Sara Riley, a respectable coloured woman who still continues when she can obtain work to earn a living by whitewashing, scrubbing &c although over 80 years of age, a Flannel Petticoat and muslin chemise."[105]

Typical 18th-century Philadelphia "Trinity" Houses—Author Photograph

The Society also taught women spinning skills and provided basic education to their children. The records show that in its twenty-three years of existence, members visited and helped 11,977 sick and poor and gave 6,262 articles of clothing to the poor. (One of its favorite projects was the education of children.)

Even as the city continued to grow and prosper, poverty continued to increase among its residents as waves of immigrants continued flooding into the city. Those arriving were poor and were forced to live in the worst possible conditions. Many houses that were abandoned by the affluent members of society deteriorated into cheap boarding houses or tenements. Small row houses—three stories high, with only one room per floor (each about ten feet by twelve feet), termed "Trinity" or "Father, Son and Holy Ghost houses"—lined many courts and alleys running off secondary streets. Others lined dead-end walls behind larger houses facing on the street, accessed only by means of narrow passageways between the larger houses.

Julianna Randolph (1794-1876), photograph, The Library Company of Philadelphia

As a way of creating the idyllic "green country home" effect of his original plan for the city, William Penn had desired that each house have sufficient land and be a comfortable distance from its neighbors. But a century later, when the rapid growth of the city dictated the need for vastly more houses, builders quickly bought up land along the small alleyways and put up modest townhouses for the city's poor population. While most of those early townhouses have since been demolished, many of the much smaller trinity houses have survived. It would have been impossible for the poor families who huddled in those modest dwellings in the eighteenth century to imagine their being valued today at $300,000 and higher.

Edward expands his business to real estate acquisitions

Numbers 2000, 2002, and 2004 Arch Street in 1879—From "Short Account of Our Ancestry and Genealogy" Arranged and Written for Rachel S. J. Randolph by William H. Jenks, Philadelphia, 1883— Courtesy of the Historical Society of Pennsylvania

Anna Julianna Steele Randolph died in Philadelphia in 1810, when she was only forty-seven years old. Edward found strength and comfort in the love of his family, especially of his daughter Rachel and her husband, Oliver Parry. Captain Edward Randolph never remarried. Three years after Anna died, Edward expanded his business in the city, purchasing from Captain Anthony Cuthbert and John Jones property with its five contiguous frame dwellings near the Schuylkill River: on the full city block between Mulberry (now Arch) Street and Filbert Street, (the part of which is now John F. Kennedy Boulevard) on the west side of 20th Street. [106] In 1780 Captain Cuthbert served in the 6th Company of the Artillery Battalion in Philadelphia, under Lieutenant Colonel Robert Knox. He also fought in the Battle of Princeton, and is believed to have crossed the Delaware River with George Washington on that fateful early Christmas morning in 1776. Edward Randolph and Anthony Cuthbert served on Philadelphia City Council together, Edward for only one year, Cuthbert for three decades, during which he was responsible for supervising the construction (beginning in 1801) of the Market Street Bridge over the Schuylkill River.[107] Cuthbert was also known as a master shipbuilder. A narrow street extending from the Delaware River west to just one block short of the Schuylkill River is named after him. Cuthbert Street runs south of Arch Street along the western side of the property that he had sold to Edward Randolph. Rachel (Edward's daughter) and Oliver Parry also owned two properties on that block. Edward and his family resided at 212 North 2nd St., and later at 11th and Master Streets. Ann Evans Randolph had the building at 2000 Arch Street constructed on land that she had inherited from her grandfather, Edward Randolph. In order to be near his mother, Evan Randolph built the home next door (2002 Arch St.) following his marriage to Rachel Story Jenks Randolph. Rachel occupied the house until 1907, when she moved to Chestnut Hill. In 1869, William H. Jenks (Rachel's brother) built the house at 2004 Arch St., desiring proximity to his parents.

By 1833 horse-drawn trams ("horse cars") connected 2nd Street with the Schuylkill River,[108] making travel across the city faster and much more convenient; only four years later, at the time of Edward's death, nearly every major street in Philadelphia had been connected by public transportation services. The Coates & Randolph Company became one of the largest exporters of goods to the East Indies. They owned their own ships. Edward was a friend and ardent supporter of George Washington. He continued well into old age to exercise his right to vote. Hope Carson Randolph relates an Election Day story about the "old Quaker," Captain Edward Randolph:

> In his day all elections were held in the State House where crowds of voters stood in line awaiting their turn to vote. When the former Captain, then in Quaker garb, drove up to the polling place, it was customary to pass him ahead to the voting window because of his age and military history. Upon one occasion a raw Irishman stood in line who did not know the old Quaker and his custom, so he demurred to the proceeding saying: 'Where was the likes of you anyhow, old Quaker, when fighting was done and this nation was made that we should stand back for you?' Turning his one good eye upon him, Captain Randolph replied, 'Well friend, I was where thee would not have dared to show thy naked nose.'[109]

Edward and Anna Julianna had fifteen children, three of whom died in infancy. Edward Randolph died in 1837, at the age of eighty-three, and was interred in "Friends Grounds," at the corner of 16th and Race Streets in Philadelphia.

Julianna Randolph Wood (1810-1885)

Julianna Randolph Wood (1810-1885), photograph, The Library Company of Philadelphia

Richard Davis Wood (1799-1869), photograph, The Library Company of Philadelphia

Captain Edward Randolph's granddaughter, Julianna Randolph, the daughter of Edward Randolph and Mary Taylor, married Richard Davis Wood on October 16, 1832 at the Friends Meetinghouse in Philadelphia. Born on March 29, 1799, Richard was the son of Elizabeth Bacon Wood and Richard Wood III; his father was a farmer, cooper, store owner, an elected member of the Assembly of the State of New Jersey, and a direct descendant of Richard Wood of Bristol, England, who arrived in Philadelphia in 1682. Richard and his brother, George Bacon Wood, exhibited strong self-confidence and dynamic personalities early in their lives. When their parents died they refused to accept any of their inheritance, preferring that it be awarded to their younger siblings and to their older half-brother, David Cooper Wood. Richard and George were confident that they could be successful without the inheritance. David was the son of Richard Wood from his marriage to his first wife, Anna Cooper, of Trenton, New Jersey, who died in 1783, only three years into their marriage.

Dr. George Bacon Wood becomes a Prominent Physician and Distinguished Author

George Bacon Wood, the eldest son, was born in Greenwich, New Jersey, in 1797, where his father had extensive landholdings and was a wealthy farmer. At the age of twelve George persuaded his father to send him to New York City so he could pursue a liberal education. When he completed his studies there, he moved to Philadelphia where he earned a Bachelor's degree from the University of Pennsylvania when he was eighteen, and his MD degree just three years later. Dr. Wood was an attending physician at the Pennsylvania Institute for the Deaf and Dumb (1822-1844) and at Pennsylvania Hospital (1835-1844). He was also appointed head of the chemistry department at the Philadelphia College of Pharmacy. In 1835 he was named Chair of Medicine and Pharmacy at the University of Pennsylvania, serving in that role until 1850, when he was promoted to the position of Chair of Theory and Practice of Medicine; five years later he served one term as president of the American Medical Association. Dr. Wood was widely respected for his artistic talent in producing extremely accurate teaching aids: illustrations of pathological lesions of the organs, and casts and models of a number of types of diseases.

He had his own conservatory, in which he cultivated medicinal plants. Coauthored with Franklin Bache and published in 1833, his first book, *The Dispensatory of the United States of America*, a systematic description of the drugs and preparations used in medicine, distinguished Dr. Wood for the excellence of his research and knowledge. Fourteen printings of *The Dispensatory* were published, totaling more than 120,000 copies in his lifetime. Dr. Wood praised the merits of the dispensatories existing at the time (published in London and Edinburgh) but cited the need for an American counterpart that would include plants and chemicals existing only in America. In the first edition to this voluminous work, Dr. Wood explained the necessity for its publication:

> In the history of our commerce in drugs, and of the nature, growth and collection of our indigenous medical plants; is the chemical operations of our extensive laboratories; and in the modem of preparing, dispensing and applying medicines, which have gradually grown into use among us; there is much that is peculiar, a knowledge of which is not to be gained from foreign books, and is yet necessary to the character of an accomplished American pharmacist. We have, moreover, a National Phamacopoeia, which requires an explanatory commentary in order that its precepts may be fully appreciated and advantageously put into practice. On these accounts, it is desirable that there should be a Dispensatory of the United States which, while it embraces whatever is useful in European pharmacy, may accurately

represent the art as it exists in this country, and give the instruction adapted to our peculiar wants.[110]

A twenty-fifth edition of the work was published in 1960, and remains a valuable resource nearly two centuries after its original publication. Dr. George Wood's writings on history— ranging from the *History of the University of Pennsylvania* and the *History of Girard College*, to the *History of Christianity in India*, and the *History of the British Empire*—are just a few of his books.

After his retirement from the University of Pennsylvania in 1870, he was named Emeritus Professor and elected a member of the board of trustees, serving as chairman of its Committee on the Medical Department. Dr. Wood also served for thirty-eight years as president of the distinguished American Philosophical Society from 1859 until his death in 1897, the board having refused to accept his resignation in 1870, recognizing him as "the most worthy representative it could have, not only where it holds its meetings, but in its correspondence with other learned bodies like itself."[111]

Richard Davis Wood embarks on a career in industry

While George Bacon Wood was pursuing his profession in medicine, his brother, Richard, followed in their father's footsteps by pursuing his career as a merchant. By the time he was twenty-one years old, Richard had opened his first grocery store in Salem, New Jersey. By 1822 he had become so successful that he was able to form a partnership in a dry goods business with William L. Abbott and Samuel C. Wood (under the name Wood, Abbott and Wood). But his talent and drive led him to far more diverse and profitable ventures. As a director of the North American Insurance Company, for example, he soon became heavily involved in the trading of railroad stock, especially with the Pennsylvania Railroad, taking a special interest in the company's planned extension of its railway from Philadelphia to Pittsburgh.[112]

Always with a sharp eye on future economic development, Richard turned his interest to investments, becoming a stockholder and active player in the operations of the Schuylkill Navigation Company. The Delaware River had long been the focus of commerce, but by the beginning of the nineteenth century, the potential use of the Schuylkill River, on the west side of the city had become a development which caught the interest of the State Legislature as a means of transporting valuable anthracite coal from Pottsville, Pennsylvania, far north of the city. The coal was critically needed for the efficient operation of the mills. In 1815 the legislature approved the charter for the Schuylkill Navigation Company to construct a system of canals and dams from Mill Creek, north of Pottsville, to Philadelphia, a distance of about a hundred and fourteen miles. Richard Wood was an early stockholder in the project, which soon attracted major investors, such as Stephen Girard, who, in 1823, loaned the company nearly a quarter of a million dollars. The Schuylkill River became known for its major role in the shipping of anthracite coal, remaining so for nearly fifteen years. Despite numerous setbacks and continuously increasing costs, the project was a success, and Richard had another lucrative investment under his belt. The company's domination ended when the Philadelphia and Reading Railroad opened in 1842. After floods and droughts and the overwhelming challenges of the Civil War, in 1870 the Schuylkill Navigation Company leased its entire operation to the Philadelphia and Reading Railroad.

The Union Mill Dam, Millville, New Jersey, in 2018—Author Photograph

In the early 1840s Richard turned his attention to his half-brother David's business operations in Millville, New Jersey, which were experiencing serious financial difficulties. David had been a partner with Joseph Wood in the Smith and Wood Company of Philadelphia. They had purchased the Union Mill and the Union Estates Company in 1813, and immediately began to expand the canal that had already been constructed there. Next, they built a blast furnace, which produced cast iron water pipes, then in great demand by a national market responding to the rapid growth of cities. Not only had the aged, traditional wooden pipes deteriorated as the cities expanded, but many water supplies were then being located outside the cities, thus requiring much greater lengths of piping in addition to their desired permanency. The cast iron product provided an ideal solution.[113]

David bought out his partner, Joseph Wood in 1822, becoming sole owner of twenty thousand acres which today comprises most of Millville. After two decades of successful operation, his business began experiencing financial problems in 1844, but could still manufacture the much needed iron castings there, producing more than eight hundred tons of castings until 1849, when the manufacture of iron directly from the ore was discontinued. By switching to the process of smelting and molding iron from pig iron, which produced heavy castings, he vastly increased production to four thousand and five thousand tons annually.[114] David continued to rely on Richard's help until the following year, when, in order to save the dire financial situation that plagued him, he sold the furnace and land to Richard outright through a bankruptcy and sheriff's sale. An entry in Richard's diary on January 6, 1856 reveals that he had reviewed David's accounts and found his brother's debts to be "larger than I expected—about one-third of all my estate." Toward the end of the year, Richard noted again that he "he had several interviews with George T. Campbell, in regard to D. C. Wood's affairs, which require much time and thought."

In 1869 Richard built a dam in order to provide the power for his entire manufacturing operations. (David had earlier constructed a dam that created the largest man-made lake in the State of New Jersey at the time.) Richard added a bleachery and dye house soon afterwards. The Maurice River Recollections Project (1993) describes Richard's project as follows:

> The industrial complex was united under the name of Millville Manufacturing Company, and grew to be one of the region's most extensive manufacturing facilities.

The need for increased power was remedied in 1869 when Wood built a new dam over the mill's pond. His project created the 890-acre Union Lake Park, one of the largest man-made lakes in New Jersey.... The Maurice River Company, one of the Wood family's divisions, maintained control of Union Lake and the dam until they sold it to the State of New Jersey in 1981.

The Project explains how the state's ownership and investment breathed new life and purpose into the Wood Family's historic and extensive creation:

In 1987, NJ Governor Thomas Kean approved a $15 million appropriation to replace the spillway and earthen dam. In 1989, the Conti Company completed construction on Union Lake's concrete gravity dam. This modern dam has sluice gates to control water levels at the lake, a spillway and an emergency spillway and an aluminum fish ladder. Jane Galetto shed some light on the addition of the fish ladder. 'For nearly120 years spawning anadromous fish (i.e. Alewife, or blue rock herring) were not able to make their migrations to the headwaters of the Maurice River,' Galetto said. 'With the new structure these historic migrations have resumed. Today during the springtime herring run, we can witness fishermen on the bridges of downtown Millville catching these prize fish.[115]

The City of Millville was essentially created at Union Lake, where the mills had been built at the mouth of the nearby Maurice River. Long before Union Lake was constructed, the northern section of the river was known as Shingle Landing. Millville was incorporated as a city by the New Jersey State Legislature in 1866, its name originating from the large number of mills already operating there and others being planned for the city. David built the Millville Cotton Mill, which began operating in 1854; at its peak in 1870 it employed six hundred people. In December of that year, Richard (by then the owner of the mill) noted in his diary that he "looked around the premises, and found that the cotton mill had made considerable progress," and that the "Furnace [is] working pretty well."

Richard is also noted for his having expanded the capacity of the Maurice River Canal, which later led to the completion of the original Maurice River Dam.

The Panic of 1857

But even as Richard's business was experiencing growth, the international economy began to decline and the US economy, which had become increasingly interconnected with the world economy, had over-expanded, creating the first worldwide economic crisis in the latter part of 1857. The panic was made even worse when the SS *Central America*, carrying much needed gold to New York, sank during a hurricane. Businesses across the country began to fail and thousands of employees lost their jobs.

> In his diary on December 2, 1857, Richard described the dire financial conditions that existed at the time: The remembrance of this year will long continue with me. It has been full of commercial losses and difficulties, owing to an immense contraction in the currency in the last half of the year, and, in the first half, from having to meet engagements that were entered into without sufficient consideration. The value of investments of every description has fallen greatly. The rise in cotton, and reduction in the prices of manufactured goods, caused the working of the mill to be unprofitable, and added to the loss by sales to parties who have become bankrupt, rendered this part of my business almost disastrous.[116]

Richard Wood hires Lincoln to help collect delinquent debts from customers

As the economy continued its decline, customers were increasingly unable to pay their bills. To help collect past-due debts from customers, Richard recruited the services of a little-known young country lawyer named Abraham Lincoln. Early in his career as an attorney, the future president was often hired by businesses and families to track down deadbeats and collect the money they owed, or turn them over to officials. It was not until 1867 that a federal bankruptcy law was passed. Daniel W. Stowell describes the young Mr. Lincoln's early work (from 1836 to just before his presidency), as follows:

> Rather than specializing, Lincoln practiced general law, and so we see him taking on both civil and criminal cases, with breaches of contract and patent infringements sharing space with bootlegging, assault and even murder cases. Much of his work concerned debt collection, for which Lincoln was known well beyond Illinois, and these cases provide a unique window on nineteenth century businesses. Lincoln also went on the road twice yearly to try cases in the state's circuit court.[117]

To be sure, Abraham Lincoln himself was no stranger to debt. When he was twenty-three years old, he and a business partner, William Berry, took a chance on buying a small shop in New Salem, Illinois. Lacking sufficient funds to pay his half of the down payment, he had to borrow the money. Their venture failed in less than a year, creating a small financial crisis for Lincoln. When Berry died three years later, in 1835, Lincoln was forced to assume his partner's debt as well, creating an even greater financial nightmare for the future president. To help pay off his debts, he got a job as postmaster of the town of New Salem. Then he started working as a surveyor, lawyer and state legislator. Lincoln later jokingly referred to his financial woes as his "national debt." (His debt would later grow to an overwhelming amount because of his wife's widely known compulsive shopping.)[118]

As the economy worsened in 1857, Richard and Julianna were grieving the loss of their youngest daughter, Caroline, nineteen years old, who had fallen from her horse and died near their home in Malvern, Pennsylvania.

When the economy began improving over the next several years, Richard not only expanded his mills and furnace, but also launched a new enterprise: creating cranberry bogs at one of his properties in Cumberland County. Richard had looked after David's business affairs and rescued him frequently when his brother faced the worst financial problems of his life. On October 6, 1859, as Richard and his family were dining at home, his brother Horatio arrived to tell them that David had been found dead in the street. Two days later Richard noted in his diary:

> In the afternoon at three-o'clock, the family met in the library [of their home], the corpse being in the parlor. We went to the Western burying ground, and deposited the remains of our brother, David. I hope his soul is in heaven.[119]

David's sudden death compounded the family's sorrow. Just two days earlier they had been mourning the second anniversary of Caroline's death.

Following David's death, Richard formed a new company, the R. D. Wood Company. He continued his negotiations with the New Jersey State Legislature and the West Jersey Railroad Company, which received its charter in 1853 and was planning the creation of a railroad linking Millville with Camden and Philadelphia. In her *Biographical Sketch of Richard D. Wood*, Julianna describes Richard's efforts in bringing the railroad line to fruition:

> Desiring to increase the value of his property, he caused a bill to be introduced into the legislature of New Jersey, chartering the railroad from Camden toward Cape May, which would run through his lands. The bill was opposed by those in the interest of the Camden and Amboy Road, as this company desired to retain it unrivalled influence in railroads in the State. It was finally arranged that the Camden and Amboy Company, under the charter of the West Jersey Railroad Company, should rebuild the road to Woodbury, and extend it to the town of Glassboro, eighteen miles from Camden, and that from this point it should be made to Melville [sic], a distance of twenty-two miles by the Melville and Glasswort Railroad Company. In this latter company my husband took controlling interest, at the same time desiring to interest the property owners generally in the enterprise.

Julianna recorded that she and Richard would take frequent drives to and from Millville, very thoroughly canvassing the area on such occasions, trying to educate the property owners about the meaning of the railroad: how it would increase their property values and be of benefit to them to purchase stock in the new company. She proudly recounts the completion of the railway:

> These roads were completed in 1860. The Melville [sic] and Glasswort is remarkable as having cost less than its estimate in every particular, and was constructed at a lower price per mile than perhaps any other road in the United States.[120]

Many of the employees who worked in Richard's mills lived in houses built by the Wood family in the area surrounding the mills. Also, as in many other company towns during that time, the employees shopped at the company store. Company records provide detailed accounts of transactions with the employees, including wages and subtractions for store purchases, coal, wood and rent. In 1899, wages for machinists and laborers were a paltry ten cents an hour, while most foremen were paid a whopping four dollars an hour. Workers averaged sixty hours a week during a normal six-day workweek.[121] Eventually the Wood Company constructed a bridge over the Maurice River to make commuting to work easier for its employees (many of whom lived across the river on the poorer west side) to get to work on time. Some of those employee houses have survived to this day. The mills were located across the street from the Wood Mansion, and the company's general store was right next door. The Millville Historical Society reported, in 2018, that one of the two foundries is still standing along Columbia Avenue, although it was reduced from two and a half stories to one and a half stories in the early 1900s. (The photograph below shows the mill operations as they appeared in 1929.)

Millville Manufacturing Company, mill buildings and Manatico bleachery, aerial view, Hagley ID #9214_015, Courtesy of the Hagley Museum and Library

Richard Wood rescues the Cambria Iron Company from financial ruin

While Richard focused his attention mainly on the company's Millville operations, he had been keeping a close eye as well on the business activities of the Cambria Iron Company, in Johnstown, Pennsylvania. It was an innovative company, being one of the first to use the steel-making processes invented by William Kelly and Henry Bessemer. Richard had invested $40,000 in the company. Founded in 1852, by the 1870s it had become the largest steel foundry in the United States. Richard's brother, Dr. George Wood, noted: "Though he never participated directly in the management of the works after they assumed their present form, he may be considered the founder of the company, as without his cooperation in its organization, it is doubtful whether the concern would have risen to its present condition, as the most extensive of the iron rail manufacturing establishments in the world." In 1916 the still- prospering company was purchased by Midvale

Steel and Ordnance, and seven years later acquired by Bethlehem Steel. As pointed out half a century earlier, the Cambria Iron Company might never have survived without the efforts of Richard Davis Wood.

In her diary, Richard's wife, Julianna vividly describes her husband's appearance:

> He was fully five feet eight inches in height, weighing from one hundred and thirty to one hundred and forty-five pounds; erect in his carriage, and well made in person, and although very rapid in walking and in all his movements, was calm and courteous in his manners. Until after middle life, he had luxuriant soft brown hair. His eyes were a blue-gray, so quiet in their habitual expression it was a rest to look into them. His voice was usually low and soft; and this, as his brother, Dr. Wood, says in some manuscript reminiscences he has kindly given me, "was an excellent quality, admirably adapted to one necessarily subjected to many trials of temper; it being scarcely possible to speak angrily with a low, soft voice."[122]

Julianna recounts the wide scope of activity that Richard was able to sustain on a regular basis. He traveled frequently to Allentown, Pennsylvania (a distance about one hundred and ten miles from his home) in conjunction with his board position as investor and board member with the Allentown Iron Works. As a member of the board of directors of the Philadelphia National Bank, he not only attended its board meetings without fail, but he also faced the unenviable task of haggling with state senators in Harrisburg on the renewal of the bank's charter. Added to these responsibilities were his important roles with the Schuylkill Navigation Company and the North American Insurance Company. All of these intense involvements occurred while he was running one of the largest industrial complexes in New Jersey. His energy seemed boundless as he traveled many hundreds of miles throughout New Jersey and Pennsylvania, sometimes taking the canal to Reading, and occasionally making business trips to Milwaukee, Baltimore, Boston and (more frequently) to Washington, DC, where he was a regular guest of the Willard Hotel, and to New York City, where he enjoyed frequent stays at the Astor House. Weather conditions or illness rarely curtailed his travel.[123]

Yet, with all of his business travel and varied obligations (several farms, for example, the largest of them being the two hundred-acre Burnt Ground Farm), he still took the time to visit his sons George and Edward at Haverford College, in suburban Philadelphia; take his wife and children out for dinner frequently; and pay visits to relatives in Philadelphia and Cape May, where they enjoyed summer holidays at the shore. He attended services at the Arch Street Meeting House in Philadelphia on most Sundays. Julianna preferred Episcopal services at Christ Church, where, at times, he accompanied her. He and Julianna would often go to lectures in the city, visit the Pennsylvania Academy of the Fine Arts, and see the latest science exhibits at the Franklin Institute. They traveled on family vacations to Lombardy Grove, Virginia. She cites numerous entries in Richard's diary recounting their visits with the Parry family in New Hope. Oliver Parry was a leading real estate developer and lumber merchant in Philadelphia; he and his wife, Rachel—Julianna's aunt—owned a country home in New Hope, where Oliver's father, Benjamin Parry, operated several mills.

In 1865 the Millville Manufacturing Company was incorporated under New Jersey State law. The company later purchased Richard Wood's cotton mill. Then, in 1867, the company gained control of the Mays Landing Water Power Company, in nearby Atlantic County, where they constructed a cotton mill. By 1884, the company had organized an expansive network of multiple trips to shuffle goods among ports. For example, trips to Kingston, Jamaica would first stop at Savanah, Georgia to pick up lumber. In Kingston, the lumber would be unloaded from the boat, which then was loaded with fruit from Jamaica. The fruit would be taken to Savannah, were it was unloaded, and, in turn, replaced with lumber for shipment to Philadelphia. There, the shipment of lumber would be unloaded and replaced with pig iron for shipment to Millville.[124]

Julianna felt compelled to preserve her loving memories of Richard for the edification of generations to come. Published in 1871, two years after Richard's death, her two-volume *Biographical Sketch of Richard D. Wood* preserves for history his massive contributions to the development of the nation. Julianna closed the introduction of her book with the following words, perfectly summarizing his lifestyle:

> After coming to the city he was at one time for weeks dangerously ill of typhoid fever, and that he was, as before stated, very closely devoted to business, which he always

pursued most vigorously during the day, and that his evenings were now occasionally passed in cultivating social relations with some of the pleasantest families of our city; that, as a rule rarely varied from, he went twice on Sunday to a place of divine worship— habitually Friends—and that he kept for daily perusal the large plain bible—that we still use—in his chamber: now no longer in his store, but a large and pleasant front room.... His movements in walking, dressing, eating, etc. were always remarkably rapid. So much so that S. Beetle, Senior, one day arresting him on the street by catching hold of his coat, exclaimed, 'Do stop for one moment, Richard Wood! And tell me if thee ever expects to find time to die.'[125]

Undoubtedly to the surprise of S. Beetle, Sr., he actually *did* die. But Richard's seemingly endless energy, vast success in business and industry, and his abiding love for Julianna and their family continued to impact all who knew Richard Davis Wood long after his improbable death on April 1, 1869.[126]

Richard's son George completed his education at Haverford College in 1860. George married Mary Hunn in 1864, afterwards residing in the Wood Mansion from 1864 to 1870, looking after the cotton mill and bleachery. He kept the mills updated and contributed to the continued development of Millville. The records of R. D. Wood & Company show the extent of the shipments that were made by the company. Schooners traveling from Millville carried many tons of pipes to New York, Philadelphia, Virginia, Maine and a wide variety of other ports, including (in later years), as many as four trips to Boston every month. Ships to Cuban ports delivered pipes and in turn loaded up sugar for delivery to New York. After a number of reorganizations, in 1912 the company became the George Wood, Sons & Company. Following is a summary of the company's history after that time:

> Gradually George Wood assumed responsibility for the cotton mill and his brothers Walter and Stuart for the iron works. The iron works passed out of the family when Walter died childless in 1934. The company faced financial difficulties after World War II when the U.S. textile industry migrated southward. The Mays Landing

Mill was closed in 1949; spinning and weaving were discontinued in Millville in 1958, and finishing operations at that site ceased in 1963.[127]

The David Wood Mansion, Millville, N.J.—Author Photograph

The National Register of Historic Places cites the Wood Mansion, and the family's significant contributions to the history of Millville, as follows:

> Built about 1814, the Wood Mansion House in Millville, Cumberland County, New Jersey is locally significant under criterion B as the residence most strongly associated with the Millville careers of industrialists David C. Wood, his half-brother Richard D. Wood, and Richard's son George Wood, who successively owned and stayed in the house when visiting Millville to oversee their multifaceted industrial operations there. As the result of the visions of these three individuals, Millville, grew from a small village settled in the late 1700s on the Maurice River to one of the largest industrial centers in the 1800s among New Jersey's three southernmost counties of Salem, Cumberland, and Cape May.[128]

The Millville Historical Society notes that the bell on the lawn in front of the Wood Mansion had originally been installed on the top of the north stair tower of the four-story cotton mill building across the street. It was removed from the tower just before a disastrous fire destroyed the two hundred-year-old mill in 1976. The Historical Society is currently creating a museum to the city's history at this location.

George Wood and the formation of the Wawa food enterprise

Wawa Store, 6th & Chestnut Streets, Philadelphia, in 2018—Author Photograph

George Wood moved his residence from New Jersey to Delaware County, Pennsylvania in 1890, when he was forty-eight years old. He bought a summer home on a thousand acres of land in Chester Heights. There he developed a keen interest in dairy farming and soon began importing cows from the British Crown dependency island of Guernsey, eventually building a small milk-processing plant, where, in 1902, he began turning out dairy products. Noted for its quality and cleanliness, and for its pasteurized processing of milk, the company delivered milk directly to their customers' homes. Using the slogan "Buy health by the bottle," the company flourished. But the popularity of home milk-delivery service waned in the 1960s as supermarkets expanded and people preferred buying milk in stores. So the company, named Wawa Dairy Farm (after the site of its first milk plant and corporate headquarters in Wawa, Pennsylvania) began building its own stores. George's grandson, Grahame Wood, opened the first Wawa Food Market in 1964.

In 1968 the Millville Manufacturing Company merged with Wawa Dairy Farms, becoming incorporated as Wawa, Inc. in 1974. The image of the Canada goose was chosen as Wawa's corporate logo because of the company's core operating principles of "teamwork, group consensus and encouragement"—analogous to Canada geese, which fly "as a team" in V-shaped formation. The name "Wawa" is derived from the Ojibwe word for the Canada goose. The Ojibwe (also known as the Chippewa) live in

Michigan, Wisconsin, Minnesota, North Dakota, and Ontario. They speak a form of the Algonquian language and are closely related to the Ottawa and Potawatomi Indians. Wawa supplies its own manufactured beverages to schools, colleges, universities, hospitals, nursing homes, restaurants and hotels. The company still produces its own milk and also manufactures various juice products. Wawa stores also serve fresh food and snacks. Many of their sites include gas stations, and the company is currently in the process of adding charging stations for electric vehicles and installing solar panels on some of their buildings.

In 2018 Wawa was ranked 25th on the Forbes Magazine list of the largest privately-owned companies in America, ahead of such prestigious companies as World Wide Technology and Bloomberg. Their total revenue that year was more than ten and a half billion dollars, its employees numbering more than thirty-one thousand in more than eight hundred locations in Delaware, Maryland, New Jersey, Pennsylvania, Virginia, Maryland, Washington, DC, and Florida. Wawa's employees own forty percent of the company through an employee stock option program. Its headquarters continues at its original location in Chester Heights. Richard D. Wood, Jr. succeeded his first-cousin Grahame Wood as chairman of the board of Wawa in 1981, serving until 2012. Chris Gheysens, the current president, was appointed that year.

In 2018, Wawa opened its largest store in the world at the corner of 6th and Chestnut Streets, Philadelphia, directly across the street from Independence Hall. Wawa is the lead sponsor for the City of Philadelphia's annual Welcome America celebration, commemorating Independence Day by providing free educational and entertainment events during the week leading up to the Fourth of July. The Wawa Foundation has donated sixty-six million dollars to various causes.[129] The Foundation provides grants to hospitals with a focus on pediatric institutions, assists local food pantries, enables Feeding America Food Banks to increase the number of communities it serves, and assists military heroes and first responders in local communities.

The same corporate charter that created the Millville, New Jersey textile business that George Wood inherited from his father, Richard Davis Wood, governs Wawa, Inc. to this day.

Jacob Randolph, MD (1796-1848)

Jacob Randolph, M.D.—
Courtesy of the Historical
Society of Pennsylvania

Julianna Randolph Wood's uncle, Jacob Randolph, was born on November 25, 1796. He received a classical education at the Friends School on 4th Street in Philadelphia, afterwards studying medicine with Dr. Joseph Woollens, a Philadelphia physician. He received the degree of Doctor of Medicine from the University of Pennsylvania at the age of twenty-one, shortly thereafter accepting a position as physician on a ship bound for China. Severe seasickness forced him to abandon the trip on the ship's first stop, in England, where he remained for several months before deciding to travel to Scotland, then to France, where he was impressed with that country's medical practices.[130] (Years later he would return to Paris to study innovative surgical procedures being developed by physicians in the hospitals there.)

In 1822 he married Sarah Emlen Physick, daughter of the eminent and revered Philadelphia physician Philip Syng Physick, the "Father of American Surgery," who persuaded Dr. Randolph to specialize in the practice of surgery. Dr. Physick was one of the leaders of Philadelphia's medical community who had answered the desperate calls to treat victims of the Yellow Fever epidemic in 1793, risking his own health in the heroic relief effort. He was the son of Edmund Physick and Abigail Syng. Edmund was a successful entrepreneur in early Philadelphia, noted as a "keeper of the Great Seal and receiver general of Pennsylvania." He was later an agent for William Penn's family during the Revolutionary War, watching over their interests in the colonies. Abigail's father, Philip Syng, Jr., was an expert silversmith. Many of his creations in silver and gold were prized possessions of the wealthiest families in Philadelphia. But his most notable claim to fame was the Syng inkstand, which was used for the signing of the Declaration of Independence in 1776, and, in 1787, for the signing of the United States Constitution. (As noted earlier in this book, Benjamin Randolph, an ancestor of Dr. Jacob Randolph, built the desk upon which Thomas Jefferson wrote the Declaration of Independence.)

In 1830, Jacob was appointed surgeon to the Almshouse Infirmary, where his father-in-law had been named Surgeon Extraordinary during the Yellow Fever epidemic, the ordeal of which, historian Simon Finger writes,

> had a profound effect on the city and the country. It was one of several factors in Philadelphia's decline relative to rising ports like New York City.... And throughout the country, and the broader Atlantic World, medical men struggled to understand a foe that thwarted their best efforts.[131]

In that same year, Jacob became a lecturer at the School of Medicine at the University of Pennsylvania. Henry Simpson, in his *The Lives of Eminent Philadelphians Now Deceased* (1859), notes that Dr. Randolph "was an impressive and agreeable lecturer, and exhibited that skill and ability as a teacher in all practical details."[132] In 1831 he introduced lithotripsy (a surgical procedure to remove gallstones from the bladder) in the United States, performing twenty-two such surgeries during his career. In 1835 he was elected to be a surgeon of Pennsylvania Hospital.

The Hospital, America's first, was founded by Benjamin Franklin and his longtime friend Dr. Thomas Bond. It was Franklin who had convinced the city's most prestigious citizens of the need for such an institution. He obtained the signatures of thirty-three citizens and submitted the petition to the General Assembly. On May 11, 1751, Lieutenant Governor James Hamilton, son of the prominent Philadelphia lawyer Andrew Hamilton, signed into law the bill that provided the charter establishing Pennsylvania Hospital. Franklin was so pleased with the outcome that he later stated in a letter: "I do not remember any of my political manoeuvres, the success of which gave me at the time more pleasure."[133]

From 1752 to 1755, prior to the hospital's construction, patients were cared for by a small hospital staff in temporary quarters at the home of Judge John Kinsey on Market Street which had become available following the judge's death. Samuel Rhoads, a master builder and designer (and a good friend of Franklin) was selected to build the hospital. It was constructed in three sections, beginning with the east wing in 1756, the hospital accepting its first patients that same year. The west wing was added in 1797, and the center building was completed in 1804. The three wings comprise the Pine Building, widely considered to be one of the finest examples of eighteenth-century colonial architecture. Dr. Bond regularly took his medical students on "ward rounds" in the building, and that practice began the clinical study—outside the classroom—of medicine in America. The surgical amphitheater was housed under the dome of the center building (on Pine Street, pictured below). Dr. Philip Syng Physick operated on his patients in that famous amphitheater, as did his son-in-law, Dr. Jacob Randolph.

In 1831 Dr. Physick performed surgery on Chief Justice John Marshall, seventy-six at the time, who had developed a severe case of bladder stones. The stones were so tiny that Dr. Physick is reported to have removed a thousand of them from Justice Marshall's bladder.[134] Other famous patients treated by Dr. Physick included Presidents John Adams, James Monroe and Andrew Jackson. Pennsylvania Hospital has retained the amphitheater and the hospital's extensive medical library, which in colonial times was the finest library of its kind. The pharmacy, which has also been preserved, displays a large portrait of Dr. George Bacon Wood, author of the *Dispensatory of the United States of America*.

Pennsylvania Hospital, Philadelphia—Author Photograph

Nicholas B. Wainwright, author of "The Age of Nicholas Biddle—1825-1841" (in *Philadelphia—A 300-Year History*) cites Dr. Randolph's continuation of the work of Dr. Physick:

> Philadelphia was still the most advanced medical center in America, with the oldest and largest medical schools, hospitals and libraries .... after the death [in 1837] of the famous Dr. Physick, his son-in-law Dr. Jacob Randolph became the leading surgeon.[135]

Jacob's article in the *North American Medical and Surgical Journal* recounting his treatment of a "femoral aneurism" by tying of the patient's external ilia artery was only the second incidence of that kind of procedure performed in Philadelphia. Dr. George W. Norris, a surgeon and close friend of Dr. Randolph, noted that his colleague's most extensive paper appeared in the *American Journal of Medical Sciences*, a procedure on the amputation of the lower jaw in a case of osteosarcoma.

As earlier discussed, it was Dr. Physick who had convinced Jacob to leave his general practice to become a surgeon. Of his closest friends and colleagues, Dr. Physick is said to have admired his son-in-law most of all, especially for his achievements in the zealous pursuit of his surgical career. When Dr. Philip Syng Physick died in 1837, it was Jacob who selected the epitaph for his tombstone: "He gave his honours to the world / His beloved part to heaven and slept in peace."

The Physick-Randolph House, Philadelphia—Author Photograph

Jacob and his wife, Sarah, inherited Dr. Physick's house, at 321 S. 4th St., and the Randolph Mansion (formerly known as the Laurel Hill Mansion), the doctor's country home in Fairmount Park. The mansion had been built in 1767 by Rebecca and Samuel Shoemaker (who served as mayor of Philadelphia in 1769-71); for ten years they spent summers there away from their home in Germantown.[136]

Dr. Physick purchased Laurel Hill in 1828 from William Rawle, the son of Rebecca and her first husband, Francis Rawle. Sarah and Jacob Randolph added the octagonal addition to the home sometime after 1837.[137] The Randolphs entertained many of Philadelphia's famous residents including the novelist James Fenimore Cooper. Perhaps at one of their dinner parties they discussed the fact that Cooper's grandfather, James Cooper, had once owned land in the "Manor of Moreland," at the time a township of Philadelphia County. The manor was later owned by the Parry Family, in-laws of Jacob Randolph. Jacob's sister, Rachel, married Oliver Parry, the son of Benjamin Parry, known as the "Father of New Hope" for his having been a leader in the early nineteenth-century development of that historic town. Jacob and Sarah were regarded as wonderful hosts, and many of the old Philadelphia families who maintained summer residences near Laurel Hill were lavishly entertained by them. Numerous distinguished guests from all walks of life were feted in the spacious halls of both Randolph residences.

Dr. Jacob Randolph's abrupt death in 1848 at age fifty-two ended his brilliant medical career. George Norris's remarks, in his obituary for Dr. Randolph, recount why Jacob was so admired:

> Dr. Randolph was straightforward and considerate, of a gay and amiable disposition, open and unobtrusive in manner, of the strictest veracity, warm in his friendship, firm in his resolution, cautious in the expression of his opinions, and not allowing those that he had deliberately formed to be easily shaken; he was endeared to all who had the happiness to know him well. In the prime of his life and in the midst of a useful cause, he was taken suddenly from us on the 29th of February 1848. During his short illness, he was collected and in the full possession of his mind. He prepared for death without fear, doubtless "sustained and

soothed by an unfaltering trust" in the principles of that Society in which he had been educated.[138]

Dr. Jacob Randolph left behind his beloved wife, Sarah, and their three children. Their daughter, Elizabeth, married Louis Wister. Their twin sons, Samuel and Philip, were both admitted to the Philadelphia Bar. Samuel Randolph later married a cousin, Ann Lewis, sister of the prominent American artist Edmund Darch Lewis, known early in his life for his watercolors and oil paintings of marine subjects. He exhibited two of his landscape paintings at the Pennsylvania Academy of the Fine Arts when he was just nineteen years old, and was elected to the board of directors of the Academy five years later.

Underscoring the close family interrelationships, Edmund's sister, Mary Darch Lewis, married her first cousin, Philip Syng Physick Conner, a nephew of Dr. Physick. Being a member of a prominent family (with its attendant access to Philadelphia's upper class) clearly enhanced the career of the well-connected young artist.[139] Samuel's son, Philip Syng Physick Randolph, only seven years old at the time of her death, inherited the house at 321 S. 4th St. He married Maie Fetherston in 1888. They had six children. In 1895 they sold the house to Philip's cousin, Elsie Keith, a great-granddaughter of Dr. Physick. After her marriage, in 1883, to Charles Penrose Keith, the couple completed extensive renovations to the house, including the installation of an elevator on the south side years later when Elsie became ill and required a wheelchair to get around. When Elsie died in 1941, two years after Charles' death and with no offspring, Pennsylvania Hospital inherited the house with the understanding that it would never be demolished.

During the Second World War, Dr. Physick's house was used as a hospital for servicemen. Then it was utilized as a dance school. Later, George Fairfax Kearney, a former editor of the *Public Ledger* newspaper, lived in the house for several years. Vacant and deteriorating for years, the Physick house, through the generosity of the Walter H. Annenberg Family, was renovated and donated to the Philadelphia Society for the Preservation of Landmarks. The house at 321 S. 4th St. stands today in tribute to Dr. Philip Syng Physick, the Father of American Surgery, and to the illustrious Randolph family.

Laurel Hill Mansion, Philadelphia—Author Photograph

A widow for twenty-five years, Sarah Randolph died in 1873, outliving all three of her children. The City of Philadelphia acquired the Randolph Mansion in Fairmount Park, in 1869. From 1900 to 1915 the Philadelphia Chapter of the Colonial Dames of America occupied and maintained the house. They were the first to have the exterior of the house painted. The Women for the Bicentennial, later the Women for a Greater Philadelphia, restored the Randolph Mansion to its original elegance—and original name ("Laurel Hill Mansion")—in 1976.

In a March 1901entry in his family records, Rachel's son Richard Randolph Parry refers to the home as "Uncle Jacob Randolph's country seat." The mansion is currently under the care of the Philadelphia Parks & Recreation.

Dorothy Randolph's husband is appointed Treasurer of the United States

Dorothy Randolph, the granddaughter of Jacob and Sarah, married Philadelphia banker John Fell in 1910. He later changed his name to John Ruckman Fell II. In the year following her divorce from John in 1923, Dorothy married Ogden Livingston Mills, a businessman heavily involved in politics. Elected senator for New York State in 1914, he resigned in 1917 to enlist in the U.S. Army, rising to the rank of captain. He was selected as a delegate to the Republican National Conventions of 1912, 1916 and 1920. Although losing to Al Smith in the race for governor of New York in 1924, Mills' political career blossomed again when he was appointed

Undersecretary of the United States Treasury, serving Secretary of the Treasury Andrew W. Mellon from 1927 to 1932. When Mellon resigned, President Hoover appointed Mills to the position. He later became an ardent opponent of Franklin D. Roosevelt's New Deal, writing two books, *What of Tomorrow* and *The Seventeen Million*, both of them detailing his views and offering guidance to those who opposed Roosevelt's policies. After leaving government service, Mills directed some of the largest companies in the United States, including the Lackawanna Steel Company, the Shredded Wheat Company, and the Atcheson, Topeka and Santa Fe Railway. Mills died in New York City in 1937 at the age of fifty-three.

Emlen Physick Jr., MD (1855-1916)

Emlen Physick, Jr., M.D.—Courtesy of Mid-Atlantic Center for the Arts & Humanities

Sarah and Jacob Randolph's nephew Emlen Physick Jr. was born in Philadelphia on June 5, 1855, the son of Emlen Physick and Frances Ralston. Although his parents were not married, Emlen was legitimized by an Act of the General Assembly of the Commonwealth of Pennsylvania, which granted Emlen "all the rights and privileges, benefits and advantages of a child born in lawful wedlock."[140] (In the twentieth century, U. S. Supreme Court decisions held that most disabilities imposed upon illegitimacy were invalid as violations of the Equal Protection Act Clause of the Fourteenth Amendment.) Emlen graduated from the University of Pennsylvania's

School of Medicine in 1878, but for reasons unknown he never practiced medicine.

Although Emlen had inherited his father's fortune, which included the family's summer home in Cape May, when he was only three years old, he never visited the house until he was an adult. When he finally had the opportunity to see it, he decided not to live in it, preferring to build a summer home more to his own liking. The Mid-Atlantic Center for the Arts & Humanities believes that he hired world-renowned architect Frank Furness to design his new Victorian-style home at 1048 Washington St., directly across from his father's house. Furness, who at the time also owned a house in Cape May, had gained prominence for his design of the Pennsylvania Academy of the Fine Arts (1871-76) in Philadelphia. (He designed more than five hundred buildings in Philadelphia during his long career.)

In 1879 Emlen moved into his new home with his mother, Frances, and her two sisters, Emilie and Isabelle Parmentier. A very knowledgeable botanist, Frances ordered the construction of two greenhouses to be added to the side of the house, and hired a full-time gardener to attend to the estate's magnificent gardens and shrubs. The house across Washington Street that was built by Emlen's father is now a bed-and-breakfast lodging, known as the Ralston-Physick House.

Emlen spent much of his time raising horses, chickens and other animals on his twenty-acre estate on Washington Street, while also enjoying life as a gentleman farmer on his two farms in Cape May. His love for animals was evident in his devoted work as president of the Cape May Society for the Prevention of Cruelty to Animals.

Emlen was active in the real estate business in Cape May, owning a number of properties in the city. He was also heavily involved in the city's civic and social life. In an article on May 25, 1904 the *Philadelphia Record* newspaper reported that Dr. Emlen Physick had pledged twenty-five thousand dollars to help save the First National Bank of Cape May from going bankrupt; unfortunately, even his generous efforts were unable to save the struggling financial institution, which failed that year. He participated in public meetings, frequently offering recommendations to the planning commission. Dr. Physick also donated the land at 1819 Delaware Avenue in Cape May for the construction of the Corinthian Yacht Club, still popular more than a century after his death.

Dr. Physick's Study, the Emlen Physick House—Author Photograph

In the last year of his life Emlen enjoyed fussing over his latest possession, a 1915 Model T Runabout, keeping it in the carriage house behind his home.

Having cherished a close bond with his mother all his life, Emlen was devastated by her death in 1916. Within the same year, he too died, at age sixty-one, from a cerebral hemorrhage. After his Aunt Isabelle died, his Aunt Emilie lived alone in the Physick House until her death in 1935. Frances Brooks and her family, who were friends of Emilie, lived across the street and took care of her when she grew ill. Emilie had bequeathed the house to Frances. The estate was sold multiple times after Frances's death, eventually falling into a sad state of disrepair. The exquisite Frank Furness creation faced an uncertain future in the 1960s when developers who acquired the house sought to tear it down and build tract housing on its grounds.

To avert the disaster, in 1970 a coalition of concerned citizens in Cape May formed the Mid-Atlantic Center for the Arts & Humanities (MAC). After forestalling the demolition, MAC obtained grants that allowed the City of Cape May, in 1973, to acquire the entire estate and lease it to MAC. Since then, MAC has undertaken an extensive restoration of the property, funded largely by money raised from tours and numerous community fund-raising events.[141]

The Emlen Physick House, Cape May, N.J.—Author Photograph

Frank Furness designed not only Dr. Physick's house, but also much of the furniture that adorns it. As a proponent of the Esthetic Movement, the legendary architect himself designed the woodwork and ceiling decor and all the woodwork throughout the home—even the very hinges on the doors. An example of his style is seen in the design of the beds, showing the structure: The stiles, rails and panels that make up the headboards are immediately apparent. The ornamentation consists of reeding, bulls-eyes and other geometric decoration, all of which emphasizes rather than hides the actual structure of the beds. The wood is left lightly varnished to show off its grain. The stained glass in the bedroom windows shows the same design as the headboards.[142] The Physick Estate includes not only Dr. Physick's house, but also the original carriage house he lived in while his home was under construction (afterwards becoming his workshop). Also preserved are the four small barns used for housing and feeding the "ponies, peacocks and doves."

Today during the summer season, Emlen's prized Model T can still be seen parked in front of the Physick House.

Rachel Randolph Parry (1804-1866)

Oliver and Rachel Randolph Parry, c. 1837—
Courtesy of New Hope Historical Society

Dr. Jacob Randolph's sister, Rachel, was the youngest of thirteen children. Her marriage to Oliver Parry on May 1, 1827 produced twelve children, significantly growing the already extensive family tree. Indeed, by the middle-to-late nineteenth century in Philadelphia, it seemed that no matter in what direction a person turned, one would most likely discover a Parry or Randolph active in one or another kind of business or profession. Rachel's husband, Oliver Parry, and her nephew, Nathaniel Randolph, began developing the Spring Garden neighborhood during the city's mid-century western expansion. Even before undertaking that massive project, they and their families had become directly involved in improving the social fabric of that part of the city. Oliver was a life member of the Philadelphia City Institute, which was organized in 1852 to establish a free library for the residents of Philadelphia.

In 1846 Rachel and her sister Julianna are founding members of the Western Association of Ladies for the Relief and Employment of the Poor

Julianna became the first treasurer of that important community service organization, the Western Association of Ladies for the Relief and Employment of the Poor, successor of the Female Society for the Relief and Employment of the Poor (thought to have been the first job-training program for women in the Unites States). Both sisters also participated on the association's Acting Committee.

Parry family records show that Julianna had inherited from her father, Edward Randolph, a number of properties on Poplar Street, in the Northern Liberties neighborhood of Philadelphia, and a property at what is now the northeast corner of 22nd and Market Streets. The role of the committee members of the Association was to visit applicants regularly and recruit them for the training programs at the House of Employment. They conducted numerous home visits for that purpose. The Association organized the effort to provide relief and employment of the suffering and deserving poor of the western part of the city. The difficulty of procuring employment, the enormous price of fuel, high rents and high-cost markets were all taking a widening toll on the city's poor families. In 1854 the Association opened a House of Employment, which by the end of the year had furnished relief to one hundred and sixty-five women and children. In its year-end report the Association proudly noted that

> from the garrets of our great city, from its cellars too, those sepulchers in which the living lie! unsunned, unaired, unvisited and unwarmed—their lonely occupants come forth, to be cheered, comforted, morally elevated and instructed in our bright and cheerful Work Room. Soon it became a cherished home to them.... In conformity with rules relative to personal cleanliness, long indulged habits of self- neglect, gradually give place to comparative neatness.[143]

Women were instructed in sewing, and their children were placed in a nursery on S. 16th Street, where volunteers cared for them. Setting a new standard for services to the poor, this organization appears to have been one of the first job-training and childcare programs in the history of Philadelphia, if not of the nation itself. The number of those applying to its various programs increased so much that, in only its second year, the Association was petitioning the city to purchase a plot of ground to erect a suitable building to accommodate the growing demand.

The Association's 1855 records show that the Parry and Randolph families were among the financial contributors to the programs. Nathaniel Randolph, Rachel's nephew and the business partner of her husband, Oliver, were among those donating to the Shoe Fund. A total of 202 pairs of shoes were distributed that year, the Association having to appeal to its members for even more donations because of the growing need. Julianna Randolph, along with two of Rachel and Oliver Parry's children—Julianna and Richard—were also contributors. The Association's by-laws indicate that it had established a "Form of Bequest" for designating in wills the donation of funds and property. (At the time, the Parry family resided at 633 Arch St., and that the Randolph family lived at 674 Chestnut St.)

Julianna Randolph continued to support the Association for the rest of her life. She passed away on August 28, 1876, leaving one thousand dollars for its programs. She also demonstrated her concern for the poor by committing funds to the Association for the Care of Colored Orphans, the Home for Colored Children (near the Woodland cemetery), and to the Old Men's Home of Philadelphia.

The Western Association of Ladies for the Relief and Employment of the Poor was the major provider of social and educational services for the disadvantaged families in Philadelphia in the second half of the nineteenth century. The "House of Employment"—as they called the building where they served the needy, teaching them sewing and seamstress skills, and selling the clothing they made there to earn additional funding to expand the training program—is now the site of One Liberty Place, a sixty-one-story office building located at 19 S. 17th St., is now also home to a men's clothing store on its ground floor.

In the 1855 report, the Association recorded that one hundred and nine women were working at the House of Employment, and thirty of their children were being cared for in their nursery. The production report for that year shows an output from those employed that included eight hundred garments, two hundred and ninety-nine "comfortables" (quilts or comforters), twenty silk skirts and ten large bed quilts, all of the fabric and materials for which were donated by residents, churches and businesses. These items were sold at the Association's store which was located at 10 S. 16th St. Total receipts for the year 1855 were $2,685.41 ($80,000 in today's currency), an increase of nearly twenty percent over the previous year. The Association later added a Visiting Housekeepers Bureau, thereby expanding the types of assistance they were providing to poor families in Philadelphia.[144] When Rachel died in 1866, the Association, in its Twentieth Annual Report, recorded the following tribute:

> It is with saddened hearts that we enter upon our duties this coming season, for we have been sorely stricken. One who has ever been in the foremost ranks, has been taken from us, taken from a life of usefulness, with a heart alive to sympathy and sorrow; and a hand ever open to freely give; pleasant and cheerful in her address, and amiable and kind to all. These endearing qualities made the presence of our dear friend, Rachel Parry, ever welcome; welcome to the young, whom she so cordially assisted with her advice and council, and welcome to those more advanced in life, for her good judgment and her readiness to assist and sustain. She has borne the "burden and the heat of the day" in this society, being one of the few among us who were its earliest members, has nursed it in its infancy, and with an interest unchanging, was a faithful worker until she was called away from works to reward. One of the strong pillars has been removed from among us; may her example be an incentive to those who follow after, and then, "although dead, she yet liveth."[145]

The Western Association of Ladies for the Relief and Employment of the Poor served Philadelphia's poor and needy for more than one hundred and fifty years after Rachel's death. In 2017, the Association dissolved, its services transferred to a number of city and nonprofit agencies that continue the work of Rachel Randolph Parry and her sister Juliana.

Oliver Parry and Nathaniel Randolph spearhead the development of Philadelphia's Spring Garden Neighborhood

In the middle of the nineteenth century, Philadelphia was struggling to gain its momentum following the tumultuous years of the Industrial Revolution. Roving gangs of marauders and the absence of any viable law-enforcement effort presented untold challenges to residents and visitors alike. The police and fire departments were reformed and expanded. The city was growing well beyond its original Revolutionary War footprint. In fact, the population of Philadelphia in 1800—41,220—had increased to 565,529 (almost fourteen-fold) by 1860.[146]

In 1826 the city had taken stock of the condition of its water supply system and acted to rebuild and improve it. The failing water system in the Spring Garden neighborhood was one of the first to be addressed. In slums that cropped up around the city, thousands of its citizens lived in filth, infestation and squalor. As the city grew dramatically, an even greater need arose for decent and safe housing. The extensive poverty of its citizens presented Philadelphia with an urgent challenge to promote the creation of affordable dwellings.[147]

While Philadelphia was working to improve its water supply, Oliver Parry and Nathaniel Randolph responded to the city's need for more housing by concentrating their real estate development efforts in what is now the Spring Garden Historic District of Philadelphia. Bush Hill, part of that neighborhood, encompassed more than one hundred and fifty acres on what was originally the estate of Andrew Hamilton, considered the first "Philadelphia lawyer" because of the shrewd advice he gave to William Penn and his sons in the course of their numerous land acquisitions and disputes. Unfortunately for Hamilton, he died in 1741—just one year after his manor at Bush Hill was completed. Bush Hill was also, for a time, the home of the Vice President John Adams. The "country" home was located in the area that is now Buttonwood Street, between 17th and 18th Streets.

Strolling through the shaded and peaceful streets in the Spring Garden section of the city today, it is hard to imagine the neighborhood's sordid history. When yellow fever began claiming thousands of lives in the 1790s, it was becoming impossible to address the dire health issues its victims presented. Dr. Benjamin Rush, a physician and signer of the Declaration of Independence, had diagnosed the disease, believing that yellow fever was carried to the city by an infected refugee from what is now Haiti in the wet spring of 1793. The symptoms of the deadly fever included nausea, skin eruptions, black vomit, incontinence and jaundice. Fearing the spread of the virus, the directors of the city's only hospital and almshouse refused to admit yellow fever victims.

Patients had at first been moved to a building at 12th and Market (then High) Streets—at that time the "outskirts" of the city. But when that site became overwhelmed, the decision was made to move the masses of yellow fever victims farther outside the city—to Hamilton's house on Bush Hill (just behind what is now the Free Library of Philadelphia), which had steadily deteriorated following its sale in 1814. What had once been the grand residence of Pennsylvania's greatest lawyer, and confidant of William Penn, had become the repository of the sick and dying.

Dr. Philip Syng Physick devoted much of his time tending to the fever victims hospitalized there. By the end of 1793, when the epidemic had finally relented, it is estimated that about five thousand Philadelphians—more than ten percent of the city's population—had died. Half of the population of the city had fled, and government had ground to a halt. Richard G. Miller writing in *Philadelphia, a 300 Year History*, reported that the federal capital had become a ghost city:

> On an average August day in Philadelphia there would have been three to five burials. On August 24 there were seventeen, on August 28, twenty-two, on August 29, twenty-four, and thereafter slight declines in burials were quickly followed by alarming increases. Though business at first went on as usual, the lassitude, glazed eyes, depression, even the yellow complexion and seizures of vomiting and delirium symptomatic of the disease could be found everywhere in the streets. By the end of the month Rush [Dr. Benjamin Rush] was advising 'all the families that I attend, that can move, to quit the city.' Jefferson, living beyond the town at Gray's Ferry, wrote to Madison that 'Everybody who can, is flying from the city, and the panic of the country people is likely to add famine to the disease'—that is, fresh produce was coming in only in a trickle.[148]

Almost four decades after the yellow fever epidemic had people fleeing the city, Philadelphia by 1830 was reinventing itself and about to expand its boundaries dramatically. Rachel Randolph Parry's nephew, Nathaniel Randolph, and Rachel's husband, Oliver Parry, were business partners who pioneered the early development of the westward expansion of Philadelphia in 1851—three years before the city's consolidation. The Act of Consolidation brought under the city's jurisdiction those townships and districts that had been established outside the original boundaries William Penn had designated for the city.

Parry and Randolph had already begun purchasing property in the Spring Garden section of the city. Their efforts drew numerous architects and developers to the expanding neighborhood. They purchased land on the south side of Pratt Street, and on the north side of what is now Fairmount Avenue near Nixon Street. Two years later, in January 1853, they bought land on both the north and south sides of Green Street, on the east side of both 17th and 18th Streets, and on the west side of 17th Street. They continued their investments by buying two parcels of land on the west side of 16th Street to Washington Street, leasing each of them for $630 annually. They purchased two parcels on the west side of 17th Street to Washington Street, which they leased for $630.50 per year.[149] These transactions were followed by their purchase of two smaller parcels, one on the north side and one on the south side of 17th St. to Centre Street, each of which they leased for ninety dollars yearly.

The Parry and Randolph homes were mostly in the Italianate style, which typically featured a rusticated basement and embellished window-and-door surrounds. Other features included double-leaf doors, elaborate bracketed cornices, and arched and rounded forms. Red brick and marble were the major materials used in the construction. Crisp, white marble entrances and marble lintels, sills and steps graced the front of the homes. The availability of mass-produced iron work for railings, fences and gates (through local manufacturers) stimulated their extensive use by Parry and the other developers in the burgeoning Spring Garden neighborhood.

Townhomes, the 1700 block of Green Street, Philadelphia, built by Parry and Randolph—Author Photograph

Townhomes, the 2100 block of Mt. Vernon Street, Philadelphia—Author Photograph

Machine-carved marble and woodwork (produced locally) were used to enhance the building facades; those exquisite ornamental features continue to grace the Spring Garden houses to this day. Most of the buildings are three stories high, others rising an additional story. Parry and Randolph sold some of the parcels to other local developers, who in turn brought their individual architectural styles to the neighborhood. The variety of architectural designs is most prominent on Green Street and Mount Vernon Street, where the north and south sides of the streets exhibit a wide array of architectural styles. Notable architects who joined the Parry and Randolph team's investment in the neighborhood include Hiram Miller, Josiah Haines, Charles Budd and Cyrus Cadwalader.

As the Spring Garden neighborhood's attractiveness and popularity grew, it began to draw more of Philadelphia's elite developers and professionals. The Philadelphia City Directory of 1866 reported that half of the physicians in the city were based on Green Street, indicating the high regard for the neighborhood with its wide, tree-lined streets. Thomas Eakins, one of the most noted artists in the history of American art (and certainly one of the most popular hometown artists in Philadelphia history) resided at 1729 Mount Vernon St. A realist painter and sculptor, Eakins painted hundreds of portraits of friends and family, featuring some of the most prominent people in Philadelphia society. The preeminent manufacturer of fine hats, John B. Stetson, built his home at 1717 Spring Garden St., and Stephen F. Whitman, the pioneering chocolatier most famous for his "Whitman's Sampler" (with its "candy map" so chocolate-lovers could identify each of the selections in the box), lived at 1701 Spring Garden St. The Pittsburgh Paint and Glass magnate, John Pitcairn, Jr., made his home at 1634 N. 16th Street.

The most impressive home in the Spring Garden district is the Bergdoll Mansion, constructed in 1882 by famed Philadelphia architect James H. Windrim, who followed the successes of Nathaniel Randolph and Oliver Parry in the neighborhood. The massive Beaux Arts, Italianate mansion—its fourteen thousand square feet comprising eight bedrooms, ten bathrooms, and two kitchens—in most of the rooms feature carved mahogany woodwork, and hand-painted ceilings, gold fixtures, and fireplaces. Typical of the Beaux Arts style, there are frescoes and mosaics decorating the home. The goddess Diana holds a cornice as her sculpture is integrated with the exterior architecture. Windrim built the luxurious Brownstone Mansion on the northwest corner of 22nd and Green Streets, in one of the city blocks where pioneers Parry and Randolph had constructed rows of Italianate homes two decades earlier.

Louis Bergdoll was a German immigrant who founded a brewery in the Brewerytown section of the city, just north of Spring Garden. The Bergdoll brand quickly became one of the most popular beers in America, making Louis a very rich young man. In celebration of his wealth, he soon began planning a mansion in Philadelphia that would rival in its sumptuousness the Vanderbilt home on New York City's Fifth Avenue, commissioning Windrim to accomplish the task.

Nine years earlier, Windrim had completed the building for which he has ever since been most famous for, the Masonic Temple in Philadelphia, at 1 N. Broad St. His reputation includes the Academy of Natural Sciences, and he was named the architect for the Stephen Girard Estate, where he designed a number of buildings for Girard College, located a few blocks north of the Spring Garden neighborhood.

The Bergdoll Mansion is listed in the National Register of Historic Places. In 2015 *Philadelphia Magazine* deemed it "the most beautiful rental in Philadelphia." Louis's grandson, Grover Cleveland Bergdoll, grew up in the Bergdoll Mansion but had no interest in brewing beer, instead becoming a playboy, aviator and auto-racing enthusiast. He was widely disparaged as a momma's boy who dodged the draft in World War I.[150]

The spacious homes and landscaped neighborhoods that Parry and Randolph created stood in stark contrast to the dire, cramped and filthy conditions that helped foster the rapid growth of the Yellow Fever epidemic only three decades earlier. Unfortunately, in 1849 Philadelphia and a large part of the nation suffered from an outbreak of another insidious disease, cholera. The deadly disease was originally thought to have entered the United States in December 1848 via passenger ships from Ireland to New York and New Orleans. It spread rapidly from the wharfs to the city's population, its victims suffering through days of diarrhea, vomiting, muscle cramps and dehydration, the skin of the hands and feet of many of them becoming wrinkled, cold, and bluish.

President James Polk, who was traveling through New Orleans at the time of the cholera outbreak, contracted the disease and died on June 15, 1849, just a few months after leaving office. More than a thousand people in Philadelphia lost their lives from the dreaded disease in 1849. Terrible as that was, however, the number of victims who died in New York City was four times as great (though NYC's overall population at the time was only about one and a half times as great). Philadelphia's much smaller number of deaths was at first attributed to the city's using water from the Fairmount Reservoir (adjacent to the Spring Garden neighborhood) to clean the city's streets, but it was soon discovered that the city's clean drinking water—not cleaner streets—had helped stop the cholera from claiming more lives. Other smaller outbreaks occurred in the city during 1854, 1866 and 1891. Despite the fact that Nathaniel Randolph had resided in a neighborhood with a clean environment, and clean drinking water, Nathaniel died in his residence at 1709 Green St. on Friday, September 4, 1858, following a severe case of cholera. He was forty-one years old. While it is not known how he contracted the disease, it is possible that on one of his many trips to areas of Pennsylvania and New Jersey outside of Philadelphia, he was infected by contaminated drinking water. After Nathaniel's death, the responsibility for the operation of the extensive Parry and Randolph developments fell on the shoulders of Oliver Parry.

Sixteen years later, on February 20, 1874, Oliver Parry died in his townhome at 1721 Arch St. in Philadelphia. He was laid to rest at the Solebury Friends Burying Ground in Bucks County, Pennsylvania, just outside the Borough of New Hope, his birthplace. His townhome was sold to William T. Taylor in the following year. It was demolished in the latter part of the twentieth century to accommodate the construction of the mammoth Bell Atlantic/Verizon Tower that now soars above the old Quaker neighborhood on Arch Street between 17th and 18th Streets (not nearly as expansive as the Quaker enclave that at one time had stretched from 4th to 20th Streets).

Oliver's son, Richard Randolph Parry, who had returned from his business ventures in Mankato, Minnesota in 1862, continued expanding the Parry business in Philadelphia until shortly before his death in 1928.

The value of Oliver Parry's estate in today's economy would be well over five million dollars. In his will he bequeathed a generous sum of cash and a townhouse on Mount Vernon Street to each of his eight surviving children. (Richard Randolph Parry inherited 1614; Edward Randolph Parry, 1618; Emma Randolph Parry, 2122; Helen Randolph Parry, 2124; Jane Parry Winslow, 2132; Mary Randolph Richardson, 2134; Julianna, 2138; and George Randolph Parry inherited 2144.)

In addition to those residences, the children were bequeathed shares in rents from properties at the following locations: Bodine Street near Columbia Street; Clayton Street east of 23rd street; the west side of Phillips Street south of Diamond Street; Clayton Street west of 22nd Street; the southeast corner of Norris and Mercer Streets, and the southwest corner of Norris and Mascher Streets. The entire city block encompassing the houses that Parry and Randolph had built on the south side of Mount Vernon Street remains occupied today in one of Philadelphia's most popular neighborhoods.

Oliver Parry's obituary was published in the *Philadelphia Inquirer* in February 1874:

> This gentleman, though retired for many years from the busy walks of life, was, in his day, a most active and useful citizen, and to his and to his nephew and partner, the late Nathaniel Randolph, the city of Philadelphia is indebted for the fine improvements made on Green and other streets in "Bush Hill" in the north-western section

of the city, they having purchased much of the ground in that section, and either had it improved for themselves or sold land to others, whom they induced to have buildings erected upon it, the result being the conversion of what was once a barren waste of vast gullies, into one of the handsomest and most attractive neighborhoods of which Philadelphia can boast of at the present day. Born a member of the Society of Friends, he lived and died in that faith, walking through life with a singleness and direct honesty of purpose which made the name of Oliver Parry synonymous with truth and honor. At the close of a long and well spent life he rests from his labors. And is at peace, his soul having gone, we have every assurance, back to the God who gave it. Long will he be missed and long will he be remembered by the near ones whom he has left behind to mourn his loss, and who will keep the fragrant recollection of his memory green for themselves and their children's children.

The Spring Garden Historic District includes within its boundaries two of what had been the most historic estates in early Philadelphia history. On the west side of 19th Street, "The Hills" estate was owned by the Revolutionary War financier Robert Morris, and at one time was referred to as Morrisville. On the east side of 19th Street, the "Bush Hill" estate, considered among the most prominent seats of the eighteenth century, was once owned by Andrew Hamilton.

Oliver Parry and Nathaniel Randolph built at least three hundred homes in the Spring Garden neighborhood.[151] Scores of those handsome redbrick townhomes, with their marble stairways and doorways, still provide some of the most desirable residences in the city. Beginning in the 1980s, many of them have been renovated and converted to luxury condominiums. Parry's vision of a spacious neighborhood with wide streets and places for gardens and trees continues to enhance the Spring Garden neighborhood of Philadelphia.

Major Edward Randolph Parry (1832-1874)

Major Edward Randolph Parry. *(New Hope Historical Society)*

Major Edward Randolph Parry—Courtesy of New Hope Historical Society

While their father, Oliver Parry, focused his business development on the westward expansion of Philadelphia, his sons Edward and Richard saw as their great opportunity the prospect of the westward expansion of the nation as a whole. Edward Randolph Parry was the oldest of the four sons born to Rachel Randolph and Oliver Parry. They had twelve children in all. In 1856, when he was twenty-four years old, Edward moved to Mankato, Minnesota with his brother Richard, who was three years younger. Shortly after their arrival they purchased property located at 316 S. Front St. One year later, they opened Parry and Brother Bank, the first commercial bank in Mankato's history. They were also known for their other major business: Parry and Brother, Land Agents and Brokers. Although Edward and Richard were out of their father's and uncles' sight, the brothers were always on their minds, as Oliver Parry's letter of Nov. 11, 1857, written when the financial panic of that year was sweeping through Philadelphia and threatening the rest of the country, clearly shows: "Much care will be necessary to avoid difficulty; as the disastrous state of affairs in the east will assuredly reach the west in a greater or lesser degree and I want you to be prepared for the worst," Oliver writes. "We hope the worst is over here, but there is very little perceptible improvement in anything. Our business is pretty much confined to furnishing lumber for our own buildings which are getting pretty well advanced—we are urging them forward as fast as possible knowing that if they had to be sold unfinished there would be a great sacrifice made on them." (This letter and all of the others quoted in this section have been provided by the Minnesota State University, Mankato Library, Southern Minnesota Historical Society.) [152]

Uncle Richard Randolph wrote to them from Philadelphia four months later (March 7, 1858), congratulating them on their good fortune in Minnesota:

> You speak of six percent [interest] a month for money as a mighty little affair. What a pity you have not got a million to put out on such like terms. I'll tell you what I am willing to do, if you encourage me to do it—I will try to furnish one or two thousand dollars for you to invest in good securities so as to make up some of my losses here.

In a letter to the editor of the *Chester County Times,* published on August 11, 1859, Edward tells of the continued success of his business affairs and how the business climate in the Midwest had improved. He also writes admiringly of Mankato, his new home,

> situated in the great south bend of the Minnesota and St. Peter River, about 90 miles southwest of St. Paul, and one hundred and eight miles directly west of the Mississippi; it is the county seat of Blue Earth and occupies one of the most central positions of any point in the State, is surrounded by a rich agricultural district extending south to the Iowa line and to the west for a hundred miles, rivaling in richness the great grain growing in Chester Valley of Pennsylvania.

His enthusiasm about business prospects in Mankato and the Midwest was so intense that Edward had written an earlier letter to another uncle, Charles Knowles, about the need for more grist mills, attempting to entice him to move out there and establish a mill. Edward recounted his efforts in a letter to his Aunts Ruth and Jane (October 24, 1858):

> I want him to come out and put up a steam flowing mill in our town. He would make more money out of it in one year, than he could in the East in three of them. We are

very much in want of some grist mills, flour has to be hauled clear from Iowa.

In a letter to his Uncle Richard, also in 1858, Edward wrote of his attempt to have the local physician in his old hometown move to Mankato:

> Jim Shannonhouse seems to have quite a notion of emigrating out here, and I think he couldn't do better than come, as there is a fine opening in our town for a smart physician.... and I believe he could do well, [so] I advised him accordingly. We are expecting a large emigration and no doubt he will not be disappointed. Already wagons are beginning to come in laden with families and household furniture.

Edward's letter of December 23, 1858 (again to Uncle Richard) shows he had also tried to convince his cousin Oliver Paxson to move to Mankato. Responding to his Uncle Richard's provincial assessment of the financial markets in the East, and his uncle's reluctance to invest in the rapidly developing economy of the Midwest, Edward adds:

> Thee speaks in thy letter of money being very abundant in the East, (and I will add, commanding but a shocking low interest) and is one of the results of not being sent out west for speculative purposes or for investments, it ought to be abundant when capitalists will put it into some five percent per annum railroad bond, or some bank stock that is long since sprung in the knees, and about ready to go up the spout, in preference to investing it in farming lands with soil unequaled by any on earth; I mean western farms of course, none of your eastern farms of stones and sand, and from which can be realized from fifty to one hundred percent per annum, to say nothing of a few hundred dollars that could be loaned out a high rate of interest per month as per year in the East, notwithstanding the all wise presses of the East would have you believe to the contrary.

But a reply from Uncle Richard several weeks later revealed that he was keenly aware of the Dakota Nation's struggle with the United States government, which had failed to make its payments of money, food and supplies to the Dakotas—thus violating the terms of the two treaties (1851 and 1858) with the Dakotas. Even though his nephews had been quite successful, he was clearly worried about their venture in Mankato. In the letter, Richard refers to the growing hostilities leading to the conflict, and sympathizes with the plight of the Indians:

> If I was out there I should certainly sigh for fine Chincoteague or Egg Harbor oysters. ... As you don't mention anything about venison, or prairie fowls or such like ... I suppose the Indians have devoured them all long ago. Take care they don't devour you too. That country belongs to them by right and by inheritance, and everything in it is theirs', fish, flesh and fowl.
>
> As you appear to have grown so corpulent and fat, your carcasses will furnish many a dainty feast for their bacchanalian feasts.

The closing sentence suggests that their uncle had seen Edward's brother Richard in Philadelphia when Richard had gone to Philadelphia to visit with his family. In a letter (dated April 19, 1858) to his aunts Ruth and Jane Parry, Edward refers to Richard's trip home:

> I received a letter from Dick by last mail, and he speaks of your being in Philadelphia, you happened there at a good time, as you were among the first to see his lordship. I have no doubt that much joy exists all around, for a year's absence from home, and for the first time is an intolerable long stretch.

Edward then bemoans the fact that he and his brother were tiring of housekeeping chores, and implores his aunts to find a wife for his brother:

> Can't you recommend our Richard to some nice young lady whilst he is in the east? One of us must have a wife and I guess it won't make much difference which one. This thing of living away out here with no one but yourselves to make up your beds, sweep the rooms out, etc. won't

do. What do you think of men doing chamber work? It is rather taking women's duties away from them. Is it not?

On August 11, 1859 Edward wrote another letter to the *Chester County Times*, in which he chronicles Mankato's continued growth and prosperity:

> Three years ago we had but one hotel, one school house, one church and one saw mill; to be sure the necessities of the people at that time demanded little more as there were but between one hundred and fifty and two hundred inhabitants, whilst now we must have between fifteen hundred and two thousand. Since which time we have erected five or six hotels, (great country for hotels,) nearly as many saw mills, one of which has planning and shingle machines connected with it; numerous large dwelling homes, and several three story stores with handsomely dressed stone fronts.[153]

Despite the growing prosperity of the area, Uncle Richard's fear about the hostile political environment in the Midwest became reality in 1862 with the outbreak of the Dakota Conflict (also known as "the Sioux Uprising" and "the Dakota War of 1862"). After Minnesota became a state in 1858, the land belonging to the Dakota Indians (one of the three main subcultures of the Sioux Nation) was portioned off to the growing number of white settlers as part of treaties between the United States in 1851 and 1858 with Dakota Chief Little Crow. The government agreed to payments of money, food and supplies to the Dakotas in exchange for their valuable hunting grounds. However, the government's decade-long failure to honor its treaties with the Dakotas led first to hunger, then to increasing starvation and death among their people.

On the evening of August 17, 1862, violence broke out when four young Dakotas, foraging for food on the property of white settlers, got into a skirmish that ended with the killing of all five of the white family members. Hostilities quickly escalated after the young rebels and their sympathizers convinced Chief Little Crow that it was time to go to war. As historian Douglas Linder writes:

> Events moved quickly. Forty-four Americans were killed in the first full day of fighting.... Nearly two-hundred additional whites died over the next few days as Dakota massacred

farm families and attacked Fort Ridgely. By mid-September, the initiative had shifted to the American forces. Penned in to the north and south, facing severe food shortages and declining morale, many Dakota warriors chose to surrender. Together with those taken captive [including many women and children], the ranks of Dakota prisoners welled to 1,250. A decision had to be made soon what to do with them.[154] After trials by a military court, thirty-eight of the Dakota men were sentenced to be hanged.

The Execution of 38 [Dakota] Sioux Indians by U.S. Authorities, Mankato, Minnesota, Friday, December 26

Following is part of a correspondent's eyewitness account of the hangings, which appeared in the *New York Times* on the very day of the execution, December 26, 1862:

> The street was full, the house tops were literally crowded, and every available place was occupied. There were from three to five thousand persons present. The reports of

a probable attempt by a mob to take possession of the remaining prisoners and inflict summary punishment upon them, induced authorities to provide a large military force for protection ... in all about 1,500 men.

Precisely at the time announced—10 A.M.—a company, without arms, entered the prisoners quarters, to escort them to their doom. Instead of any shrinking or resistance, all were ready, and even seemed eager to meet their fate. Rudely they jostled against each other, as they rushed from the doorway to the gauntlet of troops, and clambered up the steps to the treacherous drop. As they came up and reached the platform, they filed right and left, and each one took his position as though they had rehearsed the programme. Standing round the platform, they formed a square, and each one was directly under the fatal noose. Their caps were now drawn over their eyes, and the halter placed about their necks. Several of them feeling uncomfortable, made severe efforts to loosen the rope, and some, after the most dreadful contortions, partially succeeded. The signal to cut the rope was three taps of the drum. All things being ready, the first tap was given, when the poor wretches made such frantic efforts to grasp each other's hands, that it was agony to behold them. Each one shouted out his name, that his comrades might know he was there. The second tap resounded on the air. The vast multitude were breathless with the awful surroundings of this solemn occasion. Again the doleful tap breaks on the stillness of the scene. Click! Goes the sharp ax, and the descending platform leaves the bodies of thirty-eight human beings dangling in the air.[155]

President Abraham Lincoln prevented an even greater tragedy from occurring by pardoning two hundred and sixty-five Native Americans, claiming that they had legitimately defended themselves against the United States forces.

In April 1863, the remaining Dakotas were expelled from Minnesota to Nebraska and South Dakota. The war was used as a pretext to seize all of the remaining Dakota land. As historian Dee Brown notes, "Previous treaties were abrogated, and the surviving Indians were informed that they would be removed to a reservation in Dakota Territory."[156]

That was a totally different world than the one portrayed more than half a century later by Sinclair Lewis in his novel *Main Street*, in which the heroine, Carol Milford, is a former resident of Mankato. The novel's narrator describes the city as

> not a prairie town, but in its garden-sheltered streets and aisle of elms is white and green New England reborn. Mankato lies between cliffs and the Minnesota River, hard by Traverse des Sioux where the first settlers made treaties with the Indians, and the cattle-rustlers once came galloping before hell-for-leather posses.[157]

The Golden Globe-award-winning Swedish film *The New Land* (1972) presents a chilling account of the tragic execution of the Dakotas that took place there. Two years later, however, the long-running television series *Little House on the Prairie* (1974-1983), presented an idealistic version of the interaction between the Dakotas and settlers in Mankato during the Dakota War.

Both Edward and Richard had left Mankato before the tragic execution of the Dakotas occurred. By then they had designed an addition to the city in an expanded neighborhood that bears their family name. Today, Parry Street commemorates their contributions toward the early development of the city. When the Civil War broke out in 1861, Edward was the first volunteer from Mankato to enlist in the army. Richard continued his work in Mankato until May 31, 1862, brokering lands for the expansion of the railroads through the Midwest; then he returned to Philadelphia, where he continued his business career as a merchant.

Richard Randolph Parry was one of the pioneers of Minnesota in its territorial days, and later played an important role in bringing the territory into the Union in 1858. Over the years following his return to Philadelphia, he became the family's unofficial historian, gathering family documents and correspondence. Most of the family correspondence, however, was lost or destroyed when the Parry family home was sold in 1966. Fortunately, some of the surviving letters—along with and numerous other documents—have been preserved by the New Hope Historical Society and by the Spruance Library in Doylestown, Pennsylvania.

Parade on Front Street, Mankato—Courtesy of the Minnesota Historical Society

The Parry Mansion, New Hope, Pennsylvania in 2018—Author Photograph

The above photograph was taken in 1872 on Front Street in Mankato, Minnesota, near what ten years earlier had been the office of Parry and Brother.

Edward was commissioned first lieutenant in the Eleventh United States Infantry Regiment, the only person from Mankato known to have received a commission. After serving as adjutant general of the regular brigade for three years, he was promoted to captain in 1864, then to major "for gallant and meritorious service."

Parry commanded Forts Jackson and St. Philip in Louisiana, located on the west and east banks of the Mississippi River respectively. The forts had been retaken by the Union troops in 1862, when a Confederate army mutiny (at Fort Jackson) enabled Admiral Farragut's fleet to win the Battle of Fort Jackson and Fort St. Philip (April 16-28) and move on from there to seize New Orleans.[158]

Parry was present at Appomattox Court House, Virginia on April 9, 1865, when Confederate General Robert E. Lee surrendered to Union General Ulysses S. Grant. Major Parry continued his service in the military, in 1869 becoming commander of Fort Ripley, an army outpost on the upper Mississippi River in north-central Minnesota. The fort's military reservation took in ninety square miles on the east side of the river, and one square mile on the west side (where the garrison was housed). He resigned from the army due to poor health in 1871, at age thirty-nine. Three years later, on April 13, 1874, Major Edward Randolph Parry, having suffered a continuing illness from the hardships he endured during his military service, died peacefully in New Hope, Pennsylvania at the Old Parry Mansion, his boyhood home. He left behind his widow, Frances Dimick Randolph Parry, and their one child, Catherine.

Richard Randolph Parry—Courtesy of New Hope Historical Society

As his grandfather Captain Edward Randolph had done during the Revolutionary War, Major Edward Randolph Parry distinguished himself for bravery and service during the American Civil War.

Captain Oliver Randolph Parry (1873-1958)

In the first thirty years of the twentieth century the population of Philadelphia underwent unprecedented growth, skyrocketing by more than 650,000 to a total of 1,950,000 residents. Hundreds of thousands of immigrants from Europe joined many thousands of African-Americans from the Southern States who were streaming into the city during those decades. Housing, once again, grew scarce and overcrowded. To accommodate the ballooning population, streets were widened, and boulevards connecting isolated neighborhoods of Philadelphia were constructed. Beginning his career amid this rapid and unparalleled growth, Oliver Randolph Parry, the grandson of Oliver and Rachel Randolph Parry, worked to further his family's legacy in Philadelphia.

Captain Oliver Randolph Parry, c. 1912—
Courtesy of New Hope Historical Society

After completing his early home-tutored education, he was enrolled in Saint Luke's School in Wayne, Pennsylvania, near the site of the Battle of Paoli, where his great-grandfather, Captain Edward Randolph, had fought so bravely. He continued his education at the Bordentown Military Institute, in New Jersey. Oliver Randolph Parry, like many Randolph family members before him, enrolled in the University of Pennsylvania. Enrolled in the Class of 1896, he majored in architecture but (for reasons unknown) did not complete his studies for the degree.

Soon after leaving the university he became a partner in the architectural firm of Witmer and Parry; by the time he was twenty-five years old, he had already designed several projects. His works are included in the Philadelphia Record and Builders Guide in 1905. The 1909 city directory lists the location of the Witmer and Parry firm as

1723 Chestnut St., just half a block west of what is now One Liberty Place. With the success of his varied projects requiring additional office space, Oliver moved his office two blocks east, to 1524 Sansom Street by the mid-1920s. For a brief time, Oliver resided at 1604 Pine St. with his first wife, Lida Mae Kraemer (a former New York City chorus girl) and their only child, Margaret Parry Lang. Lida died in 1944 and is buried in the Morris Cemetery in her hometown of Phoenixville, Pennsylvania.

The Philadelphia Architects and Buildings database shows that, at the peak of his career, Oliver Randolph Parry maintained offices in Philadelphia and New York City, and that he was president and director of the Bay Court Estates Company in Great Neck, Long Island. He was known for being the architect for several New York and New Jersey companies. Parry designed a significant number of industrial buildings featuring the use of reinforced concrete materials, a construction material he had championed and for which he earned a national reputation. Some of his notable buildings in Pennsylvania that demonstrate the wide diversity of his work are the Protestant Episcopal Church Mission, in Chestnut Hill; the Bucks County Country Club, in Jamison; the Old York Road Country Club, in Montgomery County (since demolished); and the T. J. Stewart High School, in Norristown, a suburb of Philadelphia.

Parry was selected in 1908 as the architect and supervisor of construction for the complex of apartments and related buildings on fifteen acres along Lansdowne Avenue (site of what had been the Joshua L. Bailey Estate, later the J. C. Wilson Estate) in Darby, a suburb of Philadelphia. Also in 1908, Parry was commissioned by Wilkie Brothers to design the plans and specifications for the construction of eighty-four dwellings and stores to be built (at an estimated cost of $400,000) on the southeast corner of 54th Street and City Line Avenue, site of the old Black Horse Hotel, which, according to Parry's notes, was to be demolished to accommodate the massive development project. Plans for the project were eventually abandoned, however. Today the land is part of the campus of St. Joseph's University.

The Wills-Jones, McEwen Company Dairy—26th Street between Jefferson and Oxford Street, Philadelphia—Courtesy, New Hope Historical Society

Oliver designed and built a large modern dairy in what became known as the Brewerytown neighborhood of Philadelphia for the Wills-Jones, McEwen Company in 1912. He boasted that the design of the building paid special attention to construction costs, space utilization, and efficiency of facility operations. He ensured a low cost of maintenance by using reinforced concrete.

More than one hundred years later, Parry's dairy structure is home to a large private electrical contracting firm. In New Jersey, he designed additions to his alma mater, the Bordentown Military Institute, and later completed a movie theater in Cape May, New Jersey, the ocean resort town where his family had enjoyed for generations.

Oliver Randolph Parry's service in World War I

Like many of the Randolphs and Parrys before him, Oliver served his country in the military with distinction, attaining the rank of captain while assigned to the Army Corps of Engineers. He was a member of the Military Order of the Loyal Legion and of the Military Order of the World War. He served as captain of "D" Company, 304th Engineers (Combat) Organized Reserves, 79th Division. He was an active member of the American Legion, serving as Commander of the Taylor E. Walthour (later, Ingersoll Walthour) Post Number 282. After completing his service to the country, Parry returned to Philadelphia to continue his architectural pursuits, one of which included heading the firm of E. P. Gardner and Company, Scranton, Pennsylvania.

Oliver was a member of the Philadelphia Art Alliance, the Pennsylvania Society of the Sons of the American Revolution, the Penn Athletic Club, the Pen & Pencil Club, the Concrete Institute, and the Plays and Players Theater Club. He was also an original member of the Old York Road Country Club. He and his second wife, Carmita de Solmes Kennedy, were contributors to a number of charitable causes in Philadelphia, including the Philadelphia Museum of Art (PMA), to which several of Carmita's paintings were bequeathed. In April, 2008, to benefit its acquisitions fund, the PMA's board of trustees sold a set of Chinese export porcelain (circa 1790) that had been donated by the Parrys.

So extensive were Oliver Randolph Parry's social activities that a Philadelphia journalist for *The Evening Ledger* felt compelled to write (in April 1915): "Architect, author and multi-clubman Oliver Randolph Parry is so popular he has had a beverage named after him—The Parry Toddy. (He belongs to nearly everything and knows nearly everybody.)"

In 1938, following the death of Carmita that year, Parry retired to his boyhood home at the Parry Mansion in New Hope. Ever the architect, he set about designing an addition to the 1784 Georgian-style mansion: a modern kitchen for himself and his two spinster sisters, Gertrude and Adelaide. During his twenty years of retirement, he continued writing and accepting public speaking engagements. On April 22, 1958 Oliver Randolph Parry died peacefully in his sleep at the Parry Mansion. He was eighty-five. Two days later, in a front-page article noting his death, the *New Hope Gazette* wrote that Parry was "a proud and colorful figure [whose] death marks the end of an era."

Captain Oliver Randolph Parry's only surviving sister, Adelaide, died within a few months of her brother's death. Margaret Parry Lang, Oliver's only child, inherited the Parry Mansion. After residing there for ten years, she and her husband, Oliver Paul Lang, sold the home in 1966 to the New Hope Historical Society, which has restored the elegant mansion, creating a museum of early American history, art and culture.

Evan Randolph (1822-1887)

EVAN RANDOLPH
Randolph & Jenks
Cotton Merchants

Evan Randolph, Philadelphia and Notable Philadelphians by Moses King, 1902

Evan Randolph was the son of William Randolph and Ann Evans, and the grandson of Captain Edward Randolph and Anna Julianna Steele. Evan's marriage to Rachel Story Jenks linked the renowned Randolph family to one of the oldest and most colorful and important families in the history of Bucks County, Pennsylvania.

Rachel's great-great-great grandmother, Susan MacPherson Jenks, the matriarch of the Jenks family (whose Welsh ancestry is traced back to William the Conqueror) arrived in Bucks County from England with her five-year-old son in 1703. Whether her husband, Thomas, had died before they set sail for America or while on board the ship during the course of their journey is not known. She and Thomas Jr. settled in a little log cabin in Wycombe, Wrightstown Township, Bucks County. Five years later, in 1708, Susan married Benjamin Wiggins, a widower who had moved from New England to Wycombe; a son, Bezaleel (there are various spellings of his name), was born sometime within the next two years, during which period Susan passed away and was buried in the cemetery of the Wrightstown Meeting House. Bezaleel married Rachel Hayhurst in 1734 (as recorded by the Middletown Monthly meeting). They had five children: Benjamin, Isaac, Joseph, Elizabeth and Mary, about whom we know only that his daughter Elizabeth married John Eastburn. Bezaleel died in 1794. His wife is not mentioned in his will, and probably predeceased him. No further record exists of either Bezaleel or his wife.[159]

The smallest section of the home shown in the photograph was built by Benjamin around 1722. A large addition to the home was built by the Smith Family in 1771, on the site of the original log cabin where Susan had lived with her son Thomas. The larger addition to the house was built by the Smith Family around 1789. Susan's first son, Thomas, grew up on that farm.

The Susan Jenks Wiggins farmhouse (from the back), Wycombe, Pa. as it appeared in 2018—Author Photograph

Thomas Jenks purchased land from William Penn's sons

In 1733 Thomas Jenks took possession of a tract of land from its proprietors, John, Thomas and Richard Penn, the three sons of William Penn by his second wife, Hanna Margaret Callowhill (whom Penn had married in 1696, two years after the death of his first wife, Maria Springett). William Penn had a total of sixteen children from his two marriages—John, Thomas and Richard being the longest surviving offspring.

Penn's sons took over the governance of Pennsylvania after his death in 1718. Fourteen years later they began selling off some of the land—in the countryside north and west of Philadelphia—and were trying to make peace with a number of the local Indian chiefs who, by that time, were unfamiliar with the treaty that William Penn had negotiated decades earlier.

In 1732 the three Penn brothers signed an order to create a commission to establish the boundary between Pennsylvania and Maryland in accordance with an agreement they had reached with Charles Calvert, the 5th Lord of Baltimore. The commission included (among others) James

Logan, William Penn's trusted agent; and Andrew Hamilton, who had helped Penn get out of prison after returning to England and finding himself unable to settle the massive gambling debts and other outstanding bills accumulated by his son William Penn, Jr.

Disputes about the boundary arose between Charles Calvert's son, Frederick (the 6th Lord Baltimore) and Penn's sons—and continued for nearly four decades. The final boundary between Pennsylvania and Maryland was not determined until 1769, when King George III approved the boundary (known as the Mason-Dixon Line) established by Charles Mason and Jeremiah Dixon, who had been hired by the 6th Lord Baltimore and the three Penn brothers.[160]

In 1740, Thomas Jenks sold the one hundred and ninety-two-acre farm to the Van Horn family, who then sold it to the Smith family in 1756. Descendants of the Smith family still live there today, more than two hundred and sixty years later.

Thomas Jenks joined the Society of Friends in 1723. By the time he married Mercy Wildman, in 1731, he had already become a very prosperous businessman in Langhorne, Pennsylvania, having constructed many buildings in the area. In that same year, the thirty-two-year-old Thomas purchased six hundred acres of land on which, several years later, he built his home, naming it Jenks Hall. He added a fulling cloth mill along nearby Core Creek, where many farmers during that time would go to process the wool from their sheep. Indeed they would continue using that mill for the next hundred years.[161] Raw wool would be taken to the mill for cleaning, where, in the process known as "fulling," it was kneaded with "fuller's earth" (a finely granulated clay) to wash out the grease, oil and lanolin from the wool, which could later be narrowed into thread on spinning wheels for making "homespun" cloth.

During the American Revolutionary War, a group of Loyalists from the Light Horse Dragoons and the Bucks County Volunteers raided the mill and stole the cloth that had been ordered by George Washington for his troops in Valley Forge. The mill was later used as a stable for horses. Fulling Mill Road exists today at the northern end of what is now Core Creek Park.

Lake Luxembourg (a part of which is shown in the photograph below as it appeared in 2018) was created in 1975 by the Neshaminy Valley Water Authority when it damned Core Creek, a stream that winds through southeast Bucks County and empties into Neshaminy Creek ("Neshaminy" from the Lenape "Nischam-hanne," meaning "double stream").

The 166-acre lake was named for the Grand Duchess of Luxembourg (Charlotte Aldegarde Elise Marie Wilhelmina, Duchess of Nassau, Princess of Braganza and of Bourbon-Parma). She was married to Prince Felix Marie Vincent de Bourbon-Parma. Using the names Charlotte and Felix de Clervaux to protect their identities, they bought nearly three hundred acres in the area of what had once been the old Jenks property. At the time of purchase, it was owned by the Watson family, and known as the "Old Watson Place."[162]

The Grand Duchess and her husband had fled Luxembourg before the Nazis invaded the country during World War II. They established a government in exile in England before going to the United States where the land on what is now known as Lake Luxembourg became the Royal Family's home and private farm.

Lake Luxembourg in Core Creek Park, Middletown, Pa.—Author Photograph

In his *History of Bucks County, Pennsylvania*, General W. W. H. Davis describes Thomas Jenks as one who

> led an active business life, lived respected, and died on May 4, 1797 at the good old age of ninety-seven. He was small in stature, but sprightly, temperate in his habits, and of great physical vigor. At the age of ninety he walked fifty miles in a week, and at ninety-two his eye-sight and hearing were both remarkably good. He had lived to see the wilderness and haunts of wild beasts become the seats of polished life.[163]

Thomas and Mercy Jenks had three daughters, Mary, Elizabeth and Ann, and three sons, Thomas, Jr., John and Joseph. Thomas, Jr. became a member of the Constitutional Convention in 1790. That same year he was elected to the Pennsylvania State Senate, serving in that position until his death in 1799.

Joseph Jenks continues the work of his father

The Bridgetown Mill, Bridgetown, Pa., depicted in "Short Account and Abstract of our Ancestry and Genealogy," Arranged and Written for Rachel S. J. Randolph by William H. Jenks, Philadelphia, 1883—Historical Society of Pennsylvania

Joseph followed closely in the footsteps of his father, becoming widely known as a major agriculturalist in Bucks County. He purchased the Bridgetown Mill that had been built by Jonas Preston in 1704, around the time that Joseph's grandmother, Susan Jenks, arrived in the area. Joseph also operated his father's fulling mill and cleared fifty-one acres east of Bridgetown (now Edgemont), land farmed by Joseph's only son, William. In 1791 Joseph built a grist mill and a mansion on the land. gifting both to William and his daughter-in-law, Mary Hutchinson Jenks. Before his death in 1818, William Jenks gave the homestead and mill to his sons Joseph and Charles. (William's widow, Mary, received half ownership of the mill house, two horses, two cows, sufficient firewood and an allowance of six hundred dollars per year.) Joseph continued to operate the Jenks mills until the mid-1840s. In 1847, having amassed considerable wealth as a merchant miller, he sold the mill and the mill house, living twenty-two years in retirement before dying in 1869. Samuel Comfort, who purchased the property, continued to operate it until 1876, when it was sold to Benjamin Woodman. It was operated as a mill until 1939.

The Bridgetown Mill House Inn, 2018—Author Photograph

Left vacant and deteriorating for over half a century, the mill house and the ruins of the old mill, along with the surrounding eight acres, were purchased for commercial use in 1995. Of the original eight hundred-acre Jenks homestead, only the mill house has survived, reincarnated in 1998 as the Bridgetown Mill House Inn. It flourishes today as an elegant country inn for locals and tourists in one of the most historic towns in Bucks County.

William Pearson Jenks (1807-1886)

WILLIAM PEARSON JENKS
Randolph & Jenks
Cotton Merchants

William Pearson Jenks, *Philadelphia and Notable Philadelphians* by Moses King, 1902

William Pearson Jenks, the son of William Jenks and Mary Hutchinson Jenks, was born in 1807 and grew up on the Jenks homestead in Bucks County. After he finished school, William moved to Paterson, New Jersey, where he trained to be a machinist at a manufacturing business in the town. He was one of many hundreds of talented young men drawn to Paterson at that time. The industrial city was the dream of Alexander Hamilton, who, during the Revolutionary War, picnicked with George Washington and Lafayette at the Great Falls (in the area that later became the City of Paterson). As they lunched on what historian Ron Chernow described as "cold ham, tongue and biscuits,"[164] Hamilton was struck by the sheer power of the falls. (Two billion gallons of water at the bend of the Passaic River plunge seventy-seven feet over the falls every day.)

When Hamilton later developed his vision of America as a giant manufacturing nation that would rival England, Paterson was the place that he settled on as the foundation for fulfilling his dream. In 1791 he and his Assistant Secretary of the Treasury, Tench Coxe, encouraged the development of a manufacturing society that would have the support of the government. It would, they thought, be a type of laboratory for new and progressive ideas in manufacturing, but their arguments for the creation of the manufacturing mecca fell on deaf ears in Congress. His vision undaunted, Hamilton turned to the private sector to launch his ambitious venture. He and Coxe created an association of private investors, which they named the Society for Establishing Useful Manufactures (S.U.M.). They envisioned a manufacturing town that would produce a wide variety of goods—from paper to shoes to cotton, beer, and much more. It would occupy six square miles.

The ensuing town was named Paterson, after Governor William Paterson, a signer of the Declaration of Independence. Hamilton's intent in honoring the governor was likely coupled with the hope of winning the governor's support for the establishment of his manufacturing model. He succeeded. With Governor Paterson's support, the New Jersey Legislature voted that the Society for Establishing Useful Manufactures be forever exempt from county and township taxation. The State Legislature also gave the Society the right to hold property, improve rivers, and build canals. Surprisingly, the legislature also authorized S.U.M. to raise one hundred thousand dollars through the use of a lottery. The Society's investors quickly bought up real estate on which to set up their factories. The town's easy access to major roads that connected the country's two largest cities, Philadelphia and New York, was another critical factor in its success. In Kull's *New Jersey: A History*, we read:

> The company had paid-in capital of some $160,000 by October 1, 1792, and brought Nehemiah Hubbard down from Middleton, Connecticut, as superintendent at $2,000 per year. $20,000 was appropriated for a canal (as the falls had an elevation of 104 feet above the water); $5,000 for a weave shop and equipment; the same for the cotton manufactory; and $12,000 for a print work. For the workmen, the founders projected 50 houses costing $250 each, generously planned to cover 24 x 18 feet with cellar and garret both. These very presentable structures were offered to married mechanics on a lease system permitting them to buy the homes in installments.[165]

Alexander Hamilton's creation, The Society for Establishing Useful Manufactures, continued to function in Paterson until 1945, when the city purchased its property and charter.

After learning the machinist trade at a firm in Paterson that specialized in the manufacture of equipment for the spinning and weaving of cotton goods, William Jenks developed an interest in manufacturing cotton yarns. He left Paterson in 1828 and moved to New Hope, where the entrepreneur William Maris was operating several mills, including a cotton mill. The time was ideal for Jenks to be leaving Paterson, for it was there, in the same year that the nation's first-ever strike by factory workers broke out. Being on the job from very early in the morning, the cotton workers felt that the company's changing their lunch hour from noon to one o'clock created an unacceptable hardship. The workers also demanded that the workday be reduced from thirteen and a half to twelve hours. Abandoning their looms, they were joined in the strike by other workers in the city (including carpenters, masons and mechanics), the work stoppage thus becoming in addition the first recorded incidence of a "sympathy strike." In the end, all they got from the company was its agreement to restore the lunch hour to noon.[166]

According to Davis, William Jenks and his firm provided the machinery for William Maris's cotton mill in Solebury (now New Hope), Pennsylvania; he remained employed by Maris in that capacity until 1832. During that time, Maris became embroiled in a protracted lawsuit (lasting more than ten years) in the Bucks County court against Benjamin Parry, another New Hope industrial giant and patriarch of the renowned Parry Family. Parry's mill was located about a mile downstream from the Maris mill. In the lawsuit, Maris accused Parry of altering the flow of the Aquetong Creek (which they both used to power their mills) in such a way as to give unfair advantage to Parry. In the end, the court ruled in favor of Parry. William Maris, in the meantime, had overextended himself financially, so shortly after he lost his court battle, Maris surrendered all of his property at sheriff's sale and returned to Philadelphia.

After leaving his position with Maris's mill in 1832, William Jenks returned to the firm in Paterson. The Morris Canal had opened by then, and the city was crisscrossed with railroads. Because of its vastly increased accessibility, Paterson had become a significantly greater industrial center than when William left it four years earlier.

Located on the north bank of the Ohio River, the industry in Madison, Indiana was booming at the time, and the successful investors in Paterson's cotton mill saw Madison as a logical expansion of their business. Occupying the Madison waterfront in the 1830s were steam-powered mills producing cotton, flour, castor oil and lumber. Business there also benefited from the heavy steamboat traffic. William relocated to Madison when the company in Paterson assigned him to a project that was created there to establish a factory for the manufacture of cotton goods.

In 1835, following two successful years working in Madison, William Pearson Jenks was appointed manager of the Union Factories, near Ellicott Mills (now Ellicott City), Maryland. The Baltimore and Ohio (B&O) Railroad, the first chartered railroad in American history, opened its rail service from Baltimore to Ellicott Mills that same year, and expanded its connection to Washington, DC, the nation's capital. William continued working at the Union Factories until the fall of 1846, when poor health forced him to resign. He had been instrumental in making it the largest cotton-manufacturing mill south of New England.

Ellicott City had developed from the original Ellicott Mills founded by the Ellicott Family. The patriarch, Andrew Ellicott, left his home in Devonshire, England when his business began experiencing severe problems. He and his son, Andrew, arrived in Buckingham, Bucks County in 1730. They lived near the Buckingham Friends Meetinghouse, just a few miles west of the town of Wycombe, where William Pearson Jenks would later be born and raised. Although Andrew had intended to return to England, his son met Ann Bye, a local Bucks County woman, and they married. Tragically, after fathering five children, Andrew died from pleurisy at the age of 33. Andrew's father, having abandoned his plan to return to England at the behest of his newly-married son, purchased land in Buckingham and soon started his own wool-carding and combing mill business. Andrew's grandsons—Joseph, the eldest; and Nathaniel, Andrew, John and Thomas—all began working at the mill in Bucks County, building the largest mill in the area (most probably the Maris Mill, where William Pearson Jenks would much later provide his services as a machinist toward the beginning of his career).

Following Andrew Ellicott's death, Joseph traveled to England to claim his grandfather's property in Devon, returning to Bucks County with a considerable fortune. A short time later, all of the brothers except Thomas moved to Howard County, Maryland, where they bought property, built their own mills (on the banks of the Patapsco River near Baltimore) and developed what is now known as Ellicott City.

Thomas Ellicott remained in Bucks County, where he built and operated his own mill. Later, the Ellicott brothers built roads connecting the Ellicott Upper and Lower Mills to Baltimore and Frederick, Maryland. But they had not yet finished. They became the first mill owners in the country to grow their own wheat for commercial production. They became major producers of flour as well. By 1800 the mill industry had generated a variety of other business ventures. That is when Ellicott Mills was named Ellicott City. It was a major industrial area in the eastern United States. It is easy to imagine how delighted Alexander Hamilton would have been to see in America industrial cities rivaling those in England—his dream become reality.

The B&O Railroad Bridge over Main Street, Ellicott City, Md.—Courtesy of Creative Commons

An additional point of interest about the Ellicott Family must be included in their story. Yet another Andrew Ellicott, Joseph's son (also born in Buckingham) became intrigued by his father's mechanical ability at an early age and seemed to have inherited Joseph's skills. John Richardson, in his book *Solebury Township Bucks County*, refers to Andrew's talent: "Father Joseph was a genius at fancy clock-making.... Young Andrew, at the early age of fifteen, was giving important help to his father and they are both credited with having worked on their most famous four-faced musical clock."[167]

Having gained his elementary education at the Quaker Meetinghouse in Buckingham, Andrew Ellicott went on to study in Philadelphia. After his marriage to Sarah Brown in 1775, he and his new bride moved to Maryland to join their family in the bustling new Ellicott City.

Andrew was widely known for his knowledge of astronomy, mathematics and geography. In 1786 he was elected a member of the American Philosophical Society (APS), having impressed both Benjamin Franklin and Thomas Jefferson with his talent. "I have long known Mr. Andrew Ellicott as a man of science," Franklin writes of him on August 10, 1789, "and while I was in the Executive Council [of APS] have had frequent occasion in the course of Public business of being acquainted with his abilities in Geographical operations of the most important kind, which were performed by him with the greatest scientific accuracy."[168]

When Thomas Jefferson deemed Major Pierre Charles L'Enfant's plans for the new capital city of Washington, DC unacceptable, the disgruntled Frenchman left the country, taking his rejected plans with him. Jefferson turned to Bucks County, Pennsylvania native Andrew Ellicott to create the design for the new city.

William Pearson Jenks' daughter, Rachel Story Jenks, was born at Ellicott Mills, Maryland in 1845, the year before William became seriously ill. In 1847, William joined his family in Philadelphia after returning from Brazil, where he had gone for several months to recuperate. Later that year, he and his son-in-law, Evan Randolph, formed a business partnership known as Randolph & Jenks.[169]

John Story Jenks, William H. Jenks, and Rachel Story Jenks (1849), the Carson-Randolph Papers—Courtesy of the Historical Society of Pennsylvania

Randolph & Jenks

The offices of Randolph & Jenks were located at 101 S. Front St., and later at 238 Chestnut St., in Philadelphia (the latter location is now part of the site of the National Museum of the American Revolution). Among the city's most extensive and profitable cotton merchants, the firm purchased, in 1876, the Frogmore (also spelled "Frogmour") Cotton Mills, one of the largest such mills in Philadelphia at the time. The original mill was built in 1848 by Robert Garsed and his brother, John, a captain in the Union Army during the American Civil War. Captain Garsed had provided ten thousand dollars' worth of cotton to the army during the war and was reimbursed for his expenses by an act of Congress. As had William Pearson Jenks, Robert Garsed trained at the mill in New Hope. Robert began his training there at the age of nine, William not starting there until he was twenty-one.

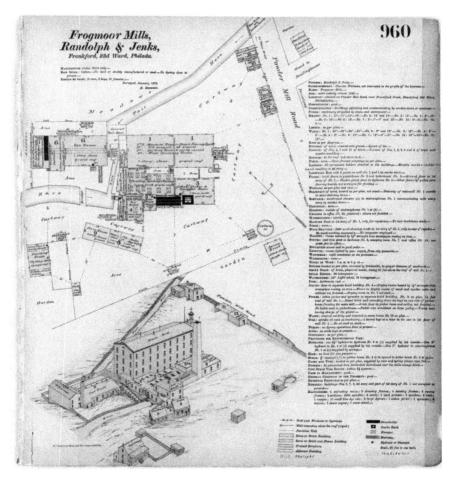

"*Frogmour [Frogmore] Mills*," Hexamer General Surveys, Vol. 11, Plate 960, 1876 (colour litho). Hexamer, Ernest (1827-1912), Free Library of Philadelphia/ Map Collection, Free Library of Philadelphia/Bridgeman Images

Evan was a traveler and an adventurer. In the Randolph-Carson Papers, his daughter, Hope Carson Randolph, recounts fascinating stories her father told her about his trip to North Dakota with friends in April 1858, when they traveled by train to Chicago, St. Paul and Minneapolis. From there they continued on horseback and wagon—stopping at various army forts, and camping out on the prairie—until finally reaching their destination in Medora, North Dakota, where they delighted in the popular sport at the time: hunting buffalos. They returned from Sioux City, cruising down the Missouri River, eventually arriving in St. Louis, where they took the train to Cincinnati, arriving back home in Philadelphia on June 14th, nearly two months later. A hint of intrigue occurs in her papers, as when she shares stories that her mother told her about Evan's interaction with President Lincoln:

> My mother used to tell me that my father knew Abraham Lincoln and that he made several trips to the south during the war between the states, at the request of Mr. Lincoln, ostensively to buy cotton but at the same time to pick up all the information he possibly could regarding Confederate armed forces and the general condition of the Confederate government. According to my mother, my father was never given any instructions in writing but Mr. Lincoln told him by word of mouth what he wanted father to report on, and such reports were always made by my father verbally to Mr. Lincoln so that there is nothing in writing to prove any of this.[170]

While it remains true that no written evidence exists of Evan's having performed reconnaissance missions for President Lincoln, several factors lend credence to the claim. Julianna Randolph Wood, a first cousin of Evan, was the wife of Richard Davis Wood, who had hired Abraham Lincoln during the Panic of 1857 to collect delinquent debts from Wood's customers when the future president was still a young lawyer. So, Lincoln had been acquainted with the Randolph family several years before he was elected President. Also, as a partner in one of the largest cotton firms in the country during the Civil War, it is certain that Evan's duties with the firm included numerous trips to the Confederate States to purchase cotton. In that capacity he would have been in a very advantageous position to observe troop buildups and movements. Additionally, as president, Lincoln is known to have used former slaves in his espionage effort. In her 2016

National Geographic story, "Harriet the Spy: How Tubman Helped the Union Army," journalist Becky Little writes: "The use of former slaves as spies was a covert operation—President Abraham Lincoln didn't event tell the Secretary of War or the Secretary of Navy about it."

With their 1876 purchase of the Frogmore Mills complex, Evan and William were acquiring a totally rebuilt mill. By then, Frankford, the neighborhood in which the mill was located had become a vital part of Philadelphia's nineteenth-century reputation as the "workshop of the world." The mills were located between Powder Mill Lane and the Frankford Creek, whose rapid-running waters provided energy generated by a fifty-two-foot, seventy-horsepower waterwheel (their steam engine providing about ten more horsepower).

Historian Emily T. Cooperman describes the mills as follows:

> In 1869 over forty manufactures lay within Frankford's borders, with the products ranging from the woolen carpets of the Tremont Carpet Factory to the steel merchandise of the Philadelphia Steel Works. During the late 1860s, Frankford's industries were still primarily textile-focused.... The machines used steam and water power to create wool and cotton textiles. The factory was the largest of the three owned by the Garsed Brothers. It was a large complex of brick and stone buildings. One large stone building held the spinning, weaving and cotton picking and spreading, warping and finishing and carding operations. There were also separate structures containing a dye house, a waste house, a carriage house, a stable and a coal pit.[171]

William Pearson Jenks retired from the company in 1860 and became president of the Bucks Mountain Coal Company, in Northeastern Pennsylvania. While travelling in Europe with his family in the summer of 1887, Evan Randolph suffered a paralytic stroke, forcing them to return home early. Evan died on December 3rd of that year after suffering a second stroke.

Randolph & Jenks continued with William's sons, John Story Jenks and William H. Jenks, joining Evan Randolph's son, Evan, Jr. William was a director of the Girard Trust Company, the Franklin National Bank, and the Philadelphia Saving Fund Society (PSFS). He was also a director of two railroad companies and a mortar-manufacturing company. In 1869, William married Hannah Mifflin Hacker, daughter of the revered Philadelphia Quakers Jeremiah and Beulah Morris Hacker. Hannah had spent many summers of her youth at the family's late-18th-century summer retreat, "Woodside," in the Germantown section of Philadelphia, the home remaining in the family until 1904.

John Story Jenks continued his duties as a merchant with Randolph & Jenks while also serving as director of Pennsylvania Hospital, the Philadelphia Trust Company, the Western Savings Fund Society, Western National Bank, and the Insurance Company of North America (INA). Today, the J. S. Jenks Academy for the Arts & Sciences, a public school in Chestnut Hill, Pennsylvania (originally the John Story Jenks School), stands as a lasting tribute to John Story Jenks, named after him by the School District of Philadelphia for his civic-mindedness. Its several hundred students are afforded specialized programs for life skills, inclusion/learning support, and gifted support.

Located near the academy is John's summer residence, Inglewood Cottage, a Gothic Revival villa designed by Thomas Ustick Walter, Fourth Architect of the United States Capitol. Built in 1850 for Cephas Childs, director of the Chestnut Hill Railroad, the residence remained in the Jenks Family until 1986.

Walker and Richman owned the Frogmore Mills in 1889. A fire destroyed the huge main building in the late 1890s, but by 1906 the rebuilt Frogmore Mills was back in the Randolph Family again (owned by Rachel and John Randolph). From 1925 to the early 1980s, the Philadelphia Felt Company, one of the few mills of its kind that produced felt and textiles for distribution throughout the country, were owners of the complex's only remaining building.

Romano's Catering Company purchased the building in 1986, converting it into one of the most unique banquet facilities in the city. In deference to the mill's great history, the owner named one of the ballrooms "The Felt Factory," retaining some of the original wood and steel structures as part of the interior design. Romano's website boasts that "Our three beautiful ballrooms give all of our guests the feeling of a foundational history with the combined designs of both modern and vintage flare, making it an ideal wedding venue in Philadelphia."

Evan Randolph Jr. (1880-1962)

Evan Randolph, Jr.—
Courtesy of the Historical Society of Pennsylvania

Evan Randolph Jr. was the son of Evan Randolph and Rachel Story Jenks, the daughter of William Pearson Jenks, who had grown up in the old Jenks homestead in Bridgetown, Bucks County, and Elizabeth Story Jenks.

Evan was born in Philadelphia and attended the Penn Charter School and the Delancey School. In 1907, four years after graduating from Harvard, Evan married Hope Carson, the daughter of Hampton Lawrence Carson, attorney general of Pennsylvania from 1903 to 1907. Evan and Hope had five children: Hope, Evan III, Hampton Carson, Rachel, and David. In partnership with Herbert W. Goodall, formerly a stockbroker with Isaac Starr, Jr. and Company, Evan Jr. formed in 1912 Evan Randolph and Company, a banking and brokerage business. Two years later, he was named vice president of the Girard Bank. Located on S. 3rd Street, Girard Bank's building had once housed the First Bank of the United States, founded by Alexander Hamilton. When that bank's charter expired in 1811, Stephen Girard purchased the building and nearly all of the bank's stock. The wealthiest man in the nation at the time, Girard helped finance the United States War of 1812. He continued operating his private banking business ("Girard's Bank," as it was called) in Philadelphia until his death in 1831.

The bank building was leased the very next year to a new state-chartered bank ("Girard Bank," no relationship to Stephen Girard or to his private banking business though obviously capitalizing on his name). Girard Bank and its successor, the Girard National Bank of Philadelphia, operated until 1926, when Girard National Bank merged with the Philadelphia National Bank. Joseph Wayne Jr. was elected president and chairman-of-the-board, Evan Randolph becoming vice-president.[172]

Evan became president of the Philadelphia National Bank in 1941, succeeding Joseph Wayne Jr., who had at one time personally approved a loan of three million dollars to the city to meet the seriously overdue payroll owed to its employees (but not without a firm warning that the city straighten out its financial affairs), earning him the enduring admiration of the City of Philadelphia. Wayne had been a beloved figure at the bank and in the city for more than half a century. Even after he suffered a stroke in June 1940, people still continued to seek him out for financial advice and help. Evan Randolph—his associate, good friend and close companion for many years—was elected his successor in January 1941. Wayne died on May 26, 1942.

In his *History of the Philadelphia National Bank*, Nicholas B. Wainwright describes Evan Randolph's outstanding leadership during his six years as its president:

> The period was indeed one of extraordinary progress.... Evan Randolph had the satisfaction of leaving the Bank with its net worth at an all-time high. During his presidency the capital assets of the Bank grew from forty-four to fifty-seven million dollars, a remarkable advance.... In two respects Randolph's services had been of particular value: he was an experienced bond man, and the Bank profited by his knowledge of that field of investment; and to quote the minutes, "Not the least of his contributions to the Bank was the acquisition of capable young men for the organization."[173]

Following his remarkable success as president of the Philadelphia National Bank, Evan Randolph Jr. retired in 1947. He passed away in 1962.

PART SEVEN

The Randolph Family in the 21st Century

Evan Randolph Jr. (1880-1962) & Hope Carson Randolph (1885-1980)

▼

Hope Randolph (1908-2002) & William Platt Hacker (1904-2002)
Evan Randolph III (1909-1997) & Frances Lewis Beale (1912-2004)
▼
Evan Randolph IV (b. 1935) & Penelope Dixon (b. 1941)
Leonard Beale Randolph (b. 1937) & Sally Ann Schoettle (b. 1940)
John Randolph (b. 1947) & Alice Moffat (b. 1947)
Francis Lewis Randolph (1951-1974)
Hampton Carson Randolph (1911-1998) & Barbara Reeves (1917-1969)
Rachel Randolph (1915-1995) & Arthur Doucette (1907-1995)
David Story Randolph (1922-1972) & Hannah Wright Sullivan (b. 1923)

Evan Randolph III (1909-1997)

Evan Randolph III (with granddaughter Rachel)—Photograph by John Randolph

Evan Randolph III was the second child of Hope and Evan Randolph Jr. Although referred to in various documents as Evan Randolph III, he began referring to himself in his adult years as Evan Randolph "Jr." since his father had begun using the name Evan Randolph "Sr." following the death of *his* father.

In 1927, Evan graduated from Milton Academy, in Milton, Massachusetts, several of whose other distinguished alumni include Nobel-Prize-winning poet and playwright T. S. Eliot, Senators Robert F. Kennedy and Ted Kennedy, and animal rights activist Cleveland Amory. A four-year member of the rowing team, Evan earned his B. A. degree from Harvard, Class of 1931. He wrote his graduate thesis about Arthur Young, an 18th Century agriculturalist[174] who became famous in England after the French Revolution as an advocate of such agricultural innovations as seed drilling, improved crop rotations, and ways of enclosing of open fields.

After graduation, Evan spent a year traveling throughout Europe, writing frequently to his family members about his impressions of the culture he encountered. Shortly after returning home he married Frances Lewis Beale in Old St. Peter's Church, 3rd and Pine Streets in Philadelphia. As his father had done, Evan pursued a career in banking. During World War II he enlisted in the US Navy. Told by officials that he was "too old to serve in active duty" (he was thirty-five at the time). Evan was assigned to the Navy Price Adjustment Board in Washington, DC, an indisputably appropriate position for the experienced banker.

He resumed his banking career after the war, soon becoming an assistant vice president of First Pennsylvania Bank, managing operations at their principal branch in Ardmore, Pennsylvania. During that time, he was president of the Ardmore Businessmen's Association and served on the board of Bryn Mawr College's School of Social Work. Evan also served on the Radnor Township Planning Commission. Over the course of his career, however, the banking business had changed its focus of developing strong business relationships with local clients. Realizing that the commercial banking business was headed away from what he wanted to focus on, Evan opted for early retirement in 1971, at age sixty-two.

Just as his father was greatly admired by the Philadelphia community for the excellence of his work in the banking field, Evan is still fondly remembered by individuals and business owners in Ardmore more than two decades after his death in 1997.

Evan and Frances suffered the tragic loss of their youngest son, Francis Lewis Randolph, at age twenty-three. He died suddenly on his way to Greece in 1974 where he was traveling to receive an award for his research into the life of Lord Byron, the famous British poet and political revolutionary. As a way of coping with their loss, Francis's parents decided to pursue their dream of owning a summer home in Maine, purchasing a cottage on Connor Point, near Southwest Harbor. The following year, they, along with their son John and his wife, Alice, and newly born granddaughter, Rachel, spent the summer converting the 1907 cottage into a summer family home, much beloved by subsequent generations. The three surviving sons of Evan and Frances are Evan Randolph IV, Leonard Beale Randolph and John Randolph.

In 1976, during the Randolph family's second summer at Connor Point, Frances presented her husband with a racing shell (promptly named "Heart's Delight"), giving Evan an opportunity to return to the sport of rowing he had so much enjoyed during his college days forty years earlier. Evan went on to compete annually in the July 4th Rowing Regattas on the Charles River—and frequently won. During winter months, he practiced on his Concept II rowing machine and entered competitions sponsored by the U. S. Rowing Association. Harvard University's obituary of Evan noted that in 1995, at age eighty-six, Evan Randolph was the oldest competitor in the Head of the Charles River Regatta.[175]

Nearly every morning he would row a mile out to the #8 buoy off Southwest Harbor. Reminiscent of the physical stamina of his eighteenth-century ancestor Thomas Jenks, who is said to have walked fifty miles a week at the age of ninety, Evan participated in local Philadelphia rowing machine competitions until he was eighty-six, even at that age continuing his daily rowing practice—up to and including the very last day of his life two years later.

John Randolph (b. 1947)
Architect, Community Activist

Born in 1947, John Randolph is the third of Evan Randolph III and Frances Beale's four sons, his siblings being Evan IV, Leonard, and Francis. Their paternal grandparents were Evan Randolph Jr., and Hope Carson, of Chestnut Hill, Pennsylvania. Anna and Leonard T. Beale, of Philadelphia and Penllyn, were their maternal grandparents. After living the early part of his life in Radnor, a suburb of Philadelphia, when he attended the Haverford School and Milton Academy, John was drawn to the urban renaissance rapidly unfolding in Philadelphia in the latter decades of the twentieth century.

John Randolph, photograph by Phil Straus

In 1969 he earned a bachelor's degree from the University of Pennsylvania, and in 1972 a master's degree in architecture from Princeton, where more than two centuries earlier his ancestor Nathaniel Fitz Randolph had been the first to donate land and funds for the establishment of the university.

John began his career as an architect but quickly became interested in combining his love of design with that of building construction. He formed a company in Philadelphia that eventually became Design + Construction Incorporated, which specialized in both residential and commercial developments. With William Post Thomas, his partner in the firm, he later added residential development to his repertoire, building several townhouse complexes in the city's resurgent downtown area.

John's involvement and commitment to center city stands in sharp contrast to Oliver Randolph Parry, the grandson of Rachel Randolph (whose brother, William, was John's great-great-great grandfather). As noted earlier, Oliver, after constructing commercial properties in several of Philadelphia's center city neighborhoods in the 1940s, shifted his attention to building mansions in the posh "Main Line" suburbs as many of the city's wealthier families had begun migrating there in the 1950s.

John moved to Philadelphia's Society Hill neighborhood in 1968.

He married Alice Day Moffat, of Cleveland, Ohio in 1971. Their family includes Rachel, born in 1975 (named after Rachel Story Jenks and John's Aunt Rachel), and Kathrine ("Kate"), born in 1978 (named after Alice's mother). John and Alice are the grandparents of Esme, Zada and Matthew.

Rachel, a practicing psychotherapist, earned a bachelor's degree at New York University and master's degree in social work at Hunter College. In 2008 Kate earned an MBA degree from Presidio Graduate School, which is ranked among the country's top five programs for sustainability studies, a field that addresses complex concerns related to the impact of environmental and social issues on long-term business management. Kate is employed by Google in the company's Real Estate and Workplace Services. She lives with her daughter, Zada, in Berkeley, California.

In 1989 John Randolph launched a campaign to revitalize the east bank of the Schuylkill River in center city, at that time an area of Philadelphia described by Sarah Clark Stuart, Executive Director of the Greater Philadelphia Bicycle Coalition, as "just scrubby brush, cow paths, weeds and criminality." Clark became an advocate for the preservation of public access to the Schuylkill River Trail in center city Philadelphia. She has led fundraising activities and has lobbied successfully for legislation mandating that bicycle parking be included in every new construction project.

John envisioned the potential that the Schuylkill River held for the future development of the city. Since early in the twentieth century, planners had dreamed of creating an urban trail that would link Philadelphia's Fairmount Park with center city.

John Randolph establishes the Schuylkill River Development Council

Earlier efforts by a number of officials and proponents to develop a trail never materialized. But that began to change when John Randolph founded the Schuylkill River Development Council in 1992. He had the vision and foresight to realize that the river with its park could be a catalyst in connecting center city's business district (east of the river) with new engines of growth west of the Schuylkill River, particularly in the burgeoning University City area. At the same time, an expanded river trail would connect underserved communities to center city, providing new opportunities for employment, education, and recreational activities (biking, walking, jogging along the trail, boating on the river, and so forth).

John garnered much-needed publicity for the project, and soon the Council began receiving grants from the Pew Charitable Trust and the William Penn Foundation. His plans were significantly enhanced when federal transportation funding (under the Intermodal Surface Transportation Efficiency Act of 1991) provided money for building the kind of trails that John had envisioned for the city.

But even with funding in hand, problems involving a battle for access to the trail with the CSX Corporation (whose freight trains run alongside the proposed trail), and the municipal bureaucracy's inability to settle on a contractor for the construction work continued to delay the project.

A Section of Schuylkill River Park at Walnut Street in 2018—Photograph Courtesy of John Randolph

As a result of John Randolph's unflagging persistence, construction of the River Park finally began in 2002. The section linking more than a one-mile stretch along the Schuylkill River— from the Fairmount Park Water Works and the Philadelphia Museum of Art to Locust Street in center city—opened in 2004. A master plan encompassing the entire Tidal Schuylkill River (the part of the river that runs from the Fairmount Water Works dam to the Schuylkill River's confluence with the Delaware River and flow and depth are affected by tides) was completed. Countless residents from across the region gained unprecedented access to a neglected natural resource. As part of the process, the board of the organization John Randolph had founded was transformed from an ad hoc group of activists to a professionally managed body of corporate and government stakeholders, now known as the Schuylkill River Development Corporation.

The trail was expanded in 2014 with the opening of the Schuylkill Banks "boardwalk," a half-mile bridge along the river, connecting the trail to South Street about three quarters of a mile south of Locust Street, which a year later the *New York Times* cited as one reason for Philadelphia's ranking "third in the world" on places to visit. In that same year, in a 2015 tribute to John Randolph's vision and dedication, *USA Today* named Schuylkill River Park the "Best Urban Trail in America."

In 2018, another quarter-mile stretch was opened, connecting the trail even farther south, to Christian Street. The next phase (under construction in 2019) will span the river to link the trail to the west bank and Bartram's Garden, the forty-five-acre "outdoor classroom, living laboratory" founded in 1728 by world-renowned naturalist John Bowman Bartram. Designated in 1960 as a National Historic Landmark, it is the oldest botanical garden in North America.

The corporation's long-term goal is to connect the Schuylkill River Trail to the west bank of the Delaware River, about eight miles south of the iconic Fairmount Park Waterworks. The trail has become part of the projected one hundred and thirty-mile Southeastern Pennsylvania multi-use trail (sixty miles of which have been completed as of 2019).

In its April 5, 2019 publication "Schuylkill Revival," the Schuylkill River Development Corporation, notes how the development of the Schuylkill River Park had been proposed as far back as 1967 by John Collins of the Delta-T Group. But even after the southern portions of Pine and Spruce Streets had been built in 1978 and 1987 respectively, another delay occurred:

> Progress halted until 1989, when John Randolph, on a walk along the riverbank pondered what it would take to bring the long-held vision for a river esplanade to reality. He began by convening neighbors to envision a future

river park. Doors began to open, a new source of federal funding became available, local foundations supported the effort, and before long the Schuylkill River Development Council (SRDC) was founded.

In the decade that followed, SRDC created a vision for the future river park, raised the necessary funds for its construction, developed a master plan for the entire tidal river, and transformed the board from a community-based to a stakeholder-based organization.

Since the River Park's completion, two high-rise luxury condominiums have been built (and a third under construction) along the park at Race Street. In 2019 Children's Hospital of Philadelphia, located on the west side of the Schuylkill River, opened its massive Roberts Center for Pediatric Research on the east side of the river. The twenty-one-story building provides direct access to the Schuylkill River Trail at South Street for its twelve hundred employees.

Community service, a Randolph Family hallmark

In the early part of the nineteenth century, John Randolph's ancestor Julianna Randolph (daughter of Captain Edward Randolph) became a vital part of the Female Society for the Relief and Employment of the Poor. She and other members gathered clothing and food to help the neediest families in the city. Her youngest sister, Rachel, later joined her. They became founding members of the Western Association of Ladies for the Relief and Employment of the Poor, Julianna serving as its first treasurer. The Association provided job-training and employment for the poorest families in the city, and was the first job-training program for women in America. Their dedicated service to the poor is recorded indelibly in the history of Philadelphia.

More than one hundred and fifty years later, even while busily pursuing the establishment of his business, John was inspired by the involvement of his present-day family with social causes. He co-founded a homeless shelter in the basement of a church, and then later co-founded the Community OutReach Partnership (CORP) to manage several outreach programs of the Episcopal Diocese of Pennsylvania's Trinity Memorial Church. In 2013 Episcopal Community Services merged with CORP, its lessons learned inspiring other parishes throughout the state.

John Randolph Family in 2000—Photograph, Courtesy of John Randolph

Top row (from left): Evan Randolph, Andrew Randolph, Evelyn and Hampton Randolph, Ann Doucette (standing alone in center of photo), Rick Randolph, John Randolph, Joshua and Melissa Doucette, and Heath Doucette (holding Esmae, her daughter). Middle row (seated): Judy Boynton, Kyle Randolph Boynton (her son), Hope Hacker (holding Madison Doucette), Rachel Doucette with granddaughter Charlotte Doucette, Sean Doucette, daughter Isabelle in his lap. Bottom row (seated on floor): Penelope Randolph, Alyin Doucette, and Jeanie Raney.

Even in retirement, John Randolph continues to be actively involved with the causes he has long championed. He serves as a board member of Episcopal Community Services, a board member emeritus of the Fairmount Park Conservancy, and chairman of the board of the Schuylkill River Park Alliance. He and his wife, Alice, continue to enjoy living in Philadelphia and summering with their children and grandchildren at their family cottage in Maine.

EPILOGUE

When Edward Fitz Randolph Jr. left his home in England in 1630 in search of freedom and opportunity in the New World, he could never have imagined the vast impact his descendants would have on the creation of America.

Originally settling in New England, Edward and his wife, Elizabeth Blossom, later moved their family to New Jersey after the puritan theocracy there denied the freedom they had sought. In 1669 they became a founding family of New Jersey. As major landowners, Edward and his sons quickly became leaders in the development of the province, holding offices in the local and provincial governments.

Hartshorne Fitz Randolph, Edward's grandson, was an early leader in the struggle to abolish slavery as one of the founders of the first anti-slavery societies in New Jersey. His great-grandson, Nathaniel Fitz Randolph, was the first to contribute land and funds for the founding of what is now Princeton University. Edward and Elizabeth's great-grandson, Benjamin Randolph was a renowned cabinetmaker in Philadelphia, chosen by Thomas Jefferson to build the desk upon which he wrote the Declaration of Independence.

When British threats to the freedom and independence of the young colonies sparked the Revolutionary War, Fitz Randolph family members were among the first to respond. Captain Nathaniel Fitz Randolph led his New Jersey militiamen in three battles; wounded and imprisoned multiple times, he nonetheless returned to lead his men in battle, ultimately dying on the battlefield at Springfield. Captain Edward Randolph, Nathaniel's cousin, commanded the 4th picket post at the Battle of Paoli, in Pennsylvania, losing his left eye in combat and left for dead on the battlefield. He survived to fight two more years in battle, being wounded again at Germantown.

After the war, the industrial revolution in America soon defined the new nation as a major industrial and manufacturing force. Captain Edward Randolph, surviving his wounds at Paoli, returned to Philadelphia where he formed a partnership creating a prestigious shipping company in the city. His granddaughter, Julianna, married Richard Davis Wood who, with their sons, created the largest manufacturing company in southern New Jersey (by the twenty-first century morphing into a ten-billion-dollar company with 31,000 employees). Edward's grandson, Evan Randolph formed a partnership with William Pearson Jenks, creating toward the end of the nineteenth century one of the largest cotton manufacturing companies in the east.

By the middle of that century, Fitz Randolph family members were leaders in government, being elected judges, governor, congressmen, senators and, in the twentieth century, four relatives becoming presidents of the United States. Jacob Randolph, Captain Edward Randolph's son, was a leading physician in Philadelphia, succeeding "Father of American Surgery" Dr. Philip Syng Physick at Pennsylvania Hospital.

While the industrial development brought prosperity to many in Philadelphia, the great majority of the hundreds of thousands of immigrants who moved to the city became mired in poverty. Julianna and Rachel Randolph, Edward's daughters, were founding members of an organization that brought job training, employment and self-sufficiency to many of the poor in the city.

As the nation expanded westward, Captain Randolph's grandsons Edward and Richard Randolph Parry pioneered banking and land brokerage businesses in Minnesota. At the outbreak of the Civil War, Edward was the first in his city to volunteer for service in the Army; as a major, he commanded three forts in the Midwest, serving for the duration of the war. Their father, Oliver Parry, pioneered the western expansion of Philadelphia.

Evan Randolph's son, Evan Jr., was appointed president of the Philadelphia National Bank just as the country's involvement in World War II had begun, leading the bank through a period of unprecedented growth. Evan Jr.'s son Evan III followed his father in the commercial banking industry, himself becoming respected in that profession.

At the dawn of the twenty-first century, Philadelphia was experiencing an urban renaissance as the city's central core began to expand. Evan's grandson, John Randolph led the way in the revitalization of the east bank of the Schuylkill River, envisioning the river as a major force in the development of the city. His plan provided a stronger link between the center city's business district to the vastly advancing medical and educational growth on the west side of the river, increasing educational, recreational and job opportunities. While pursuing his goal to implement the plan, John Randolph and his family created programs to assist the poor and homeless in the city as their ancestors had done, a century and a half earlier.

So have they lived that nearly four hundred years after Edward Fitz Randolph Jr. arrived in America, his descendants continue to contribute to the development and welfare of their communities. Their work in community service, industry, real estate development, health care and technology has extended their pilgrim ancestor's quest for freedom and opportunity into the twenty-first century.

APPENDIX

Gerald R. Ford, Descendant of the Holley Family

Joseph Holley and Rose Allen
▼
Experience Holley and John Goodspeed
▼
John Goodspeed Jr. and Remember Jennings
▼
Samuel Goodspeed and Rebecca
▼
Eunice Goodspeed and Anselm Comstock
▼
Betsey Comstock and Daniel Butler
▼
George Selden Butler and Elizabeth Ely Gridley
▼
Amy Gridley Butler and George Manney Ayer
▼
Adele Augusta Ayer and Levi Addison Gardner
▼
Dorothy Ayer Gardner and Leslie Lynch King
▼
Leslie Lynch King Jr. (Gerald Rudolph Ford Jr.)

George H. W. Bush and George W. Bush

Peter Blossom and Sarah Bodfish
▼
Thomas Blossom and Fear Robinson
▼
Elizabeth Blossom and Peter Butler
▼
Benjamin Butler and Susanna Whiting
▼
Nathaniel Butler and Sarah Herrick
▼
Samuel Herrick Butler and Judith Livingston
▼
Courtland Philip Livingston Butler and Elizabeth Slade Pierce
▼
Mary Elizabeth Butler and Robert Emmet Sheldon
▼
Flora Sheldon and Samuel Prescott Bush
▼
Prescott Sheldon Bush and Dorothy Walker
▼
George Herbert Walker Bush and Barbara Pierce
▼
George W. Bush

Barack Hussein Obama

Nathaniel Fitz Randolph and Mary Holley
▼
Samuel Fitz Randolph and Mary Jones
▼
Prudence Fitz Randolph and Shubael Smith
▼
Mary Smith and Jonathan Dunham
▼
Samuel Dunham and Hannah Ruble
▼
Jacob Dunham and Catherine Goodnight
▼
Jacob Markey Dunham and Louisa Eliza Stroup
▼
Jacob William Dunham and Mary Ann Kearney
▼
Ralph Waldo Emerson Dunham and Ruth Lucille Armour
▼
Stanley Armour Dunham and Madelyn Lee Payune
▼
S. Ann Dunham and Barack Hussein Obama
▼
Barack Hussein Obama Jr.

ENDNOTES

Introduction, xxiii-xxv

1. Thomas J. McGuire, *Battle of Paoli*, Mechanicsburg (Pa.), Stackpoole Books, 2000, p. xvi.
2. Laura A. Hibbard, *Medieval Romance in England*, New York, Burt Franklin, 1963, p. iii.
3. Henry Simpson, *The Lives of Eminent Philadelphians Now Deceased*, Philadelphia, W. Brotherhead, 1859, p. 830.

Part One, Pages 1-7

4. L.V.F. Randolph, *Fitz Randolph Traditions—A Story of a Thousand Years*. New York Historical Society, 1907.
5. Richard Winston, *Charlemagne*, NewWordCity.com, 2015, p. 439.
6. Richard E. Sullivan, "Charlemagne. Holy Roman Emperor," Britannica.com, 2019.
7. Cicero Pangburn McClure, *Randolph-Pangburn: William Pangburn and His Wife Hannah Fitz Randolph; Their Ancestry and Descendants,1620-1909*. Pangburn Society of Allegheny County, Pa., 1909/2018 (ForgottenBooks.com), p. 12.
8. David Story Randolph, Correspondence with the author, February 4, 2019.
9. L.V.F. Randolph, *Fitz Randolph Traditions—A Story of a Thousand Years*, The New Jersey Historical Society, 1907, p. 128.
10. Oris H.F. Randolph, *Edward Fitz Randolph Branch Lines and Allied Families and English and Norman Ancestry*. Ann Arbor, Edward Brothers, Inc,1980, p. ix.
11. Oris H.F. Randolph.

Part Two, Pages 8-27

12 Charles Edward Banks, *The Winthrop Fleet of 1630*. Baltimore, Genealogical Publishing, 1930, p. 70.
13 John Buchan, *Oliver Cromwell*. Houghton Mifflin, 1934, p. 929.
14 The Pupils of Ryhall CE Primary School, Rutland and John Hayden, *Robert "Troublechurch" Browne.*, Nottingham, Barry Books, p. 559.
15 L.V.F. Randolph, *Fitz Randolph Traditions—A Story of a Thousand Years*, The New York Historical Society, 1907, p. 126.
16 Robert Charles Anderson, *The Pilgrim Migration: Immigrants to Plymouth Colony, 1620-1633*, New England Historic Genealogical Society, pages 58-59.
17 L.V.F. Randolph, *Fitz Randolph Traditions—A Story of a Thousand Years*, The New York Historical Society, 1907, p. 131.
18 L.V.F. Randolph, pages 130-131.
19 Christopher Henry Pope, *The Pioneers of Massachusetts, Drawn from Records of the Colonies, Towns and Churches, and Other Contemporaneous Documents*. Boston, 1900; Baltimore, Genealogical Publishing Co., 1965.
20 Gary Boyd Roberts, *Ancestors of American Presidents*. New England Historic Genealogical Society, 2009, p. 512.
21 Caleb H. Johnson, ed., *Of Plymouth Plantation: Along with the full text of the Pilgrims' journey for their first year at Plymouth*, from the handwritten manuscript by William Bradford. Xlibris, 2006, Part VII, pages 1-2.
22 L.V.F. Randolph, *Fitz Randolph Traditions—A Story of a Thousand Years.* The New York Historical Society, 1907, p. 127.
23 John Winthrop, *The Journal of John Winthrop*. Harvard University Press, 1996, p. 1, n. 1.
24 James Walvin, *The Quakers: Money and Morals*. London, John Murray (Publishers), 1997, p. 17.
25 New England Historical Society, *Massachusetts*. November 5, 2018.
26 Nathaniel Hawthorne, *The House of the Seven Gables*. Seattle, Amazon Classics,, p. 8.
27 James Edward Maule, *Better That One Hundred Witches Should Live: The 1696 Acquittal of Thomas Maule of Salem, Massachusetts, on Charges of Seditious Libel and Its impact on the Development of First Amendment Freedoms*. Villanova (Pa.), JEM Book Publishing Co., 1995.
28 Brenda Wineapple, *Hawthorne: A Life*. New York, Random House, 2004, p. 239.
29 L.V.F. Randolph, *Fitz Randolph Traditions—A Story of a Thousand Years.* The New York Historical Society. 1907, p. 128.
30 Middlesex County, New Jersey, Division of Arts and History Programs, Office of Arts and History.

31 David McCullough, *John Adams.* Simon & Schuster, 2001, p. 156.
32 David McCullough, p. 157.
33 Stephen Fried, *Rush, Revolution, Madness, and the Visionary Doctor Who Became a Founding Father.* New York, Crown Publishing Group (a division of Penguin Random House), 2018.
34 Middlesex County Cultural and Heritage Commission, "East Jersey Olde Towne Village," culturalandheritage@co.middlesex.nj.us

Part Three, Pages 28-36

35 John C. Glynn, Jr. and Kathryn A. Glynn, *His Sacred Honor: Judge Richard Stockton, A Signer of the Declaration of Independence.* Hereditea Books, 2007, p. 1.
36 John Glynn, Jr. and Kathryn Glynn, p. 8.
37 Martha Mitchell, "Van Wickle Gates," Encyclopedia Brunoniana, Brown University, 1993.
38 Book of Records, "Nathaniel Fitz Randolph," January 29, 1754, Princeton University Library.
39 Wanda S. Gunning, "The Town of Princeton and the University—1756-1946," The Princeton Library, ` *Princeton University Chronicles*, Vol. 66, No. 3 (Spring 2005), p. 452.
40 Nick Donnoli, "Through the gates: The Myth surrounding Fitz Randolph Gate." Office of Communications, Princeton University, May 31, 2007.
41 Andrew Brunk, "Benjamin Randolph Revisited," *American Furniture*, 2007.
42 Philadelphia Parks & Recreation, "Charms of Fairmount Park, Mount Pleasant," 2012.
43 "Jefferson to Ellen Wayles, Randolph College, November 14, 1825," in M. Betts and James Bear, Jr.,eds., *Family Letters of Thomas Jefferson.* Columbia (Md.), U of Missouri Press, 1966, p. 461.
44 Silvio A. Bedini, *Declaration of Independence Desk: Relic of Revolution.* Washington (D.C.), Smithsonian Institution Press, 1981.
45 Thomas Hamilton Ormsbee, *Early American Furniture Makers.* New York, Crowell,1930, pages 46-47 .

Part Four, Pages 37-48

46 Dorothy McCardle, "Kissinger Guests Will Be Sitting Pretty," *Los Angeles Times*, Jan. 20,1974, p. 14.

47 John P. Wall and Harold Pickersgill, ed., *History of Middlesex County, New Jersey, 1664-1920*. New York, Historical Publishing Co., Vol.1, p. 239.
48 *Biographical Directory of the United States Congress, 1774-present*. http://bioguide.congress.gov/
49 Thomas Brown, *Politics and Statesmanship: Essays on the American Whig Party*. New York, 1985, Columbia University Press, 1985, p. 20.
50 John Bobsin, *History of the Lines We Represent*, Lackawanna Coalition, December 17, 2009.
51 *Journal of the Senate of New Jersey*,1863, p. 71.
52 R. John Brockmann, *Commodore Robert F. Stockton, 1795-1866: Protean Man for a Protean Nation*. Amherst (N.Y.), Cambria Press, 2009, pages 318-319.
53 Irving S. Kull, *New Jersey, A History*. New York, The American Historical Society, 1930, Vol. III, p. 811.
54 Preserve Greystone (blog), preservegrestone.org
55 Irving S. Kull, *New Jersey, A History*. New York, The American Historical Society, 1930, Vol. III, pages 951-952.
56 L. E. Crittenden, *A Report of the Debates and Proceedings in the Secret Sessions of the Conference Convention for Proposing Amendments to the Constitution of the United States, held at Washington, D.C., in February, A.D. 1861*. D. Appleton & Company, 1864, pages 440-452.
57 Joseph F. Randolph, *The Law of Faith, With a Lawyer's Notes on the Written Law*. New York, G. P. Putnam's Sons, 1914, p. 221.

Part Five, Pages 49-75

58 Gary Boyd Roberts, *Ancestors of American Presidents*. New England Historic Genealogical Society, 2009, p. 559.
59 Gerald R. Ford, *A Time to Heal*, New York, Harper & Row, New York, 1979.
60 Louise Aymar Christian and Howard Stelle Fitz Randolph, *The Descendants of Edward Fitz Randolph and Elizabeth Blossom, 1630-1950*, East Orange (N.J.), 1950, p. 6.
61 Irving S. Kull, *New Jersey, A History*. New York, The American Historical Society, 1930, Vol. I, p. 159.
62 Irving S. Kull, p. 164.
63 Irving S. Kull, p. 208.
64 Irving S. Kull, Vol. II, p. 409.
65 Jerry Schwartz, "Oldest Corporation in U.S. History—After 314 Years," *Los Angeles Times*, September 3, 1998, p. D14.
66 Sue Kaufmann, Hidden New Jersey (blog), hiddennj.com.

67   David Webster Hoyt, *The Old Families of Salisbury and Amesbury, Massachusetts, with some related families of Newbury, Haverhill, Ipswich, and Hampton.* Somersworth (N.H.), New England History Press, 1981, Part One, pages 317-318. ("In reference to Richard Singletary who was earlier of Newbury," Hoyt writes, " is the quote 'Goodwife Singletary d. about 1638 or '9. She may have been wife of Richard.' ")

68   Joseph W. Dally, *Woodbridge and Vicinity, The Story of a New Jersey Township.* New Brunswick (N.J.), A. E. Gordon, 1873, p. 44.

69   Gary Boyd Roberts, *Ancestors of American Presidents.* New England Historic Genealogical Society, Boston, 2009, p. 512.

70   *New England Historical and Genealogical Register*, New England Historic Genealogical Society, October 1943, p. 334.

71   *Hail Specimen of Female Art! New Jersey Schoolgirl Needlework, 1726-1860*, Exhibition Catalogue, Morven Museum & Garden, Princeton, 2014, p. 50.

72   *Hail Specimen*, p. 36.

73   Shirley Moskow, "Henry Francis du Pont, Brief life of a passionate connoisseur:1880-1969," *Harvard Magazine*, July-August, 2003.

74   "Guide to the Hartshorne Fitz Randolph Family Papers (1840-1979)," The New Jersey Historical Society (Bulk 1950-1967), MG 1312.

75   Samuel M. Janney, *The Life of William Penn, with Selections from the Correspondence and Autobiography*, 6th ed. Revised. Philadelphia, Friends' Book Association, 1882.

76   "Guide to the Hartshorne Fitz Randolph Family Papers (1840-1879," The New Jersey Historical Society (Bulk 1950-1967), MG 1312.

77   Richard T. Irwin, ed., A *History of Randolph Township, Morris County, New Jersey*, 2nd ed. Township of Randolph (County of Morris, State of New Jersey), 2002, p. 18.

78   Richard T. Irwin, ed., pages 59-60.

79   Glenn Valis, "The Militia of New Jersey During the Revolution," New Jersey during the Revolution (Nov. 5, 2007 revised), doublegv.com/ggv/militia.html

80   "Old Houses: Prisons of the Revolutionary War," *New York Times*, October 14, 1872, p. 5.

81   Joseph W. Dally, *Woodbridge and Vicinity, The Story of a New Jersey Township*, New Brunswick (N.J.), A. E. Gordon, 1873, p. 252.

82   Samuel W. Pennypacker, "Historical and Biographical Sketches (1863)," Wikisource, p. 277.

83   Edwin G. Burrows, *Forgotten Patriots: The Untold Story of American Prisoners During the Revolutionary War*, New York, Basic Books, 2008, p. 91.

84   Louise Aymar Christian and Howard Stelle Fitz Randolph, *The Descendants of Edward Fitz Randolph and Elizabeth Blossom*, 1950, Notes on Nathaniel

Fitz Randolph *1630-1950*, East Orange (N.J.),, 1630-1959, Christian & Fitz Randolph,1950, p. 27.
85 *The Writings of George Washington from the Original Manuscript Sources, 1745-1799*, Vol. 18, Washington (D.C.), Government Printing Office, 1931.
86 William S. Hornor, *This Old Monmouth of Ours,*, Freehold (N.J.), Moreau Brothers, 1932, Clearfield Company, Inc. reprint by Genealogical Publishing Co., Baltimore, 1990, p. 288.

Part Six, Pages 76-166

87 Sumner Hunnewell, "The Battle of Moore's Brook, Scarborough, Maine, June 29, 1677," *The Maine Genealogist*, May and August 2003.
88 Ben H. Swett (Colonel USAF, Retired), *John Swett of Newbury, A Collection of Genealogical Research Papers*, swett-genealogy.com (accessed April 2018).
89 James David Drake, *King Philip's War: Civil War in New England, 1675-1676*. U. of Massachusetts Press, 1999, pages 1-15.
90 George Ellis and John Morris, *King Philip's War*. New York, Grafton Press, 1906.
91 Henry Simpson, *The Lives of Eminent Philadelphians Now Deceased*, Philadelphia, William Broderhead, 1859, pages 826-27.
92 Thomas J. McGuire, *Battle of Paoli*, Mechanicsburg (Pa.), Stackpole Books, 2000, p. 99.
93 Thomas J. McGuire, p. 100.
94 Hope Carson Randolph, "Randolph Family Book, and Randolph Family, a pamphlet edited by Alexander du Bin." Philadelphia (privately published),1946.
95 Letter from Edward Fitz Randolph, Randolph Family records, New Hope Historical Society.
96 George Bebbington with Alan A. Siegel (editor), "Washington Rock is Focus of Renewed Interest," in "Warren History," Vol. II, No. 3 (Spring 1995), Green Brook Historical Society, p. 3.
97 Hope Carson Randolph, "Randolph Family Book, and Randolph Family, a pamphlet edited by Alexander du Bin." Philadelphia (privately published), 1946.
98 *Republica v. De Longchamps*, 1 U.S. 111 (1784).
99 La Rochefoucald-Liancourt, *Travels Through the United States of North America*, Vol. IV. London, 1809, p. 91.
100 "Never Did I See So Universal a Frenzy: The Panic of 1791 and the Republicanization of Philadelphia," *The Pennsylvania Magazine of History and Biography*, Vol. CXLII, No. 1 (January, 2018), pages 9-10.

101 Coates & Reynell Family Papers (1677-1930), Collection 140, Historical Society of Pennsylvania.
102 "A List of City Office and Councils in 1794," *Philadelphia Inquirer*, March 28, 1876, p.
103 Henry Simpson, *The Lives of Eminent Philadelphians Now Deceased*, Philadelphia, William Broderhead,1859, p. 828.
104 Robert I. Alotta, *Mermaids, Monasteries, Cherokees and Custer: The Stories Behind Philadelphia Street Names*. Chicago, Bonus Books, 1990, pages10-11.
105 Thomas Scharf and Thompson Westcott, *History of Philadelphia, 1609-1884*. Philadelphia, L.I. Everts, 1884, Vol. III, p. 380; Vol. V, p. 392.
106 City of Philadelphia Deed Book: March 18, 1813: Sale of Property and five contiguous frame buildings, IC23 p. 472.
107 "Ogden and Cuthbert Family Papers," J. Welles Henderson Archives and Library, 1760-1830 (Call Number: Ogden, I box), Independence Seaport Museum, Philadelphia.
108 Nicholas B. Wainwright, "The Age of Nicholas Biddle, 1825-1841," in *Philadelphia: A 300-Year History*, Russell F. Weigley, ed., New York, W. W. Norton,1982, pages 280-81.
109 Hope Carson Randolph, "Randolph Family Handbook, and Randolph Family, a pamphlet edited by Alexander du Bin," Philadelphia (privately published), 1946.
110 George B. Wood and Franklin Bache, *The Dispensatory of the United States of America*,16th ed.,. Philadelphia, Lippincott, 1892, p. vii.
111 Henry Hartshorne, *Memoir of George B. Wood, M.D., LL.D.* (Read before the American Philosophical Society, October 11, 1880), Philadelphia, American Philosophical Society, 1882.
112 The Historical Society of Pennsylvania, Collection 1176, R. D. Wood & Co. Records, 1858-1910, p. 2.
113 Lucius Q.C. Elmer, "Maurice River, Millville, and Landis," in *History of the Early Settlement and Progress of Cumberland County New Jersey; and of the Currency of This and the Adjoining Colonies*, Chapter IV, Bridgeton (N.J.), George F. Nixon, 1869, p. 72.
114 Lucius Q.C. Elmer, p. 74.
115 The Maurice River Recollections Project, Citizens United to Protect the Maurice River and Its Tributaries, Inc., cumauriceriver.org
116 Julianna Randolph Wood, *Biographical Sketch of Richard D. Wood* (2 vols.). Philadelphia, Lippincott's Press, 1871; Miami, HardPress (reprint), 2017, Vol. II, Location 2254.
117 David W. Stowell, *The Papers of Abraham Lincoln: Legal Documents and Cases*. Charlottesville, U. of Virginia Press, 2008, p. 26.

118 Harry E. Pratt, *Personal Finances of Abraham Lincoln*. Chicago, Lakeside Press, 1943, p. viii.
119 Julianna Randolph Wood, *Biographical Sketch of Richard D. Wood* (2 vols.). Philadelphia, Lippincott's Press, 1871; Miami, HardPress (reprint), 2017, Vol. II, Location 2253.
120 Julianna Randolph Wood, Vol. I, Location 833.
121 R.D. Wood & Co. Records (1858-1910), The Historical Society of Pennsylvania, Collection 1176, Series 4, Personnel (1858-1896), p. 9.
122 Julianna Randolph Wood, *Biographical Sketch of Richard D. Wood (2 vols.)* Philadelphia, Lippincott's Press, 1871; Miami, HardPress (reprint), 2017, Vol. II, Locations 38 and 39.
123 123 R.D. Wood & Co. Records, pages 2-3.
124 R.D. Wood & Co. Records, pages 3-4.
125 Julianna Randolph Wood, *Biographical Sketch of Richard D. Wood* (2 vols.).Philadelphia, Lippincott's Press, 1871; Miami, HardPress (reprint), 2017, Vol. II, Locations 824 and 825.
126 Although Julianna Randolph Wood refers to Mr. "Beetle," the correct spelling is "Bettle". He is mentioned numerous times by Richard Davis Wood in his diary.
127 R.D. Wood & Co. Records (1858-1910). The Historical Society of Pennsylvania, Collection 1176, Series 4, Personnel (1858-1896), p. 3.
128 National Register of Historic Places, Reference Number 1300975, Property Name: Wood Mansion House, 821 Columbia Avenue, Millville, New Jersey, Listed, 12/24/2013.
129 Ellie Silverman, "Wawa is undergoing a huge expansion," *The Morning Call* (Allentown, Pa.), April 9, 2019, pages 12-13.
130 Henry Simpson, *The Lives of Eminent Philadelphians Now Deceased*. Philadelphia, William Broderhead,1859 p. 828.
131 Simon Finger, "Yellow Fever," *The Encyclopedia of Greater Philadelphia*, Philadelphia, U. of Pennsylvania Press, 2011, p. 2.
132 Henry Simpson, *The Lives of Eminent Philadelphians Now Deceased*. Philadelphia, William Broderhead,1859, p. 829.
133 "The Story of the Creation of the Nation's First Hospital," Penn Medicine, History of Pennsylvania Hospital, 2017. www.uphs.upenn.edu/paharc/features/creation.html
134 "Philip Syng Physick, 1768-1837," Penn People, University Archives and Records Center, U. of Pennsylvania.
135 Nicholas B. Wainwright, "The Age of Nicholas Biddle, 1825-1841," in *Philadelphia: A 300-Year History*, Russell F. Weigley, ed., New York, W. W, Norton, 1982, p. 298.

136 Aaron Wunsch, "Laurel Hill, Tired of Commuting?," *Historic American Buildings Survey*, 1995, p. 2.
137 James McClelland and Lynn Miller, *City in a Park*. Philadelphia, Temple U. Press, 2006, p. 76.
138 Frank Willing Leach, "Old Philadelphia Families,"*The North American*, Nov. 3, 1912, p. 7.
139 J. Dell Conner,"The Physick House, The Physick Family, Edmund Darch Lewis" (pamphlet), p. 1.
140 "An ACT Legitimizing Emlen Physick," *Laws of the Commonwealth of Pennsylvania*, 1857, No. 1. Section1.
141 "Cape May's Emlen Physick Estate, A Window on Our Victorian Past" (brochure), Cape May (N.J.), the Physick Estate and the Mid-Atlantic Center for the Arts and Humanities, 2012.
142 Prized Artifacts of the Garden State, www.GardenStateLegacy.com, December, 2012.
143 Hannah Ann Zell, "Report of the Board of Managers of the Western Association of Ladies for the Relief and Employment of the Poor," Philadelphia, Joseph Rakestraw Publisher, 1854, p. 6.
144 T. Elwood Zell, "Report of the Board of Managers of the Western Association of Ladies for the Relief and Employment of the Poor," Joseph Rakestraw Publisher, 1869, p. 8.
145 Hannah Ann Zell, "Report of the Board of Managers of the Western Association of Ladies for the Relief and Employment of the Poor," Philadelphia, Joseph Rakestraw Publisher, Nov.1, 1866, p. 59.
146 2005-2007 American Community Survey, U.S. Census Bureau.
147 Richard G. Miller, "The Federal City, 1783-1800," in *Philadelphia: A 300-Year History*, Russell F. Weigley, ed., W. W. Norton 1982, p. 185.
148 Richard D. Miller, p. 182.
149 Parry Family Records, Box 2. New Hope Historical Society, New Hope (Pa.).
150 Willis Thornton, "Bergdoll—The Fighting Slacker," *The Olean Times-Herald* (N.Y.), Jan. 7, 1931, p. 4.
151 "The Spring Garden Historic District, A Guide for Property Owners," Philadelphia Historic Commission, October 2001, p. 5.
152 Edward Randolph Parry (1832-1874): Minnesota State University Memorial Library Collection (1857-1867); Southern Minnesota Historical Center, Manuscript Collection 110.
153 *The Chester County Times* (Coatesville, Pa.), August 11, 1859.
154 Douglas Linder, "The Dakota Conflict Trials" (5 pages), Available at SSRN (posted Oct. 20, 2007): https://ssrn.com/abstract=1021325 or http://dx.doi.org/10.2139/ssrn.1021325

155 Stephen Riggs, "The Indian Executions," *New York Times*, December 26, 1862, p.4. (http://www.startribune.com/local/138264074.html)
156 Dee Brown, *Bury My Heart at Wounded Knee: An Indian History of the American West*. New York, Open Road, p. 64.
157 Sinclair Lewis, *Main Street*, New York, Modern Library, 1920/1999, p. 4.
158 Michael D. Pierson, *Mutiny at Fort Jackson, The Untold Story of the Fall of New Orleans*, Chapel Hill, U. of North Carolina Press, 2008, pages 112-114.
159 Pennsylvania Wills and Probate Records, 1683-1993; Bucks County, Wills, Vol. 5, 1786-1797; Ancestry.com
160 Edward Bennett Matthews, "History of the Boundary Dispute between the Baltimores and the Penns Resulting in the Original Mason-Dixon Line," *Maryland Geological Survey*, Maryland State Archives, Vol. 7, p. 355.
161 161 Jane Heimerdinger and Thomas Michener, "Core Creek Park and the Grand Duchess," Pennswood View, Fall 1984, pages 1-3.
162 Jane Heimerdinger and Thomas Michener.
163 W.W.H. Davis, Warren S. Ely and John W. Jordan, *The History of Bucks County, Pennsylvania, from the Discovery of the Delaware to the Present Time*, Lewis Publishing Company, New York-Chicago, 1905, p. 309.
164 Ron Chernow, *Alexander Hamilton*, New York, Penguin, 2004, p. 373.
165 Irving S. Kull, *New Jersey, A History*, New York, The American Historical Society, 1930, Vol. 1, p. 237.
166 Selig Perlman, *A History of Trade Unionism in the United States*. Echo Books (reprint), 1922/2006, pages 16-17.
167 John Richardson, *Solebury Township, Bucks County, Pennsylvania, A Short History of the Township and a Report on Township Officers and Affairs*, Philadelphia, Offset Service Company, 1958, p. 65.
168 Sally Kennedy Alexander, "A Sketch of the Life of Major Andrew Ellicott," *Records of the Columbia Historical Society, Washington, D.C.*, Vol. 2 (1889), pages 158-202. JSTOR. www.jstor.org/stable/40066727
169 W.W.H. Davis, Warren S. Ely and John W. Jordan, *History of Bucks County, Pennsylvania, from the Discovery of the Delaware to the Present Time*, New York, Lewis Publishing Company, New York-Chicago, 1905, p. 41.
170 Hope Carson Randolph, "Randolph Family Handbook, and Randolph Family, edited by Alexander du Bin," Philadelphia (privately published), 1946.
171 Emily T. Cooperman, "Frankford, Tacony, Wissinoming, Bridesburg" for the Historic Context Statement, Cluster 1, Preservation Alliance for Greater Philadelphia, July 2009.
172 Another bank, Girard Trust Company, later known as Girard Trust Corn Exchange Bank, and finally, Girard Bank, founded in 1835, also had no

affiliation with Stephen Girard. Girard Bank merged with Mellon Bank in 1983. (See "Girard Corn Exchange Bank," *Encyclopedia of Philadelphia*.)
173 Nicholas B. Wainwright, *History of the Philadelphia National Bank,1803-1953*, Philadelphia, William F. Fell Printers, p. 223.

Part Seven, Pages 167-175

174 Carson-Randolph Family Papers, Collection 3004, Series 3, Randolph Children, 1916-1972, Box 11, Historical Society of Pennsylvania, Philadelphia.
175 Harvard University Obituary and Death Notice Collection, Number 39.

BIBLIOGRAPHY

Published Sources

Alotta, Robert I., *Mermaids, Monasteries, Cherokees and Custer—The Stories Behind Philadelphia Street Names*, Bonus Books, Inc., Chicago, 1990

Anderson, Robert Charles, *The Pilgrim Migration—Immigrants to Pilgrim Colony, 1620-1633*, Great Migration Study Project, New England Historic Genealogical Society, Boston, 2004

Banks Charles Edward, *The Winthrop Fleet of 1630*, Boston, 1930

Betts M. and Bear, James, Jr., eds., *Jefferson to Ellen Wayles, Randolph College, November 14, 1825, Family Letters of Thomas Jefferson*, Columbia, (Md.), U of Missouri Press, 1966

Brockmann, John R., Commodore Robert F. Stockton—1795-1866—A Protean Man for a Protean Nation, Cambria Press, Amherst, (N.Y.), 2009

Brown, Dee, *Bury My Heart at Wounded Knee: An Indian History of the American West*, Holt, Rinehart and Winston, New York, 1970 (reprinted by Open Road)

Brown, Thomas, *Politics and Statesmanship: Essays on the American Whig Party*, 1985, New York, Columbia University Press New York, 1985

Buchan, John, *Oliver Cromwell*, Houghton Mifflin Company,1934

Burrows, Edwin G., *Forgotten Patriots: The Untold Story of American Prisoners During the Revolution*, Basic Books, A Member of the Perseus Book Group, New York, 2008

Chernow, Ron, *Alexander Hamilton*, The Penguin Press, New York, 2004

Christian, Louise Aymar and Fitz Randolph, Stelle Howard, *The Descendants of Edward Fitz Randolph and Elizabeth Blossom, (1630-1950)*, East Orange, (N. J.), 1950

Crittenden, L. E., *A Report of the Debates and Proceedings in the Secret Sessions of the Conference Convention for Proposing Amendments to the Constitution of the United States, held at Washington, D.C., in February, A.D. 1861*, D. Appleton & Company, 1864

Dally, Joseph W. and Gordon, A. E., *Woodbridge and Vicinity: The Story of a New Jersey Township*, New Brunswick, (N. J.), A. E. Gordon, 1873

Davis, W. W. H., Ely, Warren S., and Jordan, John W., *The History of Bucks County, Pennsylvania from the Discovery of the Delaware to the Present Time*, The Lewis Publishing Company, New York-Chicago, 1905

Drake, James David, *King Philip's War: Civil War in New England, 1657-1676*, U. of Massachusetts Press, 1999

Ellis, George and Morris, John, *King Philip's War*, Grafton Press, New York, 1906

Finger, Simon, *Yellow Fever*, The Encyclopedia of Greater Philadelphia, U. of Pennsylvania Press, 2011

Ford, Gerald R., *A Time to Heal*, Harper & Rowe Publishers, Inc., New York, 1979

Fried, Stephen, *Rush, Revolution, Madness, and the Visionary Doctor Who Became a Founding Father*, Crown Publishing Group, (a division of Penguin Random House), New York, 2018

Glynn, John, Jr. and Glynn, Kathryn, *Richard Stockton*, The Society of the Descendants of the Signers of the Declaration of Independence, 2008

Haden, John, *Robert "Troublechurch" Browne*, Barny Books, Nottingham, 2013

Hartshorne, Henry, *Memoir of George B. Wood, M. D., LL.D.*, (Read before the American Philosophical Society, October 11, 1880), Philadelphia, American Philosophical Society, 1882

Hawthorne, Nathaniel, *The House of the Seven Gables*, Amazon Classics, Seattle

Hibbard, Laura, A., *Medieval Romance in England*, New York Burt Franklin, 1963

Hornor, William S., *This Old Monmouth of Ours*, Freehold, (N. J.), Moreau Brothers, 1932, Clearfield Company, Inc., reprint by Genealogical Publishing Co., Baltimore, 1990

Hoyt, David W., *The Old Families of Salisbury and Amesbury, Massachusetts, with some related families of Newbury, Haverhill, Ipswich and Hampton*, New England History Press, Somersworth, 1981

Irwin, Richard T., editor, *A History of Randolph Township, Morris County, New Jersey*, 2nd. ed., Township of Randolph (County of Morris, N.J., 2002

Kull, Irving S, *New Jersey—A History*, The American Historical Society, New York, 1930

Janney, Samuel, *The Life of William Penn*, with Selections from the Correspondence and Autobiography, (Pennsylvania), 6th ed. Revised, Philadelphia Friends Book Association, 1882

Johnson, Caleb H., Editor, *Of Plymouth Plantation: Along with the full text of the Pilgrims' journey for their first year at Plymouth*, from the handwritten manuscript by William Bradford, Xlibris, 2006

La Rochefoucald-Liancourt, *Travels Through the United States of North America*, Vol. IV, London, 1809

Lewis, Sinclair, *Main Street*, The Modern Library, New York, 1999

Maule, James Edward, *Better That One Hundred Witches Should Live: The 1696 Acquittal of Thomas Maule of Salem, Massachusetts, on Charges of Seditious Libel and Its impact on the Development of First Amendment Freedoms*, Villanova (Pa.), JEM Book Publishing Company, 1995

McClelland, James and Miller, Lynn, *City in a Park*, Temple University Press, Philadelphia, Pennsylvania, 2006

McClure, Cicero Pangburn, *Randolph-Pangburn, William Pangburn and His Wife Hannah Fitz Randolph; Their Ancestry and Descendants, 1620-1909*, Pangburn Society of Allegheny County, Pa, 1909

McCullough, David, *John Adams*, Simon & Schuster, 2001

McGuire, Thomas J. *Battle of Paoli*, Stackpoole Books, Mechanicsburg, Pennsylvania, 2000

Miller, Richard G., "The Federal City, 1783-1800," in *Philadelphia: A 300—Year History*, Russell F. Weigly, ed., W. W. Norton 1982

Ormsbee, Thomas Hamilton, *Early American Furniture Makers*, Thomas Y. Crowell Company, New York, 1930

Perlman, Selig, *A History of Trade Unionism in the United States*, Echo Books, 2006

Pierson, Michael, D., *Mutiny at Fort Jackson, The Untold Story of the Fall of New Orleans*, The University of North Carolina Press, Chapel Hill, North Carolina, 2008

Pope, Christopher Henry, *The Pioneers of Massachusetts, Drawn from Records of the Colonies, Towns and Churches, and Other*

Contemporaneous Documents, Boston, 1900; Baltimore Genealogical Society Publishing Co., 1965

Pratt, Harry E., *Personal Finances of Abraham Lincoln*, The Lakeside Press, (1943)

Randolph, Joseph F., *The Law of Faith: With a Lawyer's Notes on the Written Law*, New York

Putnam's Sons, and London, 1914

Randolph, L. V. F., *Fitz Randolph Traditions—A Story of A Thousand Years*, The New York Historical Society, 1907

Randolph, Oris H. F., *Edward Fitz Randolph Branch Lines and Allied Families and English and Norman Ancestry*, Edward Brothers, Inc., Ann Arbor, Michigan, 1980

Richardson, John, *Solebury Township, Bucks County, Pennsylvania, A Short History on the Township and a Report on Township Officers and Affairs*, Offset Service Company, Philadelphia, Pennsylvania, 1958

Roberts, Gary Boyd, *Ancestors of American Presidents*, New England Historic Genealogical Society, 2009

Scharf, Thomas and Westcott, Thompson, *History of Philadelphia, 1609-1884*, Philadelphia, L. I. Everts & Co., 1884

Simpson, Henry, *The Lives of Eminent Philadelphians Now Deceased*, W. Brotherhead, Philadelphia, 1859

Stowell, David W., *The Papers of Abraham Lincoln: Legal Documents and Cases*, U. of Virginia Press, 2008

Sullivan, Richard E., *Charlemagne: Holy Roman Emperor,(1747?-814)* Encyclopedia Britannica

Wainwright, Nicholas B., *Philadelphia: A 300-Year History*, "The Age of Nicholas Biddle, 1825-1841," W. W. Norton, New York-London, 1982

Wainwright, Nicholas, B., *History of the Philadelphia National Bank,1803-1953*, William F. Fell, Printers, Philadelphia, 1953

Wall, John P. and Pickersgill, Harold, eds., *History of Middlesex County, New Jersey*, 1664- 1920, New York Historical Publishing Co.

Walvin, James, *The Quakers: Money and Morals*, John Murray (Publishers) Ltd., London, 1997

Wineapple, Brenda, *Hawthorne: A Life*, Random House, 2004

Winston, Richard, *Charlemagne*, Horizon, New Word City, LLC

Winthrop, John, *The Journal of John Winthrop*, Harvard University Press, 1996

Wood, Dr. George B., and Bache, Dr. Franklin, *The Dispensatory of the United States of America*, Sixteenth edition, Philadelphia, J. B. Lippincott Company, 1892

Wood, Julianna Randolph, *Biographical Sketch of Richard D. Wood* (2 vols.) Philadelphia, Lippincott's Press, 1871, Miami, HardPress (reprint), 2017

Manuscript Sources

Alexander, Sally Kennedy. "A Sketch of the Life of Major Andrew Ellicott," Records of the Columbia Historical Society, Washington, D. C., vol. 2, 1899, pp. 158-202. JSTOR, www.jstor.org/stable/40066727

American Community Survey, 2005-2007

City of Philadelphia Deed Book: March 18. 1813; Sale of Property and five contiguous frame buildings, IC23 p. 472

Coates & Reynell Family Papers (1677-1930), Collection 140, Historical Society of Pennsylvania

Cooperman, Emily T., "Frankford, Tacony, Wissonoming, Bridesburg" for the Context Statement, Cluster 1, Preservation Alliance for Greater Philadelphia, July 2009

Finger, Simon, "Yellow Fever," *The Encyclopedia of Greater* Philadelphia, U. of Pennsylvania Press, 2011

Fitz Randolph, Nathaniel, "Book of Records," January 29, 1754, Princeton University Library Department of Rare Books & Collections, Princeton, New Jersey

Frankford, Tacony, Wissonoming, Bridesburg for the Preservation Alliance for Greater Philadelphia, "Historic Context Statement," Cluster 1, July, 2009 by Emily Cooperman

Harvard Magazine, "Henry Francis du Pont, Brief Life of a Passionate Connoisseur, 1880-1869" by Shirley Moskow, Spring-Summer, 2003

Harvard University Obituary and Death Notice Collection, Number 39

Historical Society of Pennsylvania

    Collection 1176, R. D. Wood & Co. Records, 1858-1910

    Collection 3004, Series 3, Carson-Randolph Family Papers, Randolph Children, 1916-1972, Box 11

Linder, Douglas, "The Dakota Conflict Trials," http://ssrn.com/abstract=1021325 or http://dx.doi.org/10.2139/ssrn.1021325

Maryland Geographical Survey, Volume 7, Maryland State Archives, "History of the Boundary Dispute between the Baltimores and the Penns Resulting in the Original Mason-Dixon Line" by Edward Bennett Matthews, 355

Matthews, Edward Bennett, "History of the Boundary Dispute between the Baltimores and the Penns Resulting in the Original Mason-Dixon Line," *Maryland Geological Survey*, Maryland State Archives, Vol. 7

Minnesota State University, Mankato, Minnesota, Memorial Library, Southern Minnesota Historical Center, Parry, Edward Randolph, 1832-1874, Collection, 1857-1867 SMHC Manuscript Collection 110

National Register of Historic Places, Reference Number 1300975, Property Name: Wood

New Hope Historical Society, New Hope, Pennsylvania, Parry Family Papers, Box 2

New Jersey Historical Society, Newark, New Jersey, "Guide to Hartshorne Fitz Randolph Papers (1840-1879). Bulk 1950-1967, MG 1312

"Ogden and Cuthbert Family Papers," J. Welles Henderson Archives and Library, 1760-1830, Independence Seaport Museum

"Parry Edward Randolph (1832-1874)" Minnesota State University Memorial Library Collection (18571867); Southern Minnesota Historical Center, Manuscript Collection 110

"Parry Family Records," Box 2, New Hope Historical Society, New Hope, Pa.

Penn Medicine, "The Story of the Creation of the Nation's First Hospital," History of Pennsylvania Hospital, 2017, www.uphs.upenn.edu/paharc/features/creation.html

Pennsylvania Wills and Probate Records, 1683-1993; Bucks County, Wills, Vol. 5, 1786-1797. Ancestry.com

"Philip Syng Physick, 1768-1837," Penn People, University Archives and Records Center, U. of Pennsylvania

Princeton University Library, Princeton, New Jersey, Book of Records, "Nathaniel Fitz Randolph", January 29, 1754

University of Pennsylvania, University Archives and Records Center, Penn People, Philip Syng Physick, 1768-1837

Urban Archives, Samuel Paley Library, Temple University, Philadelphia, Pennsylvania

R. D. Wood & Co. Records (1858-1910), The Historical Society of Pennsylvania, Collection 1176, Series 4, Personnel (1858-1896)

Report of the Board of Managers of the Western Association of Ladies for the Relief and Employment of the Poor, Hanna Ann Zell, Joseph Rakestraw, Publisher, 1854

Report of the Board of Managers of the Western Association of Ladies for the Relief and Employment of the Poor, T. Elwood Zell, Publisher, 1869

Writings of George Washington from the Original Manuscript Sources, 1745-1799, Government Printing Office, Washington, (D. C.), 1931

Newspapers, Magazines, Periodicals and Internet Sources

American Foundation, Chipstone, *County Times*, Coatesville, Pennsylvania, August 11, 1859

Bebbington, George, with Alan A. Siegel (editor), "Washington Rock is Focus of Renewed Interest," in "Warren History," Volume II, No. 3 (Spring, 1995), Green Brook Historical Society

Bedini, Silvio, *Declaration of Independence Desk: Relic of Revolution*, Washington, (D.C.), Smithsonian Institution Press, 1981

Biographical Directory of the U. S. Congress, 1774-present

Bobsin, John, *History of the Lines We Represent*, Lackawanna Coalition, December 17, 2009

Brunk, Andrew, *Benjamin Randolph Revisited*, American Furniture, 2007

"Cape May's Emlen Physick Estate, A Window on Our Victorian Past" (brochure), Cape May, (N. J.), the Physick Estate and the Mid-Atlantic Center for the Arts and Humanities, 2012

Chester County Times (Coatesville, Pa.), August 11, 1859

Connor, J. Dell, "The Physick House, The Physick Family, Edmund Darch Lewis," fireback.com/Drphysick.com/index.html

Donnoli, Nick, "Through the gates: The Myth surrounding Fitz Randolph Gate." Office of Communications, Princeton University, May 31, 2007

Elmer, Lucius Q. C., "Maurice River, Millville, and Landis," in *History of the Early Settlement and Progress of Cumberland County New Jersey; and the Currency of This and Adjoining Colonies*, Chapter IV, Bridgeton, (N. J.), George F. Nixon, 1869

Gunning, Wanda S., "The Town of Princeton and the University—1756-1946,"The Princeton Library, *Princeton University Chronicles*, Vol. 66, No. 3, (Spring 2005)

Heimerdinger, Jane and Michener, Thomas, *Pennswood View*, "Core Creek Park and the Grand Duchess", Fall, 1984

Hunnewell, Sumner, "The Battle of Moore's Brook, Scarborough, Maine, June 29, 1677," *The Maine Genealogist*, May and August 2003

Journal of the Senate of New Jersey, 1863

Kaufmann, Sue, *Hidden New Jersey* Blog, hiddennj.com

Leach, Frank Willing, "Old Philadelphia Families," *The North American*, Nov. 3, 1912

Maurice River Recollection Project, Citizens United to Protect the Maurice River and its' Tributaries, Inc., cumauriceriver.org

McCardle, Dorothy, "Kissinger Guests Will Be Sitting Pretty," *Los Angeles Times,* January 20, 1974

Middlesex County Cultural and Heritage Commission, *East Jersey Olde Towne Village,* culturalandheritage@co.middlesex.nj.us

Mitchell, Martha, "Van Wickle Gates", Encyclopedia Brunoniana,, Brown University, 1993

Morven Museum and Garden, Princeton, 2014

Moskow, Shirley, "Henry Francis du Pont, Brief Life of a passionate connoisseur: 1880-1969," *Harvard Magazine,* July-August, 2003

"Never Did I See So Universal a Frenzy: The Panic of 1791 and the Republicanization of Philadelphia," The Pennsylvania Magazine of History and Biography, Vol. CXLII, No 1 (January, 2018)

New England Historic Genealogical Society, New England Historic Genealogical Society, Boston, October, 1943

New York Times, October 14, 1872, "Old Houses: Prisons of the Revolutionary War."

Oleans Times Herald, Oleans, New York, "Bergdoll—The Fighting Slacker" by Willis Thornton

Penn Medicine, History of Pennsylvania Hospital, Stories from Pennsylvania Hospital's Past, In the Beginning—The Story of the Creation of the Nation's First Hospital, 2017, www.uphs.upenn.edu/paharc/features/creation.html

Pennypacker, Samuel W., *Historical and Biographical Sketches* (1863) *Wikisource*

Philadelphia Parks and Recreation, *Charms of Fairmount Park*, Mount Pleasant, 2012

Preserve Greystone Blog, preservegrestone.org

Princeton University Chronicles (Spring, 2005) Volume 66, Number 66, Number 3, p. 452, *The Town of Princeton and the University—1756-1946* by Wanda S. Gunning, The Princeton Library, Princeton, New Jersey

Princeton University, Office of Communications, *Through the gates: The Myth surrounding Fitz*

Randolph Gate, Nick Donnoli, May 31, 2007 Randolph, Hope Carson, "Randolph Family Book and Randolph Family—A pamphlet edited by Alexander du Bin," Philadelphia (privately published), 1946

Riggs, Stephen, *New York Times,* December 26, 1862, "The Indian Executions" (http://www.startribune.com/local/138264074.html

Schwartz, Jerry, *Los Angeles Times,* "Oldest Corporation in U. S. History— After 314 Years" September 3, 1998

Silverman, Ellie, *Morning Call,* Allentown, Pennsylvania, "Wawa is undergoing a huge expansion"

Swett, Ben H., Colonel USAF (Retired), *John Swett of Newbury, A Collection of Genealogical Research Papers,* swett-genealogy.com (accessed, (April, 2018)

Pennsylvania Magazine of History and Biography, Volume CXLII, No. 1, pp. 9, 10 (January, 2018) "Never Did I See So Universal a Frenzy: The Panic oof 1791 and Republicanization of Philadelphia" Published by the Historical Society of Pennsylvania

Valis, Glenn, "The Militia of New Jersey During the Revolution," New Jersey during the Revolution (Nov. 5th, 2007 (revised), doublegv.com/ggv/militia.html

Wunsch, Aaron, Historic American Buildings Survey, 1995, *Laurel Hill, Tired of Commuting?*

Zell, Hanna Ann, "Report of the Board of Managers of the Western Association of Ladies for the Relief and Employment of the Poor," Philadelphia, Joseph Rakestraw Publisher, 18564

Zell, T. Elwood, "Report of the Board of Managers of the Western Association of Ladies for the Relief and Employment of the Poor," Philadelphia, Joseph Rakestraw, Publisher, 1869

INDEX

A

Abbott, William L 97
Adams, John 25, 34, 114, 127, 187, 200
Adams, John Quincy 38, 41
Admiral Warren Inn 72
Affleck, Thomas 33
Alain 4
Allen, Rose 49–50, 181
Allentown Iron Works 106
Amsterdam 14, 69
Annenberg, Walter H. 117
Appomattox Court House 144
Arbella xvii, 12–13
Arch Street Meeting House 107
Arnold, Benedict 34

B

Bank of the United States xviii, 86, 88, 165
Barbe-Marbois, Francis 85
Barnstable 16–17, 49–50
Basque xxiv
Battle of Germantown 84
Battle of Long Island 25, 69, 71
Battle of Naseby in 1645 9
Battle of Paoli xxv, 72, 80–81, 84, 145, 177, 185, 190, 200
Battle of Roncevaux Pass 24
Battle of Springfield 68, 74, 177
Battle of Staten Island 72
Battle of the Spanish Armada 14
Beale, Frances Lewis (1912-2004) 76,167–168
Beetle, S. Senior 108
Bergdoll, Grover Cleveland 132
Bergdoll, Louis 131
Bergdoll Mansion 131–132
Berkeley, John, Lord 22, 51
Berry, William 102
Bessemer, Henry 105
Bethlehem Steel 106
Bishop, Bridget 19
Bloomfield College 47
Bloomfield, Ezekiel 23, 27
Blossom, Elizabeth 10, 14–15, 26–28, 32, 38, 44, 49, 62, 177,182,188–189, 198
Blossom, Peter 16, 182
Blossom, Thomas 11, 14–16, 18
Bodfish, Sarah 16, 182
Bond, Dr. Thomas 113, 212
Book of Common Prayer 9
Bradford, Governor William 16
Bradstreet, Anne 13
Bradstreet, Simon 13
Bridewell Municipal Prison 69
Bridgetown Mill xix, 153–154
Bridgetown Mill House Inn xix, 154
Broderick, Esther (1718-1782) 37

Broomwick, Anna (1746-1767) 28
Broomwick, William 32
Browne, Robert 10
Bryant, William Cullen xxi, xxv
Burlington 22, 52, 55–56
Bush, George H. W. 3, 16, 27, 182
Bush, George W. 3, 16, 27, 182
Bush Hill 127–128, 133–134

C

Cadwalader, John 33
Callowhill, Hanna Margaret, 150
Calvert, Charles 150–151
Cambrian Iron Company, 105–106
Cambridge University, 10
Camden and Amboy Railroad 41, 42
Campyon, Anna (1770-1810) 37
Carman, Sarah Kent 38
Carson, Hampton Lawrence 165
Carson, Hope (1885-1980) 76, 94, 162, 165, 167, 170, 190–191, 194, 208
Carteret, George 22, 51
Catholics 8–11
Charlemagne xvii, xxiv–xxv, 1–2, 4–6, 60, 185, 201–202
Charles II 10, 18, 22, 51
Chester County Times 136, 139, 193, 206
Chief Little Crow 139
Chippendale 33, 35–36
Cholera 132
Church of England 4, 9–11, 16–17
Civil War xxv, 9, 41, 44–45, 61, 83, 98, 135, 142, 145, 161–162, 178, 190, 198
Coates, George Morrison 88
Coates, Josiah Langdale 87, 94
Coates, Samuel 87
Coleman, Mary (1831-1914) 37
College of New Jersey 28– 29
Community OutReach Partnership 174
Conger, Hannah (1670-1726) 27, 37
Continental Army xxiii, 33, 67, 69, 80, 82, 88–89
Coolidge, Eleanor Randolph 35
Cooper, Anna 95
Cooper, David 95
Cooper, James Fenimore 116
Cooper, Sarah Ann (1815-1904) 37
Core Creek Park xix, 151–152, 194, 206
Corey, Giles 19
Corinthian Yacht Club 120
Corlies, Elizabeth 79–80
Corlies, John 79
Cromwell, Oliver 9, 52, 186, 197
Cunningham, William 69
Cuthbert, Captain Anthony 93

D

Dakota Conflict 139, 193, 203
Dakotas xviii, 111, 137–142, 162, 193, 203
See also: Sioux Uprising, 139
de Longchamps, Charles Julien 85
Declaration of Independence xvii, 28, 32, 34, 69, 112, 127, 155, 177, 187, 199, 206
Delaware and Raritan Canal Company 41
Delftshaven 16
Dennis, Ruth (1727-1770) 49, 64
Dennis, Sarah (1799-1747) 27–29
Descartes, René 15
Design + Construction Incorporated 170
Dickinson, John 34
Dimick, Frances (1845-1914) 76, 144
Dix, Dorothea 42
Dixon, Jeremiah 151
Dixon, Penelope H. (b. 1941) 77, 167

Dodd, Joseph S. 43
Domesday Book 3–4
Doucette, Arthur (1907-1995) 77, 167
Drake, Rebekah (1655-1749) 37
du Pont, Eleuthere Irenee 62
du Pont, Henry Algernon 61
du Pont, Henry Francis 61–62, 189, 203, 207
Duane, Jonathan 55
Dunham, Jonathan 57–60
Dunham, Jonathan Singletary (1709-1748) xvii, 49, 57–60
Dunham, S. Ann 60, 183

E

Eakins, Thomas 33, 130
East Jersey xvii, 21–26, 50–53, 55–56, 58, 66, 187, 207
East Jersey Old Town Village xvii, 23, 26
E. I. du Pont and Company 62
Elfreth, Jeremiah 86
Elfreth's Alley xviii, 86–87
Ellicott, Andrew 158–160, 194, 202
Ellicott City xix, 157
Ellicott, Thomas 158
Evans, Ann (1795-1874) 76, 94
Evening Ledger 148
Eudo 4, 6

F

Fairmount Park Conservancy 175
Father of American Surgery 112, 117, 178
Female Society for the Relief and Employment of the Poor 90, 124, 174
Fenimore, Mary Wilkinson 32
First Continental Congress 34
First Pennsylvania Bank 168
Fis Randolph, Le Conte Gerard 3

Fitz Randolph, Captain Asher 74
Fitz Randolph, Benjamin (1663-1746) 27–29
Fitz Randolph, Edward (1672-1760) 49, 60
Fitz Randolph, Edward Jr. (1607-1675) xxv, 1, 4, 10, 14, 16, 20, 26–27, 32, 38, 44, 49, 60, 62, 177, 179
Fitz Randolph, Elizabeth (1657-1702) 17, 27, 45
Fitz Randolph, Ephraim (1724-1793) 37
Fitz Randolph, Hannah (1649-1743) 27, 185, 200
Fitz Randolph, Hartshorne (1723-1806) 49, 62, 64–65, 67–68,177, 189, 204
Fitz Randolph, Hope (1661-1703) 27
Fitz Randolph, Isaac (1701-1750) 28, 32
Fitz Randolph, Lewis (1757-1822) 3, 213
Fitz Randolph, Lieutenant Edward (1754-1837) xviii, xxiii, xxv, 80
See also: Randolph,Edward (1754-1837) and Randolph, Captain Edward
Fitz Randolph, Mary (1644-1649) 27
Fitz Randolph, Mary (1650-1738) xvii, 49
Fitz Randolph, Mary (1710-1779) xvii, 27, 49, 60–62
Fitz Randolph House xvii, 23–24, 26
Fitz Randolph, James (1791-1871) 37–38
Fitz Randolph, John (1652-1652) 27
Fitz Randolph, John (1653-1726) 27
Fitz Randolph, Joseph (1656-1726) 27, 37
Fitz Randolph, Joseph Jr. (1803-1873) 37, 44

Fitz Randolph, Joseph Jr. (1843-1932) 37, 46, 48
Fitz Randolph, Joseph II (1690-1750) 37
Fitz Randolph, Joseph III (1722-1782) 37, 44
Fitz Randolph, Nathaniel (1640-1640) 27
Fitz Randolph, Nathaniel (1642-1713) 49–51, 59–60, 67-69, 72-73, 75, 82, 170, 177, 183, 187, 189, 205
Fitz Randolph, Nathaniel (1703-1780) 28–30, 49–51, 67–69, 72–73, 75, 82, 170, 177, 183, 187, 189, 205
Fitz Randolph, Nathaniel (1714-1780) 49–51, 59–60, 67–69, 72–73, 75, 82, 170, 177, 183, 187, 189, 205
Fitz Randolph, Captain Nathaniel (1747-1780) xviii, 49, 67, 73, 75, 82, 177
Fitz Randolph, Prudence (1696-1766) 49, 57, 59, 183
Fitz Randolph, Richard 79
Fitz Randolph, Robert (1762-1821) 5, 37, 44
Fitz Randolph, Samuel (1668-1754) 49, 59, 183
Fitz Randolph, Theodore (1826-1883) xvii, 37–38, 43, 46
Fitz Randolph, Thomas (1659-1745) 27
FitzRandolph Gate 30–31
FitzRandolph Observatory 31
Ford, Gerald R. 3, 49–50, 181, 188 *See also*: King, Leslie Lynch, Jr.
Fourth Pennsylvania Regiment 80
Fox, George 18
Franklin, Benjamin 25–26, 54, 87, 113, 159
Franklin, William 54

Fredonian 38
French and Indian War 32
Frogmore Mills xix, 163–164, 213
Furness, Frank 120–122

G

Garden State Preservation Trust 55
Gardner, Dorothy Ayer 50, 181
Garsed, Robert 161
German Theological Seminary 47
Gheysens, Chris 111
Girard Bank 165, 194–195
Girard National Bank of Philadelphia 165
Glanville 5
Glanvill, Joseph 21
Gradual Abolition Act of 1804 66
Grant, Ulysses S. 44, 144
Great Emigration of 1630 8
Great Migration xxv, 197
Grey, General Charles xxiii, 81
Greystone Park Psychiatric Hospital 42
Griffin 17

H

Hacker, Jeremiah and Beulah Morris 164
Hacker, William Platt (1904-2002) 76, 167
Hamilton, Alexander 32, 51–53, 113, 127, 134, 151
Hamilton, James 32, 13
Hartshorne, Katherine (1682-1759) 49, 60, 62
Hartshorne, Richard 56, 62–64
Hawthorne, Nathaniel 20, 186
Heilson, Ann 14, 16
Higginson, John 18
Hightstown, New Jersey 41
Hinckley, Samuel 22

Holder Hall xvii, 30
Holland 8, 10, 14–16
Holley, Joseph 49, 181
Holy Roman Empire 1
Hunn, Mary 108
Hyde, Edward, Lord Cornbury 53

I

Independence Hall xvii, 32, 66, 111
Indian Queen Tavern xvii, 24–26
Inslee, Experience (1750-1813) 49, 67
Intermodal Surface Transportation Efficiency Act of 1991 172

J

Jackson, Andrew 38, 114
Jackson, James (1704-1750) 49, 60
Jackson, John 65
Jefferson, Thomas 32, 34–36, 112, 159–160, 177, 187, 197
Jenks, Joseph 153
Jenks, Thomas 150–152, 169
Jenks, William Pearson xix, 149, 155, 157-158, 160-161, 163, 165, 178
Jersey Blues 59
Jones, Mary (1672-1760) 49, 183
J. S. Jenks Academy for the Arts & Sciences 164

K

Kean, Governor Thomas 100
Keith, Charles Penrose 117
Kelly, William 105
Kelsey, Henry 43
Kennedy, Carmita de Solmes 148
Kent, Sarah (1790-1860) 37–38
Kler, Dr. Joseph 24
King Charles I 8
King George III 151
King, Leslie Lynch Jr. 50
    See also: Ford, Gerald R Jr

King Philip's War 79, 190, 198
Kissinger, Henry 36
Knowles, Charles 136
Kraemer, Lida Mae 146

L

Lake Luxembourg xix, 151–152
Lancaster Turnpike 89
Lang, Margaret Parry 146, 148
Lang, Oliver Paul 148
Langstaff, John 22
Laurel Hill xviii, 116, 118, 193, 209
Law of Nations Clause 85
Lee, Robert E. 44
Leiden 14–15
Lenape Indians 62
Lewis, Ann 7, 117
Lewis, Edmund Darch 117, 193, 206
Lewis, Sinclair 142, 194
Lincoln, Abraham 39, 101–102, 141, 162–163, 191–192, 201
Livingston, William 54, 73–74
Lollard movement 11
London 10, 13, 55, 64, 69, 96, 186, 190, 200–202
Lothrop, John 17
Luxembourg, Grand Duchess of 152

M

Mankato, Minnesota xviii, 133, 135, 140, 143, 204
Manning, Elizabeth Bathsheba 23
Manning, Justice Randolph xvii, 45
Maris, William 156–157
Marshall, Chief Justice John 1, 114
Maryland Militia 72
Mason, Charles 151
Mason-Dixon Line 151, 194, 203–204
Massachusetts Bay Colony 11, 13, 17
Massacre of Verden 2
Maurice River Canal 101

Maurice River Dam 101
Maurice River Recollections
    Project 99, 191
Maule, Thomas 18, 20, 186, 200
Mayflower xvii, 11–12, 14, 16
Mayflower II 14
McClure, Cicero Pangburn 2, 185
Mellon, Andrew W 119
Mendham Meeting 64, 67
Mershon, Rebecca (1710-1789) 28
Mid-Atlantic Center for the
    Arts & Humanities 120–121
Middle Dutch Church 69–70
Mills, Ogden Livingston 118
Millville Cotton Mill 100
Millville Manufacturing Company
    xviii, 99, 105, 107, 110
Millville, New Jersey 98–99, 111,
    192, 204
Mine Hill 65
Moffat, Alice (b 1947) 77, 167, 170
Monmouth County 32, 44, 62, 64, 66
Monroe, James 114, 146, 148
Morris and Essex Railroad 39
Morris, Lewis 52–54
Morris, Robert 134,
Morristown, New Jersey 44, 54
Mount Pleasant 34, 187, 208
Muslims xxiv

N

Nassau Hall 29
Navesink Highlands 63
Navigation Act 1696 52
Middleham 1, 4-5
New Brunswick 25–26, 29, 38, 44, 84,
    189, 198
New England 4, 11–12, 15, 17,18,
    21, 46, 51, 58, 142, 149, 158,
    177, 186, 188–190, 197–199,
    201, 207

New England Company 12
New Jersey Green Acres Program 55
New Jersey Legislature 42, 53, 156
New Jersey Militia 23, 54, 68, 72
New Jersey Proprietors 21, 63
New Jersey Society for Promoting the
    Abolition of Slavery 65–66
New Jersey State Constitutional
    Convention of 1844 44
New Plymouth 17
New York Central Railroad 42
New York Times 56, 69, 140, 173, 189,
    194, 207–208
Nicholas of Hereford 10
Norris, George W 115
Norris, Thomas 29
Nottinghamshire, England 4, 8

O

Obama, Barack Hussein 3, 49, 58–
    60, 183

P

Parry, Benjamin 71, 107, 116, 157
Parry, Captain Oliver Randolph (1873-
    1958) xviii, 76, 145, 148
Parry, Colonel Caleb 71–72
Parry, Edward Randolph (1832-1874)
    xviii, 76, 133, 135, 144–145,
    193, 204
Parry, Emma Randolph 133
Parry, George Randolph 133
Parry, Helen Randolph 133
Parry, Oliver (1794-1874) 71, 76, 93–
    94, 107, 116, 123, 125, 127, 129,
    131–135, 178
Parry, Rachel Randolph xviii, 76, 123,
    126, 129, 135, 145, 170, 178
Parry, Richard Randolph (1835-1928)
    xviii, 76, 118, 133, 142, 144,
    178, 187, 199

Paterson, Governor William 155
Paterson, New Jersey 65, 155
Peabody Essex Museum 18
Peace Conference of February
    1861 44
Penn, William 28, 51, 56, 63-64, 86,
    91-92, 112, 127-129, 150-151,
    172, 189, 199
Pennsylvania Abolitionist Society 66
Pennsylvania Academy of the Fine
    Arts 107, 117, 120
Pennsylvania Hospital xviii, 96, 112–
    114, 117, 164, 178, 192, 204, 207
Pennsylvania Railroad 39, 97
Perth Amboy 22, 52, 54, 84
Pew Charitable Trust 172
Philadelphia xi, xiii, xvii–xix, 25,
    32–36, 41–42, 55, 66, 71, 76,
    80–99, 103, 106–108, 110–120,
    Early job-training program for
        Women, 123–136,
    Yellow Fever epidemic, 127-128,
    Consolidation of the city, 129-
        130, 138, 142, 145–150,
        153, 155–157, 159–166,
        168–175, 177–178, 185, 187,
        189–195,
Philadelphia and Reading Railroad 98
Philadelphia Felt Company 164
Philadelphia Inquirer 133, 191
Philadelphia Magazine 131
Philadelphia National Bank 88–89,
    106, 165–166, 178, 195, 202
Philadelphia Record 120,145
Philadelphia Society for the
    Preservation of Landmarks 117
Physick, Edmund 112
Physick, Emlen 119
Physick, Emlen Jr. xviii, 76, 112, 119–
    122, 193, 206

Physick, Sarah Emlen (1801-1873)
    76, 112
Pike, John 23
Pike's Peak 23
Pike, Zebulon Montgomery 23
Pilgrim ix, 4–6, 8–12, 14–16, 21,179,
    186, 197, 199
Piscataway 21–23, 26, 28, 44
Pitcairn, John Jr. 131
Plymouth Colony xxv, 8, 14, 49–
    50, 186
Polk, President James 132
Potter Farm 29
Potter, John 29
Presbyterians 10, 47, 75
Princess Anne 52
Princeton xiii, xvii, 2, 28–32, 93, 170,
    177, 187, 189, 203, 205–208
Princeton University xiii, xvii, 28, 30–
    31, 177, 187, 203, 205–206, 208
Prisoner of War window 70
Privateers 32
Prize Law 32
Proprietors 21, 50–53, 55–56, 58,
    63–65, 72, 150
Prospect Farm 29
Public Ledger 117
Puritans 8–13, 16–22, 58, 177
Purvey, John 10

Q

Quakers 17–18, 48, 50, 52, 57, 64–68,
    71, 79, 82, 84, 87, 89, 91, 94,
    133, 159, 164, 186, 202
Queen Elizabeth I 10

R

R. D. Wood Company 103
Ralston, Frances 119
Randolph and Jenks 160, 163, 164
Randolph and Talcott 47

Randolph, Benjamin (1737-1792) xvii, 28, 32–36, 112, 177, 187, 206
Randolph, David Story xiii, 3, 77, 185
Randolph, Dorothy 118
Randolph, Edward(1754-1837) xviii, 71–72, 76,78–79, 83–85, 87–89, 93–95,123–124, 133, 135, 144–145,149, 174, 177–178, 193, 204 *See also*: Fitz Randolph, Lieutenant Edward and Randolph, Captain Edward
Randolph Captain Edward (1754-1837) 76, 79–80 *See also*: Fitz Randolph, Lieutenant Edward; Randolph, Edward (1754-1837)
Randolph, Evan (1822-1887) xix, 76, 149, 160, 163, 178
Randolph, Evan Jr. (1880-1962) xix, 76, 89, 165–168, 170
Randolph, Evan III (1909-1997) xix, 76, 167–168, 170
Randolph, Evan IV (b 1935) xiii, 77, 167, 169
Randolph, Francis Lewis (1951-1974) 77, 167, 169
Randolph, Hampton Carson (1911-1998) 77, 167
Randolph, Hope (1908-2002) 76, 167
Randolph, Jacob MD (1796-1848) xviii, xxv, 76,112, 114-119, 123, 178
Randolph, John (b. 1947) xiii, xix, 77,164, 167–175, 178–179
Randolph, Josiah Coates 87
Randolph, Leonard Beal (b. 1937) 77, 167
Randolph, Lewis V. F. (L. V. F.) 1, 3, 5, 11, 21
Randolph, Rachel (b. 1915) 167
Randolph, William (1788-1832) 76, 149

Randolph, Talcott and Black 47
Raritan River 21–22, 24, 26
Read, Ellen (1846-1916) 76
Reeves, Barbara (1917-1969) 77, 167
Rembrandt 14
Revolutionary War xi, xxv, 12, 23, 25–26, 28–29, 35–36, 54, 67–69, 71–72, 75–76, 83, 89, 112, 127,134, 145, 151, 155, 177, 189, 207
Reynell, John 87
Reynell, Mary Coates 87
Rhinelander Building 70

S

Salem xvii, 11, 13, 18–21, 97, 102, 109, 186, 200
Salem Witch Trials xvii, 18–21
Salem Witch Trials Memorial xvii, 19
Schoettle, Sally Ann (b. 1940) 77, 167
Schuylkill Navigation Company 97–98, 106
Schuylkill River xix, 89, 91, 93–94, 97–98, 170–175, 178
Schuylkill River Development Corporation 173
Schuylkill River Development Council 170–171, 174
Schuylkill River Park Alliance 175
Schuylkill River Trail 171, 173–174
Scituate 4, 14, 17
Seabrook, Rebecca (1708-1744) 28, 32
Second Continental Congress 34
Separatist Pilgrims 8–12
Shotwell, Mary (1722-1743) 49, 67
Singer, Isaac Merritt 65
Singer Sewing Machine Company 65
Sioux Uprising 139 *See also*: Dakota Conflict
Sloan, Samuel 42, 55
Smith, Mary (1717-1784) 49, 60

Smith, Robert 29
Smith, Shubal (1692-1769) 49, 57, 60
Snowden, Rachel (1758-1822) 37
Springett, Maria 150
Steele, Anna Julianna xxv, 84, 90, 93-94
Steele, Anna Margaret Ebright 484
Steele, Henry 84
Stelle, Rachel (1720-1791) 37
Stetson, John B. 131
Stockton, Richard 28
Stuart, Sarah Clark 171
Sullivan, Hannah Wright (b. 1923) 77, 167
Sullivan, Major General John 72
Swett, Lieutenant Benjamin 79
Sioux Uprising 139
Syng, Abigail 112
Syng, Philip 112, 114–115, 117, 128, 178, 192, 205

T

Talcott, Hattie (1846-1891) 37
Taylor, Jasper 22
Taylor, Mary (1789-1867) 76, 95
Thanatopsis xxi, xxv,
Thorne, William (1684-1735) 49, 60
Trevisa, John 10
trinity houses xviii, 93
Tryon, General William 83
Tyler, President John 44

U

Union Lake 100
United New Jersey Railroad and Canal Company 41
United States Constitution 20, 85, 112
University of Pennsylvania xiii, 96–97, 112–113, 119, 145, 170, 205
USA Today 173

V

Van Wickle, Augustus Stout 30
Vanderbilt, Cornelius 41

W

Washington, George 25, 33, 73, 83, 93–94, 151, 155, 190, 205
Wawa Dairy Farm 110
Wawa Food Market 110
Wawa Foundation 111
Wawa, Pennsylvania 110
Wayne, Brigadier General Anthony xxiii
West Jersey 22, 51–53, 55–56, 63–64, 66, 103
West Jersey Railroad Company 103
Western Association of Ladies for the Relief and Employment of the Poor 124–126, 174, 193, 205, 209
Wiggins, Benjamin 149
Willard Hotel 45, 106
William III 51–52
William Penn Foundation 172
William the Conqueror 1, 3, 4, 149
Wilson, Woodrow 30
Windrim, James H. 131
Winslow, Jane Parry 133
Winterthur xiii, 60-62
Winthrop Fleet 8, 12, 186, 197
Winthrop, John 12, 17, 186, 202
Wood, Elizabeth Bacon 95
Wood, George xviii, 97, 105, 108–111
Wood, Grahame 110–111
Wood, Joseph 99
Wood, Julianna Randolph (1810-1885) xviii, 76, 82, 95, 112, 162, 191–192
Wood, Richard III 95

Wood, Richard Davis (1799-1869)
    xviii, 76, 95, 97, 106, 108, 111,
    162, 178, 192
Wood, Samuel C. 97
Woodbridge 21, 23, 50, 52, 57–61, 64,
    73, 75, 79, 189, 198

Wooden, Andrew 22, 27
Wycliffe, John 10
Wycombe xix, 149–150, 158

Z

Zenger, John Peter 20

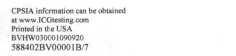